REAL-TIME 3D TERRAIN ENGINES USING C++ AND DIRECTX 9

Real-Time 3D Terrain Engines Using C++ and DirectX 9

Greg Snook

CHARLES RIVER MEDIA, INC.

Hingham, Massachusetts

Publisher: Jenifer Niles
Production: Publishers' Design and Production Services
Cover Design: The Printed Image
Cover Image: Gregory Snook

CHARLES RIVER MEDIA, INC.
10 Downer Avenue
Hingham, Massachusetts 02043
781-740-0400
781-740-8816 (FAX)
info@charlesriver.com
www.charlesriver.com

This book is printed on acid-free paper.

Gregory Snook. *Real-Time 3D Terrain engines Using C++ and DirectX 9*.
ISBN: 1-58450-204-5

All brand names and product names mentioned in this book are trademarks or service marks of their respective companies. Any omission or misuse (of any kind) of service marks or trademarks should not be regarded as intent to infringe on the property of others. The publisher recognizes and respects all marks used by companies, manufacturers, and developers as a means to distinguish their products.

Library of Congress Cataloging-in-Publication Data

Snook, Gregory.
    Real-time 3D terrain engines engines using C++ and and DirectX 9 /Gregory Snook.
        p. cm.
    ISBN 1-58450-204-5 (Paperback w/ CD-ROM : alk. paper)
    1. Computer games—Programming.   2. Three-dimensional display systems.
3. Direct3D.   4. C++ (Computer program language)   I. Title.
    QA76.76.C672S64 2003
    794.8'16693—dc21
                            2003008198
Printed in the United States of America
03 7 6 5 4 3 2 First Edition

CHARLES RIVER MEDIA titles are available for site license or bulk purchase by institutions, user groups, corporations, etc. For additional information, please contact the Special Sales Department at 781-740-0400.

This book is dedicated to my wife, Denise,
and my children Madeline, Ben, and Jon
for their incredible patience and support.

CONTENTS

INTRODUCTION

Since the first computer-controlled dots appeared on a display in the early 1950s, an elite group of programmers has been obsessed with finding ways to get those dots to hunt, fight, outwit, and destroy each other. We call these people "game programmers." Under their guidance, early computer parts designed to land men on the moon and regulate nuclear power were soon busy doing more important things: playing games. Pioneers such as Willy Higginbotham and A. S. Douglas turned a collection of oscilloscopes, vacuum tubes, knobs, and buttons into machines that could play tennis and tic-tac-toe. A little more than a decade later, men such as Ralph Baer found ways to incorporate television displays into computer-controlled games, and the first dedicated game machines were born.

These early pioneers defined what computer games are today: a way to convert expensive calculating marvels into playthings for our amusement. With each generation, the computers grew more powerful and the games more complicated. Today, programming computer games is a bona fide career choice, and there are ample game machines at our disposal. We have reached the point where gaming drives the sales of many computers, and dedicated video hardware exists to create 3D worlds for us to play in.

To bring new programmers into the field of 3D computer game programming, this book is dedicated to teaching the fundamentals of a popular 3D engine type: the Real-Time 3D Terrain Engine. Whether you are new to 3D engine programming or a seasoned veteran, this book will teach you how to use the latest advancements in hardware-accelerated rendering to create a highly detailed, real-time 3D landscape for use in your own projects. Over the course of this book, an entire 3D engine will be built to instruct the reader on the concepts behind 3D terrain systems and the methods used to represent them.

AUDIENCE

This book is written for programmers who are familiar with C++, Microsoft® DirectX®, 3D mathematics, and geometry. While this book provides an overview of basic 3D mathematics topics and using DirectX, it is not intended to be an introduction to 3D programming—nor does it provide a complete introduction to DirectX and Microsoft Windows® programming. We assume the reader has already acquired these basic skills and is ready to move into 3D engine design and real-time terrain visualization. If needed, references to reading material are provided in Appendix D, "Recommended Reading," for further background information.

ON THE CD

The complete Software Development Kit (SDK) for Microsoft DirectX 9.0 is included on the CD-ROM accompanying this book. This SDK contains tutorials and documentation designed to introduce programmers to 3D and working with DirectX. If you are unfamiliar with these topics, we recommend that you read the information provided with the SDK and explore the tutorials provided with it.

HARDWARE AND SOFTWARE REQUIREMENTS

ON THE CD

This book focuses on real-time terrain programming using C++ and DirectX 9.0. The complete DirectX 9.0 SDK is provided on the accompanying CD-ROM, but the reader must provide a compiler capable of compiling C++ source code written to use these libraries. The sample code provided on the CD-ROM was written using Microsoft Visual Studio.NET® (Visual Studio 7.0), which is the recommended compiler for working along with this book. Project files are also provided for Microsoft Visual Studio® version 6.0 for convenience. Compilers from other vendors might also be able to compile these files, but have not been tested.

Running the programs provided with this book requires a suitable PC. The minimum CPU requirement is support for the Intel® Streaming SIMD Extensions (SSE), which are available in the Intel Pentium® III (or greater) CPUs, and the AMD® Athlon™ processor family. The recommended minimum speed rating for the CPU is 1GHz, with a minimum system RAM recommendation of 256MB.

You'll also need a video card that supports hardware-accelerated pixel and vertex shaders compliant with the standards set by DirectX 9.0. These include video cards based on the NVIDIA® GeForce™ chipsets (versions 3, 4, FX, or greater) and the ATI® Radeon™ chipset (8500 series or greater), among others. Some of the sample shaders use the latest language features for programmable shaders, and might require more powerful video cards to function. In addition, as we add features to our engine over the course of the book, less powerful PC and video card combinations might not be able to maintain fully interactive frame rates.

Each programmable vertex and pixel shaders used within DirectX has its own language specification, denoted by a version number. This version number is separate from the DirectX SDK version number. Some of the shaders used in this book require the latest vertex and pixel shader versions (vs 2.0 and ps 2.0), which are currently supported on high-end video cards such as the NVIDIA GeForce FX and the ATI Radeon 9700. Whenever possible, backward-compatible versions of these shaders are provided to meet the minimum hardware requirements.

It should also be noted that DirectX 9.0 marked the end of DirectX support for Microsoft Windows 95. The source code provided with this book is intended for Microsoft Windows XP, but might also function under Windows 98, Windows ME, or Windows 2000. However, support for these older versions of Microsoft Windows is not guaranteed because DirectX 9.0 drivers might not be available for all video cards on these older operating systems.

USING THIS BOOK

Many books on programming 3D game engines exist today, but most are either too general in their approach, or too fixated on individual tips and tricks. All of the ideas presented in these books are incredibly useful, but trying to incorporate combinations of those ideas into a single design has always been a daunting task for the reader. This book takes a different approach by focusing directly on outdoor terrain rendering topics, presenting all of the tips, tricks, and ideas in the context of a single game engine.

Over the course of this book, we will build a complete 3D terrain engine from the ground up (pun intended) in order to examine key landscape rendering topics. To better facilitate this engine, we will be making use of the sample framework provided by the DirectX SDK, and the Direct3D Extension Library (D3DX). While the D3DX library is not often used in retail games, it provides a suitable, well-documented foundation for our engine to use. Taking advantage of this library allows us to move directly into terrain-related topics without the need to create low-level mathematics and geometry libraries of our own.

ON THE CD

While the accompanying CD-ROM contains the source code for the engine we will be building, we highly recommend that you write your own source code as you read the book. The source code on the CD-ROM is there for you to use and reference, but there is no better way to learn programming ideas than to code them yourself. As we progress through each chapter, incorporate the ideas presented into your own engine using the text and CD-ROM as a guide. When you have completed the book, you will emerge with a head full of rendering methods and programming concepts, and a complete 3D outdoor game engine of your own design.

Building a game engine, in practice, is not a linear task. While there is a general building order we can follow in constructing the game engine, we will often revisit previously written sections to add new functionality. In some cases, this will mean jumping around from file to file, rewriting code you might have thought was finished. We do this to see our new code in action right away, knowing that we can revisit it later to add additional features. The alternative, which we will endure from time to time, is long dry spells where we add a lot of new code, but see little change in the engine on-screen. Either way, it all pays off in the end—it just takes a little patience to get there.

The source code provided with the book also contains additional support classes created to make programming the engine a little easier. This support code provides our type definitions and a host of tools for manipulating data and managing memory. Debugging and profiling tools are also contained within this toolset. In the interest of brevity, these support classes are not discussed within the book in any detail. The source code for these classes is written to incorporate ample comments to help guide the reader through them. Appendix A, "Gaia Utility Classes," also contains a synopsis of these core libraries, and a brief explanation of the functionality provided. As you read the source code provided on the accompanying CD-ROM, refer to Appendix A for explanations of the support classes you might encounter.

ON THE CD

Many of the concepts and algorithms explained in the book are shown along with the corresponding source code. However, we do list all source code within these pages. Consider the source code on the accompanying CD-ROM as an extension of the book. The CD-ROM is provided for you to explore the remaining source code at your leisure, providing additional insight than the book alone can provide. We consider the source code an integral part of this book, and will often refer you to it for more information.

HOW THIS BOOK IS ORGANIZED

The book is divided into three main parts, each of which is geared toward a specific group of topics. Over the course of this book, we will build the engine in three major steps: foundation, basic functionality, and final product. These steps also denote the order in which we will be exploring terrain topics. We will first examine DirectX 9.0 and build our foundation classes, construct a basic terrain engine, and finally add the features that will augment the engine and bring our outdoor landscape to life. Along the way, many small demonstration programs are provided to show our progress.

In the opening chapters of Part 1, "A Foundation in 3D," we explore the basics of DirectX 9 and the D3DX library. We also discuss the High-Level Shader Language (HLSL), a new language specification included in DirectX 9.0 that allows for the creation of programmable shaders without the use of traditional vertex and pixel shader assembly code. All vertex and pixel shaders created within the book will use HLSL, so we provide a complete chapter on this language.

From this foundation, we begin building our own classes on top of DirectX and D3DX to facilitate the basic needs of our engine. In the final chapters of Part 1, we will construct the first version of our engine and build a utility application that will allow us to view models and animations using HLSL shaders.

In Part 2, "Introduction to Terrain Systems," we focus on the basic needs specific to a terrain engine: providing the geometry of the landscape itself and the textures applied to it. In the opening chapter, we explore methods to spatially organize data with our world, using a method based on traditional quadtrees to divide the expansive landscape area into more manageable sections. We examine methods to create and maintain large sets of terrain geometry, providing flexible levels of detail to maintain rendering speed. We discuss the popular terrain management methods of Real-Time Optimally Adjusting Meshes (ROAM) [Duchaineau] and Chunking Terrain [Ulrich] in addition to the traditional brute-force approach. We also expand on the Interlocking Terrain Tile method (ITT) [Snook] and show demonstrations of each method.

We end Part 2 with a chapter on texturing the terrain using various techniques. While we have not yet added realistic lighting or atmospheric effects to our engine, this part of the book provides all the underlying functionality used to manage the geometry of our terrain. We provide a demonstration at this point to incorporate the world organization, texturing, and terrain management techniques to create a view of a barren landscape.

In Part 3, "Extending the Engine," the world begins to take shape. With the basic needs of terrain in place, we focus on adding realism to the scene. In Part 3, we discuss the latest advancements in outdoor lighting techniques, including atmospheric effects. From these ideas we construct our final rendering pipeline, and begin building shaders to bring a high level of realism to our synthetic world. While dealing with the sky and sunlight, we discuss methods to display a façade of distant scenery, clouds, and the sun itself. We explore procedural methods for animating cloud cover, and the gratuitous lens flare effect commonly seen in outdoor photography.

To populate the landscape, we also examine methods to depict various types of vegetation. We discuss methods ranging from simple grass to colossal trees as we explore methods to render each type of flora interactively. We then move off the land and into the sea, building a robust ocean water shader to surround our island landscape.

We end our exploration of real-time 3D terrain rendering with a final demonstration of everything learned within the book. This completed landscape engine will allow you to further investigate your own topics of interest, providing a solid foundation for whatever type of game or application you want to build.

ADDITIONAL CONTENT

The book does not end with the final chapter. To help you further develop your application, we provide a few appendices of helpful programming reference sheets and recommended reading material. These are intended to serve as a handy way to look up various DirectX 9.0 vertex and pixel shader instructions, and seek out new techniques for further study. A full listing of the content provided on the CD-ROM is also included, along with simple instructions explaining how the CD-ROM contents can be installed on your computer for easy reference.

A FEW WORLDS ABOUT PROGRAMMING STYLE

One thing we guarantee about this book is that there will be some design decision or coding practice that you will absolutely hate. Here, we present Snook's first law of game programming: "For each programmer, there exists an equal and opposite programmer who can't stand reading the first programmer's code." Personal coding styles are just that—personal. Many programming teams have wasted weeks of development time arguing over a set of programming rules for a project. Most of these arguments usually center on naming conventions, bracing styles, and line indents. In fact, entire books have been written presenting uniform coding practices for teams to adopt. Suffice it to say, with the amount of code provided in this book, something is bound to annoy you. The solution? Change it.

As stated earlier, we highly recommend that you code your own engine along with the book. There is simply no better way to learn the concepts presented here than to code them yourself. This also gives you the opportunity to write the engine in your own personal style—no source code will ever be more useful or readable to you than your own. Therefore, while you have to endure the coding style used in the text and CD-ROM to pick up on the ideas, you should feel free to reinvent the code to suit your own taste.

REFERENCES

[Duchaineau] Duchaineau, M., M. Wolinski, D. Sigeti, M. Miller, C. Aldrich, and M. Mineev-Weinstein. "ROAMing Terrain: Real-time Optimally Adapting Meshes" (available online at *www.llnl.gov/graphics/ROAM*).

[Snook] Snook, G. "Simplified Terrain Using Interlocking Tiles." *Game Programming Gems* 2. Charles River Media, Inc., 2001.

[Ulrich] Ulrich, Thatcher. "Chunked LOD" (available online at *http://tulrich.com/geekstuff/chunklod.html*).

ACKNOWLEDGMENTS

Special thanks to the folks at Bungie for their support, advice, and patience with the writing of this book, and to Brian Harvey from NVIDIA for additional advice and support.

I

A FOUNDATION IN 3D

To build an engine from the ground up, we need to start with a good foundation. In this part, we introduce the latest advancements in DirectX 9.0 and take a thorough look at the DirectX sample framework provided with the SDK. For simplicity's sake, we will be building our engine on top of these classes provided by Microsoft. In addition, we will look at the Direct3D Extension Library (D3DX), which is also provided as part of the DirectX 9.0 SDK. This utility library satisfies our basic needs for a 3D math library, and provides useful methods for loading and maintaining our game resources.

In examining DirectX 9.0, we will also take an in-depth look at the High Level Shader Language (HLSL). HLSL is a C-like development language that allows shader authors to write vertex and pixel shaders without needing to resort to low-level shader assembly code. This is a great way to introduce 3D shader programming for today's graphics hardware. This book will focus on the use of HLSL rather than the assembly-language methods because of the ease of use and readability it provides.

For readers who want to learn the low-level assembly languages, HLSL can also serve as a useful learning aid. The command-line HLSL compiler provided with the DirectX SDK (`fxc.exe`) can convert HLSL programs into assembly language files using the `/Fc` command-line option. By coding in HLSL and viewing the corresponding assembly code, readers should be able to gain insight into these languages with the help of the DirectX SDK documentation. Periodic conversion to assembly is also a great way to monitor the efficiency of the HLSL code we will be writing.

Working with the DirectX sample framework and D3DX allows us to get our engine up and running quickly. However, while these libraries are suitable for use within a retail product, they are designed for general use and might sacrifice speed in favor of flexibility under some circumstances. When building a retail application using our terrain engine, we might discover that knowledge about our application's content or target platform might allow us to cut corners, or achieve additional speed using hand-written replacements for D3DX components. To account for this eventuality, we will build our own library atop D3DX and the sample framework to provide our own customized interface. If we later discover that our needs differ from the support provided by the Microsoft libraries, this degree of separation will allow us to write our own custom internals without having to change the high-level interfaces.

In addition to the source code built on top of the D3D sample framework and D3DX libraries, we also provide our own low-level library of utility functions and helpful classes. These core libraries provide essential interfaces for manipulating numeric values, working with floating-point numbers, and allocating memory. In addition, we also provide a set of debug and profile classes that make the coding process much easier. Together with good coding practices, these debug and profile classes will help uncover any bugs within the code before they become a problem.

ON THE CD

These support functions and classes, called the Core Library Components, can be found on the CD-ROM that accompanies this book. Their construction is straightforward, and well documented within the source code. Therefore, we will not be going over their use within the book in any detail. This allows us to devote more of our time to the task at hand: building a robust 3D terrain engine. As you encounter these classes within the source code, refer to the corresponding source code files for a better understanding of their functionality. Appendix A, "Gaia Utility Classes," also provides an overview of some of the more common utility classes, while Appendix B, "Floating-Point Tricks," explains some of the floating-point exploitation used within portions of the game engine.

Before completing this part of the book, we will have constructed all the required components for our first demo application. This application is a model viewing utility that can load models in the common Direct3D X file format (*.X), attach textures, and view animations. It also provides the ability to load and view D3DX effect files (*.fx) that contain the HLSL shaders we will be writing.

GETTING STARTED WITH DIRECTX 9.0 AND D3DX

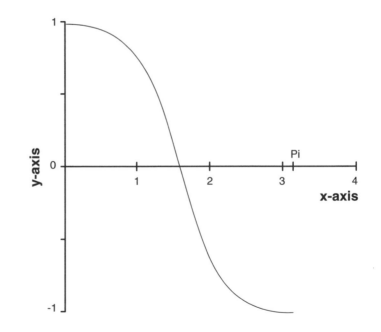

For readers who are new to programming 3D graphics on the Microsoft Windows platform, DirectX is a high-performance, low-level library that provides an application programming interface (API) to the underlying multimedia hardware. DirectX is built from components designed to speak directly to key pieces of hardware within the PC. For this engine, we are mainly concerned with only one of these components, DirectX Graphics. Moreover, we will be dealing specifically with the 3D functionality of DirectX Graphics, known commonly as Direct3D. Additional DirectX interfaces exist for reading user input, generating audio, and providing network connections, but these are not used within this book.

Readers are assumed to have a general familiarity with DirectX before progressing through this book. While we provide a brief synopsis of DirectX and the components we will be using, readers might need to investigate the documentation provided with the DirectX 9.0 SDK for a more detailed background on DirectX and 3D programming in general. Once the SDK is installed, this documentation is readily available from the Windows Start menu.

SETTING UP VISUAL STUDIO.NET

When the DirectX 9.0 SDK is installed onto a development machine, it will automatically update any installations of Microsoft Visual Studio products to use the header and library files provided with the SDK. In addition, Visual Studio.NET users are given additional DirectX debugging tools that are added to the .NET project browser. For alternate compilers, or copies of Microsoft Visual Studio installed after an installation of the DirectX SDK, the DirectX include file folders and library folders must be hand set in order for DirectX programs to compile and link properly.

There is one caveat when using compilers other than Microsoft Visual Studio.Net. The Direct3D Extension Library (D3DX) contains support for Intel Streaming SIMD Extensions (SSE) instructions, but only when compiled with Microsoft Visual Studio.Net (Microsoft Visual C++® 7.0 or greater, to be specific). This is because support for 16-byte aligned memory allocations was not supported under earlier versions of Visual C++ without the installation of an additional patch, known as the processor pack. Because the 16-byte alignment is a critical requirement of many SSE memory-access instructions, these instructions are not enabled within D3DX unless compiler support for aligned memory allocations can be guaranteed. Since the presence of the processor pack cannot be detected, the Intel SSE-aware code within the D3DX library is not enabled unless the preprocessor definition identifying Microsoft Visual C++ compilers is set to denote version 7.0 or higher.

If you are working with a non-Microsoft compiler, or if you are using an earlier version of Microsoft Visual C++, you can set this preprocessor definition yourself to enable the SSE support within the D3DX library. However, this should only be done when you are certain that 16-byte aligned memory allocations are supported by your compiler via the non-standard `__declspec(align(16))` statement used by D3DX. See your compiler documentation if you are uncertain of support for this alignment feature. Once verified, you can add the following preprocessor definition to your makefile or project settings to mimic the presence of the Visual C++ 7.0 compiler and enable Intel SSE support within the D3DX library.

```
#define _MSC_VER 1300 // mimic the presence of VC 7.0
```

The SDK dependencies reside in two key folders, named `Include` and `Lib`. These folders contain the header files required for compilation of a DirectX product and the libraries files required for linking, respectively. Both of these folders can be found within the folder where the DirectX SDK was installed. For example, if the SDK was installed in its default path, `c:\DXSDK`, the folders required would be `c:\DXSDK\Include` and `c:\DXSDK\Lib`. Setting up your compiler and linker to use these folders is a matter of adding their paths to the compiler's list of directories to search for content. See your compiler's documentation for details on adding these folders to the proper search paths. It is recommended that these folders appear first in their respective search chains. For Microsoft Visual Studio users, these instructions are provided within the DirectX SDK help file under the heading "Compiling DirectX Samples and Other DirectX Applications." The HTML file `dxreadme.htm`, located in the root folder of the SDK, also contains information on setting up DirectX for use with your operating system and compiler.

THE DIRECT3D SAMPLE APPLICATION FRAMEWORK

To provide a common foundation for all of the sample programs included with the DirectX SDK, Microsoft provides a set of simple utility classes upon which all of the DirectX samples are built. While these framework classes were not necessarily intended for use within retail products such as a game engine, they contain a core set of application-hosting classes that can handle the needs of most programs. These classes handle the mundane setup routines for DirectX, including enumerating hardware video devices, and determining the display modes and feature sets they support. They also provide an interface to the Windows operating system that relieves us of the burden associated with handling incoming window messages and smoothly transitioning from windowed to full-screen display modes. While we do not assume that the entire sample framework is an optimal and efficient means to produce a retail product, we can certainly endorse the use of the elements we plan to employ.

Our engine also makes use of the sample framework for setting up a basic DirectX-enabled application, manipulating files, and providing additional rendering support. The individual source code files of the D3D application framework have been copied into the source code folders provided with the sample engine. This was done to ensure that the sample engine would compile and link even if future versions of the DirectX SDK are installed. However, as updates to the DirectX SDK are released, the sample framework files copied into the engine source code folders might need to be updated to take full advantage of any new additions to the DirectX SDK.

The sample framework contains the file pairs listed in Table 1.1, which also shows the functionality provided within each file set. These files are included with the SDK installation folder in the `Samples\C++\Common` subfolder.

As shown in Table 1.1, we do not intend to make use of all the files in the D3D sample framework. For example, the mesh-loading functions provided by `D3DFile.h` and `D3DFile.cpp` are of no use to us. We will be loading our own data resources using a customized extension of the `.X` file format through D3DX, which we will cover later. This loading scheme will feed into our own classes for storing and displaying mesh information, so the objects provided by `D3DFile` are not needed. In addition, we use the text display capabilities provided by the `CD3DFont` class only to output debug information to screen. Should our application require a true text display, we would most likely want to devise our own method for peak efficiency. This is especially true of the 3D text display capabilities provided by `CD3DFont`, which are of no use to our application.

For simplicity's sake, we will use the same display mode dialog box used by all D3D sample applications for our engine. A retail product would most likely create its own interface for setting display mode options, but we have no need of custom interface screens for our exploration of terrain rendering. Therefore, we will make use of the `D3DSettings` files for this iteration of the engine. Using the `CD3DSettingsDialog` class does imply that we must also include the file `D3DRes.h`, which contains the resource definitions for the dialog box used, and copy the template for the dialog box

TABLE 1.1 Files Provided as Part of the Microsoft DirectX Samples Framework

FILE PAIR (.H AND .CPP)	FUNCTIONALITY PROVIDED
D3DApp	Contains the CD3DApplication class, providing the overall framework for an application using Direct3D.
D3DEnumeration	Contains the class CD3DEnumeration, an object designed to query resident video hardware and report a set of display modes and features supported.
D3DFile	A set of classes for loading and displaying CD3DMesh objects. Our application does not make use of these files.
D3DFont	Houses the CD3DFont class, written to enable easy output of 2D text over the 3D scene. Our engine uses this for debug purposes.
D3DSettings	Provides the CD3DSettings and CD3DSettingsDialog classes. These provide a method to identify the current display settings of the application and display the dialog box used by DirectX samples to change display modes.
D3DUtil	A set of utility functions for Direct3D samples to use, including a simple camera class, CD3DCamera, and a user input device called CD3DArcBall.
DXUtil	A host of useful DirectX utilities, including string manipulation functions, Registry access functions, and a simple, resizable array class CArrayList.

ON THE CD

into the resource file of our application. This is already done within the sample code provided on the accompanying CD-ROM.

The most important class we will be using is CD3DApplication. This class provides the backbone of the D3D sample framework. If you have investigated the sample programs included with the DirectX SDK, then you are already somewhat familiar with this class. All application-hosting facilities are provided here, from creating the main window and managing its message pump, to interrogating the host video card for display mode and feature support through the CD3DEnumeration class. This class also contains the central loop of the application, which is responsible for reading incoming messages from Windows and calling out to your application-specific code to update and render the scene as needed.

CD3DApplication is also user-extendable, which is why it is so useful to us. Certain member functions of the class are declared as virtual functions, allowing a programmer to derive an application-specific class from CD3DApplication and overload these members for product-specific functionality. Most, if not all, of the D3D samples are built in this manner; overloading the virtual members of `CD3DApplication` to focus on the key features the samples want to showcase. Our application is no different, as we will see a few chapters down the road as we build our own instance of `CD3DApplication` to host our engine.

While we might only need to work with the `CD3DApplication` interface directly, there are a few more framework classes used behind the scenes. Understanding the functionality of these classes provides great insight into DirectX, and can stand alone as a tutorial for the use of the DirectX SDK in general. The most notable of these classes is the `CD3DEnumeration` class mentioned earlier. For readers who are new to DirectX, this class provides a set of functions to interrogate the resident video hardware and build a list of the display modes supported. Enumeration of display modes is a key step in setting up a DirectX graphics environment. Reading through the functionality provided by this class is an excellent tutorial for enumerating these display modes.

USING THE D3DX MATH LIBRARY

As stated earlier, we will be using D3DX to provide the necessary math functions for our engine. Making use of the D3DX math library requires a working knowledge of essential 3D math topics. These include vector mathematics, the use of matrices, and quaternion rotation. A basic understanding of trigonometry is also useful when working with angles and vectors. In truth, while complex mathematics can certainly be used to augment a game, only a few key concepts need to be understood to build a basic engine.

We will provide a brief review of basic trigonometry, vectors, matrices, and quaternion rotation. The DirectX SDK documentation provides introductory information on these topics for readers who require more background reading. The recommended reading list in Appendix D, "Recommended Reading," also provides a listing of books, periodicals, and Web references for 3D math background information.

To anyone getting started in 3D engine development, this might seem like an inexhaustible amount of complex mathematics to learn. It doesn't help that people well versed in mathematics seem to have a hard time breaking the concepts down into an easy-to-understand form. Many times, academically minded authors will use formulas to express an idea, rather than the idea itself. This can be intimidating for a reader who is not accustomed to such notation. Every time a formula appears, the reader must stop and dissect each one in order to follow along.

For example, calculating the average for a set of numbers can be expressed as:

$$m = \frac{1}{n} \sum_{i=1}^{n} V_i \quad \text{For } n \text{ source values } \mathbf{V}$$

Is that really more useful than simply stating the process itself?

"Add all the source values together and divide the result by the number of source values."

Throughout this book, we provide you with equations that perform key calculations for our geometry and shading operations. Wherever possible, we break down these equations into a more readable explanation.

THE DIRECT3D COORDINATE SYSTEM

Before we can explore 3D math and geometry, we need to put everything in a uniform context. That is, we need to define the 3D space we will be using so we can be sure that the various math and geometry topics we cover will share a consistent basis. We do this using a Cartesian coordinate system. Cartesian coordinate systems are nothing more than a convention to represent space in terms of a set of axes. The axes converge at a single point, known as the *origin*, allowing the axes to define a numbering system that can be used to state locations in the defined space. This sounds more complicated than it really is.

We use coordinate systems for many common programming operations, perhaps without realizing it. Anytime we state a position as a set of *x* and *y* values to specify a horizontal and vertical position, we are using a coordinate system. Drawing pixels to the screen, or placing text on a Windows device context using the `TextOut` function, makes use of a 2D Cartesian coordinate system. In both cases, positions are stated as *x*-axis and *y*-axis distances from the origin. These often relate to the horizontal and vertical positions within the destination. Figure 1.1 shows a sample 2D coordinate system, and a point located by its *x* and *y* axis values.

When moving into three dimensions, there are two options. Given a 2D coordinate system of *x* and *y* axes, there are two possible ways to place a third axis, *z*. Using the system shown in Figure 1.1, where arrows are used to show the positive direction of the axes, the *z*-axis could either be an arrow pointing up at you, or away from you. These are called right-handed and left-handed versions of the 3D coordinate system.

The handedness idea is a very confusing way to state the two possible orientations of the *z*-axis. It was intended as a helpful way to remember the configurations using your fingers. By holding the fingers of your left hand a certain way, you can represent the left-handed coordinate system.

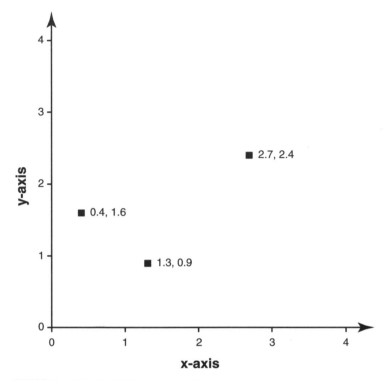

FIGURE 1.1   A Simple 2D Cartesian coordinate system.

The right-handed coordinate system can be shown using the fingers of your right hand. However, different texts present different hand positions and ways to position the fingers of each hand. Figure 1.2 shows the two common hand positions used to remember the coordinate systems. In this example, the y-axis is grasped with the thumb on the positive side. The direction that the fingers curve around the y-axis matches the rotation from the z-axis to the x-axis.

An even sillier way to remember the coordinate handedness is to picture the 2D system shown in Figure 1.1, where the positive x-axis points to the right and positive y-axis points up. Now imagine the right-handed version of the z-axis pointing up from the surface of the page. The right-handed z-axis vector is pointing directly toward you, and anything traveling in the positive z direction is headed *right* at you. The left-handed z-axis would be pointing deeper into the page, or away from you. In a sense, anything traveling along the positive direction of this z-axis has *left* you behind. Yes, it might be even stranger than using hand gestures to remember the right- versus left-handed coordinate systems, but it works.

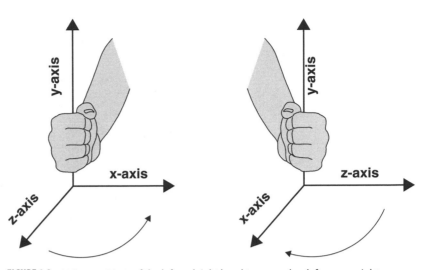

FIGURE 1.2   Using positions of the left and right hand to remember left- versus right-handed 3D coordinate systems.

To add even more confusion, most academic books use the right-handed coordinate system, while graphics APIs such as DirectX use the left-handed coordinate system. This is because showing a 3D coordinate system in print is more intuitive when drawn with the z-axis pointing toward the user. In practice, it is more intuitive to have positive z values traveling away from the 3D camera within a 3D engine. This way, as an object's z position increases, it travels farther away from the viewer. For this reason, graphics APIs will often invert the z-axis to point into the screen and use the left-handed system. This book works in the left-handed coordinate system, making it identical to the format used within DirectX.

D3DX VECTORS AND POINTS

With the coordinate system defined, we can examine two of the basic building blocks for 3D objects provided by D3DX: points and vectors. In D3DX, points and vectors are synonymous and both are represented using the D3DXVECTOR classes. To better understand the functionality of these classes, we will examine points and vectors and some of the key concepts used to manipulate them within 3D space.

Using the 3D coordinate system, a point in 3D space is defined by its distance from the origin along the x-, y-, and z-axes. This means that the position for any point can be represented as three values, which we call the x, y, and z positions of the point. In formulas, points are often represented as italic, uppercase letters such as P or Q. The individual axis values of a point are referenced by a subscript, as in P_x, P_y, or P_z.

A vector is similar to a point in many ways, but represents a different idea. Vectors represent a direction from the origin, and are said to have a magnitude equal to their distance from the origin. Although they are stored in the same manner as points (using three values to denote distances along the x-, y-, and z-axes), a vector and a point represent different things. Figure 1.3 shows a point and a vector, each with identical values for its three axes. The point defines a specific location in space, and the vector defines a direction of travel from the origin to that point.

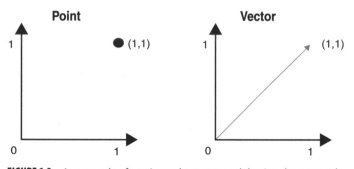

FIGURE 1.3   An example of a point and a vector, each having the same values for x and y.

However, although points and vectors are different, they adhere to the same principles and are stored in the same manner. In fact, it can be argued that a point is the destination of a vector, and that the two are essentially equal. This is why some text and graphics APIs (DirectX included) will use the terms *points* and *vectors* interchangeably.

NORMALIZING VECTORS

Recall that a vector can be considered as a direction from the origin. This direction also has a distance, which is equal to the length of the vector. The vector length is also referred to as the *magnitude* of the vector, and is often written using the absolute value brackets around the name of the vector. The length or magnitude of a vector is computed with the formula shown in Equation 1.1.

$$\|\mathbf{V}\| = \sqrt{\left(V_x^2 + V_y^2 + V_z^2\right)} \qquad (1.1)$$

Simply put, this equates to adding together the squares of all the components, and taking the square root of that sum. A vector is said to be normalized when it has a magnitude of one unit. For this to happen, the sum of all the squared components must also be 1, since the square root of 1 is 1.

Normalized vectors are often called *unit vectors*, because they are one unit long. To normalize a vector, it must be scaled to unit length. To perform the scaling, simply compute the magnitude of the vector using Equation 1.1, and divide each component by this value. This scales the vector to unit length. D3DX also provides a handy method to perform this operation on 2D or 3D vectors using the functions `D3DXVec2Normalize` and `D3DXVec3Normalize`, respectively.

THE DOT PRODUCT

The dot product is provided by D3DX for 2D and 3D vectors as the functions `D3DXVec2Dot` and `D3DXVec3Dot`. However, the dot product is a powerful operation that we will use constantly in our engine, vertex and pixel shaders. Therefore, we will take a moment to explore what the dot product actually is and why it is so useful.

Dot products are based on the directional relationship between two vectors with respect to their lengths. As a formula, the dot product is stated as the cosine of the angle between two vectors, multiplied by both of their magnitudes. In the following equations, the vertical lines placed around a vector mean that the desired value is the magnitude of the vector (the value found using Equation 1.1). The angle between two vectors, expressed in radians, is depicted by the Greek letter alpha (α) as shown in Equation 1.2.

$$\mathbf{P} \bullet \mathbf{Q} = \|P\|\|Q\|\cos\alpha \qquad (1.2)$$

However, the actual dot product value can be found without the cosine function. The dot product of two vectors can also be found by multiplying together the matching components of each vector, and adding the results. Equation 1.3 shows this alternate formula for the dot product.

$$\mathbf{P} \bullet \mathbf{Q} = \left(P_x * Q_x\right) + \left(P_y * Q_y\right) + \left(P_z * Q_z\right) \qquad (1.3)$$

By combining the two equations, we can derive an equation to compute the angle between two vectors. First, we combine the two equations. Then, we can isolate the angle value on the left side of the equation. Equations 1.4 through 1.6 show this progression.

$$\|\mathbf{P}\|\|\mathbf{Q}\|\cos\alpha = \left(P_x * Q_x\right) + \left(P_y * Q_y\right) + \left(P_z * Q_z\right) \tag{1.4}$$

$$\cos\alpha = \frac{\left(P_x * Q_x\right) + \left(P_y * Q_y\right) + \left(P_z * Q_z\right)}{\|\mathbf{P}\|\|\mathbf{Q}\|} \tag{1.5}$$

$$\alpha = \arccos\left(\frac{\left(P_x * Q_x\right) + \left(P_y * Q_y\right) + \left(P_z * Q_z\right)}{\|\mathbf{P}\|\|\mathbf{Q}\|}\right) \tag{1.6}$$

For any two vectors, Equation 1.6 will compute the angle between them in radians. However, we don't always need to do so much work to find this angle. When both vectors are normalized, their magnitudes are 1. When this is true, the division on the right-hand side of Equation 1.6 is unnecessary, leaving us with a few multiplies, additions, and one nasty arccosine.

The cosine has an interesting property that allows us to skip the arccosine computation in many cases. The cosine arc from 0 to *Pi* travels between 1 and –1, as shown in Figure 1.4. Using this information, we can deduce some basic information about the angle without performing any trigonometry.

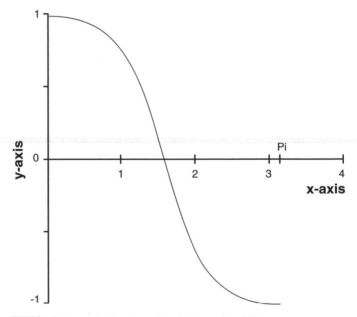

FIGURE 1.4   A graph of cosine values between 0 and Pi.

When two vectors are parallel and facing the same direction, their dot product will be 1. We know this because the angle between them would be zero, and the cosine of zero is 1. Therefore, as the dot product of two vectors approaches 1, the angle between them is approaching zero, when the two vectors will overlap.

According to Figure 1.4, we also know that when the angle between two vectors is one-half *Pi* (90 degrees), the dot product of the two vectors will be equal to zero. Again, this is known because the dot product is equal to the cosine of the angle, and the cosine of one-half *Pi* is zero. Also notice that angles greater than one-half *Pi* will yield negative cosine values and therefore negative dot products. When two vectors are completely opposite, their dot product will be –1, the cosine of *Pi*. We combine all these properties in Table 1.2.

TABLE 1.2   Properties of the Vector Dot Product

DOT PRODUCT	ANGLE IMPLIED BETWEEN VECTORS
1	The angle between the vectors is zero.
0	The vectors are perpendicular to each other.
–1	The angle between the vectors is Pi (180 degrees).

One final property of the dot product is its ability to project one vector onto another. When one of the vectors in the dot product is a unit vector, the dot product will produce a value that is equal to the projected length of the second vector along the unit vector. Figure 1.5 makes this more apparent.

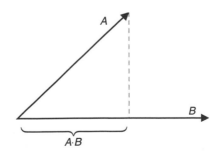

FIGURE 1.5   The dot product of an arbitrary vector **A** with a unit vector **B** produces a result that is the length of **A** projected onto **B**.

The projection is again provided by the cosine. A cosine is nothing more than the length of the adjacent side of a right triangle. Referring again to Figure 1.5, we can see that the two vectors do indeed form a right triangle when the third side is considered as the path of the projection (perpendicular to the unit vector). The side adjacent to the angle formed by the two vectors is the side containing the unit vector, allowing us to reinterpret the cosine of the angle as the length of this side.

So, how is this useful? Projecting arbitrary vectors onto unit vectors is exactly how points are rotated in 3D space. Given a point in the world, and a set of unit vectors axes representing the desired coordinate system to rotate the point into, simply projecting the point onto each axis will perform the rotation. Projecting a point onto a unit vector also provides a method to compute distances between points and planes. Given a unit vector that is normal to a plane (i.e., perpendicular to the plane), calculating the distance between a point and the plane is the same as projecting the point onto the plane normal.

THE CROSS PRODUCT

As with the dot product, D3DX provides functions for computing cross products (`D3DXVec2Cross` and `D3DXVec3Cross`) that we could simply use, but a deeper understanding of the cross product is essential for some of the shading operations we will be performing later in the book. Therefore, we take a moment to dissect the cross product and understand its use.

Unlike the dot product, the cross product does not yield a single, scalar result. Instead, the cross product of two vectors produces a third vector. This third vector is perpendicular to the plane formed by the first two vectors, and has a magnitude equal to the area formed by their parallelogram. The cross product can be computed as shown in Equation 1.7.

$$\mathbf{P} \times \mathbf{Q} = \left\langle P_y Q_z - P_z Q_y, \quad P_z Q_x - P_x Q_z, \quad P_x Q_y - P_y Q_x \right\rangle \tag{1.7}$$

However, the plane defined by vectors **P** and **Q** has two sides. So, which side is the perpendicular vector pointing in? The result of the cross product is dependent on the order of the source vectors. Cross products follow the right-hand rule, so computing the cross product of P and Q will result in the right-hand perpendicular vector. Recall the right- and left-handed systems shown in Figure 1.2. Given two axis vectors, **X** and **Y**, the third vector, **Z**, could be determined using left-hand or right-hand construction rules. Computing the cross product of the x-axis with the y-axis will yield the right-handed z-axis. Reversing the order of the x-axis and y-axis will result in the left-handed z-axis.

D3DX MATRICES

Matrices are an essential part of any 3D engine. They allow multiple vector operations to be combined into a single entity. These entities provide a convenient shorthand for a group of equations, and can be concatenated with other matrices to easily combine an even greater number of equations. Explaining the underlying functionality of matrices is beyond the scope of this book. Instead, we will cover how matrices are used for 3D transformations within the engine. For more detailed information on matrices, refer to the recommended reading section provided in Appendix D, or consult the DirectX SDK documentation.

Matrices are defined as a two-dimensional grid of numbers. This grid can be of any size, but for computer graphics, we use only a few common dimensions. The values held within the matrix are numbered by their row and column positions. In most textbooks, the values in the matrix are numbered in row-column pairs. Figure 1.6 shows the general format of a matrix.

$$
\begin{matrix}
m_{11} & m_{12} & \mathsf{L} & m_{1w} \\
m_{21} & m_{22} & \mathsf{L} & m_{1w} \\
\mathsf{M} & \mathsf{M} & \mathsf{O} & \mathsf{M} \\
m_{h1} & m_{h2} & \mathsf{L} & m_{hw}
\end{matrix}
$$

FIGURE 1.6 The general format of a WxH matrix.

Matrices provide a convenient way to manipulate points in 3D space. By arraigning values in a matrix, a model built of points can be moved, rotated, or scaled in any way desired. Because matrices are shorthand for coordinate systems, we can use them to move objects around in the world. Moving an object simply means to relocate the origin of its local coordinate system. By passing the points of a model through a matrix, a set of affine transformations (rotation, scaling, and position) can be applied to the points of the model, moving it to the coordinate system defined in the matrix.

Before we continue, we need to understand how matrices are stated within this book. There are two different ways to represent matrices in print, and some authors prefer one to the other. In this book, the matrices are listed within their grids, in left-to-right reading order, in exactly the same order in which they are stored in RAM. This is different from some popular graphics programming books that choose to print the matrices in one manner within the book, and store them in memory using the transpose of the printed order (i.e., rows and columns switched).

For example, the 4x4 grid pattern for a transformation matrix is often displayed in academic books as having the three coordinate system axes (right, up, and forward) listed as columns, followed by a final column containing the translation component for each axis. When this format is used, vectors are also treated as columns.

$$\mathbf{M} = \begin{bmatrix} Right_x & Up_x & Forward_x & T_x \\ Right_y & Up_y & Forward_y & T_y \\ Right_z & Up_z & Forward_z & T_z \\ 0 & 0 & 0 & 1 \end{bmatrix} \quad \mathbf{V} = \begin{bmatrix} x \\ y \\ z \\ w \end{bmatrix}$$

This is called the *column-major format*, and is probably the most common way to see matrices listed in print. However, it is not the most efficient order to store matrices within system memory. To take full advantage of the Intel SSE instruction set, for example, it is far more convenient to store them in the transposed order. Therefore, most 3D math libraries will store a matrix in system memory using an order that is the transpose of the printed matrix. In this format, single vectors are treated as rows. This is sometimes called the *row-major format*.

$$\mathbf{M} = \begin{bmatrix} Right_x & Right_y & Right_z & 0 \\ Up_x & Up_y & Up_z & 0 \\ Forward_x & Forward_y & Forward_z & 0 \\ T_x & T_y & T_z & 1 \end{bmatrix} \quad \mathbf{V} = \begin{bmatrix} x & y & z & w \end{bmatrix}$$

In this book, we maintain a 1:1 relationship between the matrix format used in the book, and the layout of the matrix in system memory. The row major format is used in the remainder of the book. This is far more intuitive, even if it does mean that matrix information printed in other books might need to be mentally transposed by the reader in order to line up with the matrix format used here. Many popular books on computer graphics, such as *3D Computer Graphics* by Alan Watt [Watt], use the row-major format, as does the DirectX SDK documentation, so we are not alone in using this method.

The main operation we perform with matrices is matrix multiplication. Before we begin discussing how matrices are useful, we state the process for multiplying them together. For two 4 x4 matrices, **M** and **N**, the result of their multiplication is given as Equation 1.8.

$$\mathbf{M} = \begin{bmatrix} A & B & C & D \\ E & F & G & H \\ I & J & K & L \\ M & N & O & P \end{bmatrix} \qquad \mathbf{N} = \begin{bmatrix} a & b & c & d \\ e & f & g & h \\ i & j & k & l \\ m & n & o & p \end{bmatrix}$$

$$\mathbf{M} * \mathbf{N} =$$

$$\begin{bmatrix} (Aa+Be+Ci+Dm) & (Ab+Bf+Cj+Dn) & (Ac+Bg+Ck+Do) & (Ad+Bh+Cl+Dp) \\ (Ea+Fe+Gi+Hm) & (Eb+Ff+Gj+Hn) & (Ec+Fg+Gk+Ho) & (Ed+Fh+Gl+Hp) \\ (Ia+Je+Ki+Lm) & (Ib+Jf+Kj+Ln) & (Ic+Jg+Kk+Lo) & (Id+Jh+Kl+Lp) \\ (Ma+Ne+Oi+Pm) & (Mb+Nf+Oj+Pn) & (Mc+Ng+Ok+Po) & (Md+Nh+Ol+Pp) \end{bmatrix} \quad (1.8)$$

It looks like a mess, but it is much simpler than it appears. For each location in the destination matrix, the result is the dot product of the row position within **M** and the column position within **N**. For example, the lower-left corner of the result matrix (column 1, row 4) is the dot product of row number 4 from matrix **M** and column number 1 from matrix **N**.

To transform a point (or vector) through a matrix, we simply treat the axes information within the point as a one-dimensional matrix. Standard matrix multiplication rules can then be applied to compute the new point. The point is treated like a single-row matrix, using Equation 1.9 to compute the result of each vector component.

$$\mathbf{P} = \begin{bmatrix} X & Y & Z & W \end{bmatrix} \qquad \mathbf{M} = \begin{bmatrix} a & b & c & d \\ e & f & g & h \\ i & j & k & l \\ m & n & o & p \end{bmatrix}$$

$$P'_x = (Xa+Ye+Zi+Wm)$$
$$P'_y = (Xb+Yf+Zj+Wn)$$
$$P'_z = (Xc+Yg+Zk+Wo)$$
$$P'_w = (Xd+Yh+Zl+Wp) \quad (1.9)$$

Points and vectors are typically considered to have three components: x, y, and z. To transform the vector or point with a 4x4 matrix, a fourth component, w, must be added. This adds an interesting property. As shown in Equation 1.9, the value for w controls how much the final row of matrix **M** affects the computed point. Each of the row values (m, n, o and p) are multiplied by w in order to contribute to the result. This row of the matrix contains the translation portion of the affine transformation.

The w component controls whether the translation information of a matrix can affect the point during transformation. For points, the additional *w* component is set to 1, allowing the point to be translated by the matrix. For vectors, the *w* component is often set to 0. This only allows the vector to be rotated and scaled by the matrix, not translated away from the origin. Because vectors are considered directions from the origin, allowing them to be translated by a matrix would distort their value. This is a handy trick that we will use when writing functions to transform points and vectors with matrices.

Multiplying matrices that represent affine transformations combines their transformations in the same order in which they were multiplied. For example, if matrix **M** represented a three-unit translation along the *x*-axis, and matrix **N** represented a 90-degree rotation around the *y*-axis, then the result of **M*N** would represent a shift of three units along the *x*-axis, following by the *y*-axis rotation. This process is often called *matrix concatenation*, and it is one of the most appealing reasons for using matrices in 3D.

D3DX provides a set of classes for housing matrices, as well as functions to build and manipulate them. Explanations of each function can be found in the DirectX SDK documentation. One new addition to the D3DX library in DirectX 9.0 is the 16-byte aligned matrix, D3DXMATRIXA16. This matrix provides the 16-byte alignment required by Intel SSE instructions to produce the greatest efficiency. As mentioned at the beginning of the chapter, this functionality is only provided when the application is compiled using Visual C++ 7.0. Under all other circumstances, D3DXMATRIXA16 becomes an alias for the standard D3DXMATRIX class, and no SSE-enabling alignment is provided.

QUATERNION ROTATION

As stated in the DirectX SDK documentation, a quaternion is essentially a four-unit vector whose component values represent a counter-clockwise rotation around a given axis. The values for each component of the quaternion are shown as a group in Equation 1.10. In this set of equations, the quaternion *q* has its values defined by the axis of rotation and a counter-clockwise rotation around that axis, represented by the Greek letter theta (θ).

$$
\begin{aligned}
q.x &= \sin(\theta/2) * \text{axi} \\
q.y &= \sin(\theta/2) * \text{axis.y} \\
q.z &= \sin(\theta/2) * \text{axis.z} \\
q.w &= \cos(\theta/2)
\end{aligned}
\tag{1.10}
$$

The quaternion structure is useful because it can be used to overcome the shortcomings of rotation matrices: storage space, interpolation, and the potential for a phenomenon known as *gimbal lock*. Gimbal lock occurs when two axes of a coordinate system become collinear. This can happen when transformation matrices are built from discreet Euler angles (i.e., separate rotations around each of the three cardinal axes). When this is done incorrectly, one coordinate vector becomes rotated to lie atop another of the coordinate system vectors. Applying further rotations around the free axis will yield no result, giving the appearance of the axis being "locked" or unable to rotate.

The quaternion uses a non-Euler method for storing a rotation about an axis in 3D space. This avoids the potential for gimbal lock to occur. However, it also sacrifices readability, as quaternion data cannot be visualized by most human beings. A quaternion is a complex number containing both real and imaginary numbers, a full explanation of which is beyond the scope of this book. Appendix D lists ample reading material containing complete discussions of quaternion rotations and the algebra that can be used to manipulate them.

The gain in storage space when using quaternion rotations is immediately evident. The quaternion represents a complete 3D rotation in four values, whereas a 3D rotation matrix would require nine. Although the quaternion must be converted to a suitable matrix format for use within the DirectX render pipeline, models that contain a large amount of rotation data for animation purposes can reduce their size dramatically by using quaternion representation for storage.

Like matrices, rotations can be concatenated by simply multiplying two quaternion structures. However, the quaternion representation also provides a method for interpolating between two rotations. This interpolation, called Spherical Linear Interpolation (SLERP), is far easier and more efficient to compute than interpolating between two rotation matrices. For keyframe animation of a skeletal hierarchy, quaternion data is essential for optimum performance due to the large amount of interpolation required between the various poses of the skeleton.

D3DX provides a quaternion object, `D3DXQuaternion`, and a set of functions to multiply, manipulate, and interpolate between them. Functions are also provided to convert rotations between matrix and quaternion formats. Documentation for the use of each function can be found within the SDK.

REFERENCES

[Watt] Watt, A. *3D Computer Graphics, Second Edition*. Addison-Wesley Publishers Ltd., 1993.

FUNDAMENTAL 3D OBJECTS

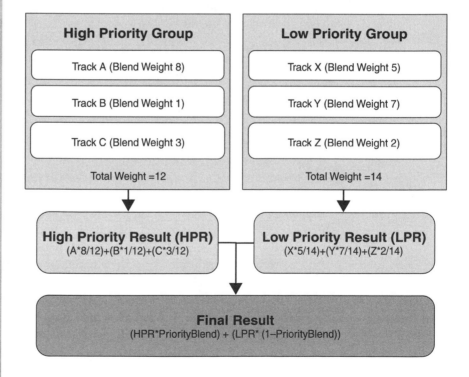

High Priority Group	Low Priority Group
Track A (Blend Weight 8)	Track X (Blend Weight 5)
Track B (Blend Weight 1)	Track Y (Blend Weight 7)
Track C (Blend Weight 3)	Track Z (Blend Weight 2)
Total Weight =12	Total Weight =14

High Priority Result (HPR)
(A*8/12)+(B*1/12)+(C*3/12)

Low Priority Result (LPR)
(X*5/14)+(Y*7/14)+(Z*2/14)

Final Result
(HPR*PriorityBlend) + (LPR* (1–PriorityBlend))

With a solid understanding of the Direct3D sample framework and the Direct3D extension library, we are ready to dig in a little deeper and discuss some of the D3DX features we will be taking advantage of in our engine. In this chapter, we discuss some of the D3DX class objects we will be using throughout our engine to load, render, and save our world models. We also discuss the two major file formats associated with Direct3D, and the objects used to receive their data. These are the Direct3D effect object and file format (.fx files), and the Direct3D X files (.x file extension). Finally, we look into creating hierarchies of these objects using the D3DXFRAME and D3DXMESHCONTAINER structures for composite objects and skeletal animation.

The ability to load model and shader information from disk is a primary need for all 3D engines. While we could devise our own proprietary format, this additional effort is not necessary given the flexibility of the file formats provided by DirectX. We also gain the use of tools already available for manipulating these DirectX files. These include exporters for most popular 3D modeling and animation packages, and tools provided with the DirectX SDK for editing and viewing .x model files and .fx effect files. Direct3D also affords us the ability to extend the X file format with our own data. This feature provides the flexibility we need, and keeps the X file format viable into the future.

BASIC DIRECT3D OBJECTS

Three basic elements are required to display an object in 3D: the model itself, the material that describes the model surface, and an optional texture map to cover the model with. Lighting and shading methods aside, these are the basic building blocks of 3D model rendering. D3DX provides helpful objects to represent each of these elements, along with a host of functions to load, manipulate, and use each one.

The tutorials that come with the DirectX SDK provide a useful introduction to the D3DX class objects used to represent these basic elements. A brief overview of each is provided here, but readers needing additional information should refer to the SDK documentation.

D3DXMaterial is by far the most succinct of the three objects. It is no more than a structure containing the D3DMATERIAL9 properties of a surface (information regarding the various hues of light reflected from the objects surface), along with an optional filename for a texture to cover the surface of the model with. Having only one texture reference makes this object a little too antiquated for our needs, but we still employ it as a storage structure for the basic lighting properties of a model.

The IDirect3DTexture9 object provides an interface to manipulate texture resources and use them during rendering. The D3DX library contains a set of functions to make working with IDirect3DTexture9 objects much easier for the programmer. One such function is D3DXCreateTextureFromFile, which can import texture information from a variety of bitmap file formats, including .bmp, .dds, .dib, .jpg, .png, and .tga. In addition to the robust file support, the various D3DX texture loading functions can also resize the image and change the color depth using a variety of filters during the import process. The D3DX library also contains a set of texture-related functions for working with 3D volume textures as well as cube environment maps. We will explore these as we dive into advanced rendering methods later in the book.

The ID3DXMesh class is the workhorse of the three. This class contains the geometry information of a model, and the fields that describe the format of the model vertices. D3DX provides several means to load mesh information from the DirectX proprietary file format known as X files. While the basic format of an X file is also rather antiquated, being based on the same one-texture-per-material policy as the D3DXMATERIAL structure, it is a user-extendable file format. We will use this extendibility to save and load our own proprietary data within the X files used by our engine later in the book.

The basic ID3DXMesh class is little more than a container for model vertices, an index buffer used to reference those vertices by polygon, and an optional attribute table that groups sets of polygons by the materials used to draw them. In most cases, the ID3DXMesh class represents the same data storage method you would likely use when creating your own geometry container, and is therefore suitable for most of our 3D engine's needs. In some cases, however, we will find that our terrain geometry does not quite fit into the ID3DXMesh storage method, and we will need to devise our own geometry format. Even when this occurs, we can still make use of the ID3DXMesh as an intermediate format for loading and saving data to disk.

D3DX meshes come in a variety of flavors, each geared toward a specific purpose. The class we have discussed so far is the basic mesh container for static geometry. In addition to this class, D3DX also provides customized classes for simplification meshes, ID3DXSPMESH, and progressive meshes, ID3DXPMESH. Simplification meshes allow the user to reduce the number of faces or vertices a model contains using weight values to control which components of the model are more important than others. As the user requests further reduction of the model, the least important elements are removed. This is a one-time operation that cannot be undone, and is therefore most usable in a stand-alone tool to prepare models for the engine.

Progressive meshes are an alternative to the strict reduction method of simplification meshes. Progressive meshes are based on the View Independent Progressive Mesh method described by Hughes Hoppe [Hoppe]. Hoppe's method records a series of triangle divisions, known as *splits*, which can be used to increase or reduce the complexity of a model in real time. By joining adjacent polygons together and recording their unions, visual complexity of a model can be reduced. By undoing these unions and splitting triangles back into their original form, surface complexity can be restored. These triangle divisions and rejoining operations can be performed iteratively, allowing the model to smoothly transform from high to low definition and back. This allows the same progressive mesh to be used in high detail when near the camera, reducing its complexity as it moves further away from the viewer.

LOADING AND DISPLAYING A MODEL USING D3DX

As shown in the DirectX SDK tutorials, loading and displaying a simple mesh using D3DX is straightforward. For readers unfamiliar with `ID3DXMeshes`, working through the DirectX SDK tutorials is an excellent way to become familiar with these objects. We will outline the basic use of the D3DX object classes here as an overview, but we will not be reiterating the in-depth coverage already provided by the SDK.

Once the application and Direct3D environment have been initialized, using the DirectX sample framework in our case, displaying a mesh is a simple matter of loading the mesh from disk, building the objects needed to render it, and using those objects to display the contents of the mesh.

The first step is to load the mesh from an X file using the D3DX function `D3DXLoadMeshFromFile`. This will load the mesh geometry, and allocate and fill a list of `D3DXMATERIAL` structures used by the mesh. Each material can contain an optional string containing the name of a texture file to load. `D3DXLoadTextureFromFile` can then be used for each valid texture name to load the bitmap data. Assuming that no texture or model geometry conversion is necessary, the data is now ready for rendering.

The simplest method of rendering the mesh is the brute-force approach. In this method, we render any meshes within the scene one at a time, making no effort to batch similar render states or otherwise increase performance through efficient ordering of our render calls. Each mesh is divided internally into *subsets*. A subset is a set of polygons that use the same material properties. Therefore, if an `ID3DXMesh` contains *n* subsets, it must be rendered using the corresponding *n* materials and *n* texture maps created during the loading process. To render a given mesh, we simply loop through the subsets of the mesh, activating the proper textures and setting the active materials. Once these objects are properly activated, we can instruct the mesh to render the given subset geometry using the member function `DrawSubset`.

USING DIRECT3D EFFECT FILES

When building a 3D engine, consideration must be given to the wide variety of hardware available in today's home computers. Rendering procedures that work well on one type of video card might be woefully inefficient, or altogether unsupported on another. The only viable solution is to provide multiple rendering procedures to ensure that your product remains viable across multiple types of hardware. Direct3D effect files provide a way to encapsulate these render methods, allowing multiple techniques to be grouped together into a single file. Each technique contained in the effect file is a high-level abstraction of a given render method, containing the render states required as well as any vertex or pixel shader instructions needed. In this manner, effect files help facilitate backward compatibility while providing a modular approach to defining render methods.

Effect files are nothing more than text files that contain a list of available techniques. Each technique can contain a number of passes, each representing the instructions and resources needed to perform a single rendering procedure. With this hierarchy, the files can be written to contain multiple techniques, one for each class of hardware supported, with each technique being able to contain specific instructions for multiple passes when needed.

The text nature of effect files makes them easy to edit and rapidly prototype. They are compiled at runtime to produce render state and shader instructions specific to the hardware on which they are being executed. Techniques within the effect file can be validated at compilation time to find the best possible technique for a given hardware configuration. This provides a highly modular system, allowing programmers to support multiple hardware configurations and even support products into the future by releasing additional effect files as new hardware becomes available.

Listing 2.1 shows the contents of a simple effect file to illustrate the technique and pass hierarchy. In this example, only texture stages are specified by the effect file for brevity. A more robust effect file might also contain vertex and pixel shader instructions to further control the rendering process of each technique. This sample file is intended to illustrate the use of multiple techniques for hardware support. Many video cards differ in the number of textures they can use in a single pass. Both techniques shown in Listing 2.1 use six textures to generate the same visual effect. The first technique uses all six textures in a single pass, while the second technique uses the same six textures in multiple passes, one of four textures and another of two. As this effect file is compiled for a given hardware platform, the single-pass technique will be deemed valid only if the platform allows six textures per pass. When fewer textures are supported, the first technique will not validate, and the program can be instructed to switch to the second technique instead.

LISTING 2.1   A sample effect file containing single and multipass techniques.

```
// Both of the techniques below use the same
// four textures, which we define using the
// following variable declarations. The program
// will set these variable to point to specific
// D3DTexture9 objects loaded.
texture tex0;
texture tex1;
texture tex2;
texture tex3;

// The first technique renders using all four
// textures at once. Four complete texture
// stages are defined to add the colors
// of all four textures.
technique t0
{
  pass p0
  {
    // all four textures are loaded
    // into the texture input parameters
    Texture[0]   = (tex0);
    Texture[1]   = (tex1);
    Texture[2]   = (tex2);
    Texture[3]   = (tex3);
```

```
        // for the first texture, the
        // color values are used as-is
        ColorOp[0]   = SelectArg1;
        ColorArg1[0] = Texture;

        // for the remaining textures,
        // their color values are Added
        // to the contents of the previous
        // texture channel
        ColorOp[1]   = Add;
        ColorArg1[1] = Texture;
        ColorArg2[1] = Current;

        ColorOp[2]   = Add;
        ColorArg1[2] = Texture;
        ColorArg2[2] = Current;

        ColorOp[3]   = Add;
        ColorArg1[3] = Texture;
        ColorArg2[3] = Current;

        ColorOp[4]   = Disable;
    }
}

// The second technique renders using the textures
// in two passes. One pass renders the first
// two textures, and a second pass renders
// the remaining two. The passes are added
// together in the frame buffer to produce the
// same result as the first technique.
technique t1
{
    // first pass. Draw two of the four textures
    pass p0
    {
        // no blending is performed in this pass
        AlphaBlendEnable = False;

        // four textures are loaded
        // into the texture input parameters
        Texture[0]   = (tex0);
        Texture[1]   = (tex1);
        Texture[2]   = (tex2);
        Texture[3]   = (tex3);
```

```
// for the first texture, the
// color values are used as-is
ColorOp[0]   = SelectArg1;
ColorArg1[0] = Texture;

// the second texture is added to the first
ColorOp[1]   = Add;
ColorArg1[1] = Texture;
ColorArg2[1] = Current;

ColorOp[2]   = Disable;
}

// second pass. Draw the reaming two textures,
// blending the result with the first pass
pass p1
{
  // blend the results of this pass with
  // the first one
  AlphaBlendEnable = True;
  SrcBlend     = One;
  DestBlend    = One;

  // two textures are loaded
  // into the texture input parameters
  Texture[0]   = (tex4);
  Texture[1]   = (tex5);

  // for the first texture, the
  // color values are used as-is
  ColorOp[0]   = SelectArg1;
  ColorArg1[0] = Texture;

  // the second texture is added to the first
  ColorOp[1]   = Add;
  ColorArg1[1] = Texture;
  ColorArg2[1] = Current;

  ColorOp[2]   = Disable;
}

}
```

To make use of an effect file within your program, D3DX provides a simple interface to load and verify the techniques within an effect. The easiest, and most common, way to use effect files is to use one effect file for each render method desired. Each effect file can contain multiple versions of the same render method as individual techniques. More demanding techniques are placed at the top of each file, and versions intended for older, less powerful hardware follow in descending order. This is the manner in which the sample shown in Listing 2.1 is constructed. Setting up your effect files this way allows the D3DX library to load the files and determine the best possible effect that will run on the target hardware.

The two D3DX functions that perform the work are `D3DXCreate EffectFromFile` and `FindNextValidTechnique`. `D3DXCreateEffectFromFile` loads an effect file from disk and compiles it for the application to use. Any errors in the file found during compilation are output via a standard `D3DXBuffer` object. If the compilation succeeds, an `ID3DXEffect` object is constructed, providing an interface to the compiled effect.

To choose the best possible technique within the effect, the member function `FindNextValidTechnique` can be used to step through each of the techniques that validate on the resident hardware. `FindNextValidTechnique` takes a handle to a technique within the file, and searches for the next valid technique that appears after the provided technique. When NULL is used as the input parameter, `FindNextValidTechnique` will search from the top of the file, returning the first valid technique found. If our file contains techniques listed in order from most demanding to least, using `FindNextValidTechnique` in this manner will return the most sophisticated version of our render method that will work on the resident hardware. Listing 2.2 shows a small snippet of code used to load and search an effect file for the best possible technique.

LISTING 2.2   Loading and searching an effect file for the best possible technique.

```
// global variables for the effect
// and the technique in use
LPD3DXEFFECT m_pEffect=0;
D3DXHANDLE m_hTechnique=0;

HRESULT loadEffectAndSetTechnique(
  const char* filename)
{

  // load the effect from the file path
  // provided. In this example, no
  // additional macro definitions or links
```

```
// to include files are necessary
LPD3DXBUFFER pBufferErrors = NULL;
HRESULT result = D3DXCreateEffectFromFile(
  g_d3dDevice,
  filename,
  NULL,
  NULL,
  0,
  NULL,
  &m_pEffect,
  &pBufferErrors );

if( FAILED( result ) )
{
  // here we can examine the pBufferErrors buffer
  // to determine the reason for failure.
  // for now, we just return the error code
  SAFE_RELEASE(pBufferErrors);
  return result;
}

// we are now finished with the error buffer
SAFE_RELEASE(pBufferErrors);

// find the best possible technique to use
// by searching from the top of the effect file
// for the first valid technique.
result = m_pEffect->FindNextValidTechnique(
  NULL,
  &m_hTechnique);

if( FAILED( result ) )
{
  // no valid techniques were found.
  // release the effect interface
  // and report the error
  SAFE_RELEASE(m_pEffect);
  return result;
}

// activate the technique chosen
result = m_pEffect->SetTechnique(m_hTechnique);
if( FAILED( result ) )
{
  // activation failed.
```

```
    // release the effect interface
    // and report the error
    SAFE_RELEASE(m_pEffect);
    return result;
  }

  // the new technique is ready for use
  return D3D_OK;
}
```

Effect files also gain a great deal of flexibility from the various types of vertex and pixel shaders that can be embedded in them. The sample in Listing 2.1 does not contain vertex or pixel shader information, implying that the fixed-function pipeline, the predecessor to programmable shaders, will be used. If desired, pixel and vertex shader source code can be placed directly into the effect file. This allows the programmer to full encapsulate the complete specification for a given render method within an effect file. Pixel and vertex shaders can be written within the effect file using either their respective assembly languages, or the new High-Level Shader Language (HLSL) available in DirectX 9.0. We will explore embedding HLSL shaders in the next chapter.

THE D3DX FRAME AND MESH CONTAINER

Each model in the game world is associated with a transform node. These nodes are essentially matrices that define the coordinate system of the model's vertices. These transform nodes, also called *frames*, allow us to position the model anywhere we want. By chaining these nodes and model together into a hierarchy, larger objects can be assembled and animated by adjusting their transform nodes over time. D3DX provides a handy pair of structures to contain this hierarchy and provide a framework that can later be animated: D3DXFRAME and D3DXMESHCONTAINER.

D3DXFRAME is a simple structure designed to represent a single transform node of a model hierarchy. It contains the transform matrix defining the coordinate system of the node, pointers to the child and sibling D3DXFRAME objects in hierarchy tree, and a pointer to a D3DXMESHCONTAINER. D3DXFRAME also contains a pointer to an optional test name for the frame itself. Frames can be named so that they can later be identified when animations are applied to the hierarchy. The layout of the D3DXFRAME structure is shown at the top of Listing 2.3.

LISTING 2.3   D3DX structures for building a hierarchy of model data.

```
typedef struct _D3DXFRAME
{
    LPTSTR Name;
    D3DXMATRIX TransformationMatrix;
    LPD3DXMESHCONTAINER pMeshContainer;
    struct _D3DXFRAME *pFrameSibling;
    struct _D3DXFRAME *pFrameFirstChild;
} D3DXFRAME, *LPD3DXFRAME;

typedef struct _D3DXMESHCONTAINER
{
    LPTSTR Name;
    D3DXMESHDATA MeshData;
    LPD3DXMATERIAL pMaterials;
    LPD3DXEFFECTINSTANCE pEffects;
    DWORD NumMaterials;
    DWORD *pAdjacency;
    LPD3DXSKININFO pSkinInfo;
    struct _D3DXMESHCONTAINER
      *pNextMeshContainer;
} D3DXMESHCONTAINER, *LPD3DXMESHCONTAINER;
```

The second structure, D3DXMESHCONTAINER, does exactly as its name suggests. The format of this structure is shown at the bottom of Listing 2.3. All ID3DXMESH objects that appear in the hierarchy are stored within D3DXMESHCONTAINER structures, and linked into the tree through the D3DXMESHCONTAINER pointers of the D3DXFRAME structure. The D3DXMESHDATA object held within D3DXMESHCONTAINER contains a pointer to the mesh itself, and an ID code identifying the type of mesh stored. Meshes can be stored as regular ID3DXMesh objects, ID3DXPMesh objects, or ID3DXPatchMesh objects.

The mesh container structure also contains pointers to the data created during the model import process. These include the materials used by the mesh, adjacency information for the model faces, and link to a structure containing data about the optional D3DXEffect object used to render the model itself. A pointer to an ID3DXSkinInfo interface is also provided, allowing the mesh within the container to behave as a skinned mesh. Skinned meshes contain weight and index values per vertex that allow the model to be deformed by multiple D3DXFRAME transform matrices within the hierarchy.

The optional skinning information transforms the linked tree of D3DXFRAME objects into a cohesive skeletal model for animation. With this flexibility, the complete hierarchy can be used as either a traditional parent-child scene graph of connected models, a complete skeletal structure for mesh deformation, or both. Additional flexibility is gained by the final member of the D3DXMESHCONTAINER structure, which is simply a link to another D3DXMESHCONTAINER. This allows multiple mesh containers to be chained to the same D3DXFRAME node, each of which may or may not contain skinning information (see Figure 2.1).

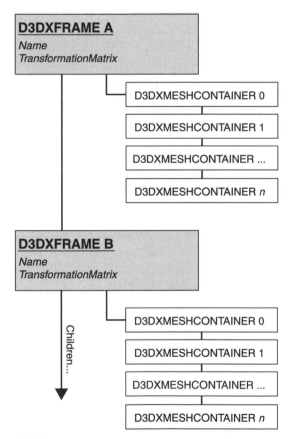

FIGURE 2.1   A sample mesh hierarchy showing skinned and rigid models coexisting on the same skeleton framework.

Building these hierarchies consists of allocating the required data structures, along with the objects they contain, and then linking them together to form the desired tree. The same ID3DXMesh loading procedures we used at the end of Chapter 1, "Getting Started with DirectX 9.0 and D3DX," can be used to read in mesh objects, their materials, and textures. These mesh objects can then be placed in D3DXMESHCONTAINERS within the tree at the desired locations. Using this method, large hierarchies of individual mesh objects can be grouped to create larger entities or complete scenes.

D3DX also provides a much simpler means to create these large data trees. Most 3D modeling packages such as discreet® 3ds max™ and Alias|Wavefront® Maya® allow users to build scenes containing multiple nodes and models. These model hierarchies can define an entire scene and allow artists to animate nodes within the scene to move rigid meshes or deform skinned objects. For most popular 3D modeling packages, including those mentioned previously, X file plug-ins are available to export the entire scene to a database of frame and mesh containers within a single X file. The D3DX library contains hierarchy loading functions such as D3DXLoadMeshHierarchyFromX that can construct an entire tree of D3DXFRAME and D3DXMESHCONTAINERS from the contents of these X files. We will cover this functionality in greater depth in Chapter 4, "Gaia Engine Overview," when we begin importing our own animated mesh hierarchies.

SKELETAL ANIMATION AND SKINNED MESHES

Information regarding skinned meshes is provided during the loading process of a D3DXFRAME hierarchy. Although the object containing the skin information, ID3DXSkinInfo, can be created by hand, it is far more intuitive to create skinned meshes in a professional modeling package and export them to the X file format. Using D3DXLoadMeshHierarchyFromX, the entire frame hierarchy is loaded into memory, along with any skinning information and animation data.

So, what is this data anyway? The ID3DXSkinInfo object contains a set of data for each vertex of a model. The model itself is stored externally, and can reside in an ID3DXMesh object, a vertex buffer, or generic system memory. ID3DXSkinInfo contains only the data needed to deform the mesh vertices using a set of matrices, which are also stored externally to this data set. What is stored within this object are the indices of the matrices used by each vertex, and scalar weight values used to control the influence each matrix has on a given vertex. This is the standard set of data used to perform indexed palette skinning.

This brings three pieces of the puzzle together. In the D3DXFRAME hierarchy, we have a set of nested transform matrices defining a local skeleton system. With D3DXMESHCONTAINER, objects can be hooked to any D3DXFRAME within the hierarchy to locate a model at the position and orientation provided by the parent. Finally, links to ID3DXSkinInfo objects within each D3DXMESHCONTAINER provide the data necessary to deform the model contained in the mesh container across a series of D3DXFRAME nodes, creating a skinned mesh. D3DXLoadMeshHierarchyFromX provides the means to load and construct the entire system, as we will see in Chapter 4. The last remaining piece is animation data, and a means to control the playback of the data over the D3DXFRAME hierarchy.

Class interfaces for animation data and playback are also provided by the D3DX library. ID3DXAnimationSet is the container class for the animation data itself, and ID3DXAnimationController provides an interface to link the animation data to a set of matrices (such as a tree of D3DXFRAME structures) that will be controlled by the animation. ID3DXAnimationController also provides playback controls for the animation and the ability to blend the effects of multiple animations.

Using these classes is very simple. D3DXFRAME nodes contain matrices that are registered with the ID3DXAnimationController using the name strings also provided with the D3DXFRAME structure. Only named matrices can be animated, because the names are used to link the matrices themselves with the animation data being played back.

The ID3DXAnimationController maintains links to one or more ID3DXAnimationSet objects, which contain key-framed animations that can be played using the controller. These key-framed animations contain information to produce rotation, translation, and scale changes to a matrix over time. These keyframes also contain the name of the matrices they are intended to affect. As named matrices are registered with the ID3DXAnimationController, their names are matched against the set of named keyframes and links are established. In this way, the matrix registered as "left knee" will be updated with the animation data with the corresponding name.

All of this matrix registration is performed automatically when using D3DXLoadMeshHierarchyFromX to load and assemble the frame hierarchy from an X file that also contains animation. The result is that the registered matrices are automatically updated by the ID3DXAnimationController as playback is performed. Figure 2.2 shows the relationship between the animation data and named matrices within the model hierarchy.

ID3DXAnimationController provides interfaces to blend the effects of multiple animation sets together, and adjust their playback parameters such as speed and blending priority. To enable playback, ID3DXAnimationSet objects must be assigned to the individual animation tracks ID3DXAnimationController. This allows each ID3DXAnimationSet to be animated independently by controlling the speed and blending weights of the tracks with which they are associated. To blend animations, the active tracks must be classified as being either low or high priority. The priority of an animation track controls how it is blended with the other tracks.

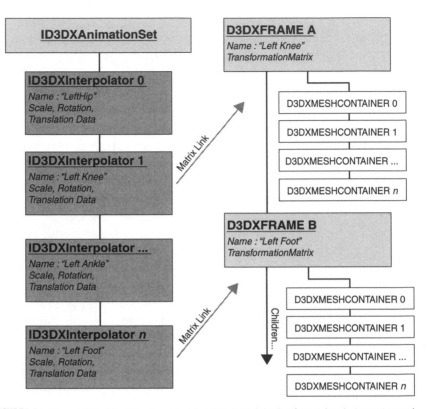

FIGURE 2.2   The relationship between named matrices and the keyframe data being animated with the `ID3DXAnimationController` class.

Setting the priority of a track is achieved using the `SetTrackDesc` member function of the `ID3DXAnimationController` to load a `D3DXTRACK_DESC` structure containing data about the track. The first parameter of this structure is a field named *flags*. Unfortunately, the documentation provided with the DirectX 9.0 SDK states that this field is unused, which is not the case. Setting this flag parameter to one of the `D3DXTRACKFLAG` enum values (`D3DXTF_LOWPRIORITY` or `D3DXTF_HIGHPRIORITY`) will associate the track with the proper group. This documentation error will hopefully be fixed in future revisions of the SDK.

The animation data of active tracks is then blended together in a three-step process. First, all tracks belonging to the low-priority group are blended together using their individual weight values. Next, all tracks belonging to the high-priority group are blended together using the weight values set for each track. Finally, the results of the high- and low-priority track blends are blended together using a scalar value set on the animation controller itself. This value can be set via the member function

`SetPriorityBlend` or adjusted over time using the `KeyPriorityBlend` function. Figure 2.3 shows the blending stages used to create a final animation pose from a set of blended animation tracks.

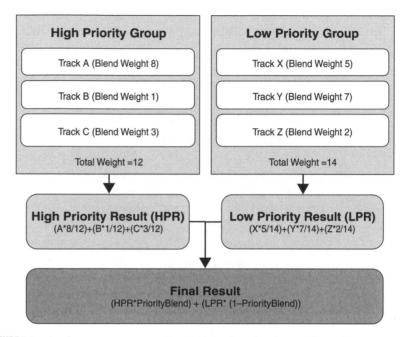

FIGURE 2.3   The three-step process used by `ID3DXAnimationController` to blend animation tracks.

We should also mention that when the individual tracks of a priority group are blended together, their weight values do not directly control the amount they contribute to the result. That is to say, setting the weight value for a track to 0.5 does not guarantee that the track will contribute 50 percent of the final result. Track weight values are relative to the other tracks within the priority group, not absolute contribution values. For example, if a priority group contains two tracks, and both are given weight values of 0.5, the blended result will be the same as if the tracks were each given weight values of 1.0. In either case, both tracks contain the same weight values so they contribute evenly to the result. If track A is given a weight of 0.5 and track B is given a weight of 0.25, track A will contribute twice as much to the result since its weight value is double the weight of track B.

To take full advantage of the skeletal animation facilities provided by the D3DX library, we will wrap these class interfaces in our own structures to provide additional interface methods. Some of these new interfaces are merely a matter of taste, but the modular design of the D3DX components allows us to add any application-specific features we desire.

For example, we would prefer to have an animation controller notify us when an animation is finished playing. The `ID3DXAnimationController` class will only report the length of the animation being played, and how much of it has currently elapsed. This puts the burden on the program to constantly monitor the animation controller or forecast when the animation will complete. To ease our development process, our wrapper will monitor the elapsed animation time itself and notify the application via a callback when the animation has completed. This creates a message system for animation feedback that makes state machine coding a little easier for our game objects.

Again, these interface additions are a matter of personal taste. Wrapping our own class around `ID3DXAnimationController` affords us the ability to add such interfaces as we see fit. In this manner, we take the ease of use provided by the D3DX classes and extend them for our own needs. In Chapter 4, we derive our own animation controller, and our own variation on the `D3DXFRAME` and `D3DXMESHCONTAINER` to augment them with our own product-specific needs. The design of the D3DX library enables us to add these customizations while still maintaining the key functionality provided by the original authors.

However, there are a few omissions from the `ID3DXAnimation Controller` that we can not remedy as easily. The `ID3DXAnimation Controller` provides a useful set of interfaces for controlling the playback of animation data over time. These member functions, such as `KeyTrackSpeed` and `KeyTrackWeight`, allow us to set dynamic keyframes on active animation tracks to increase and decrease playback speed over a time, as well as control the weighting of tracks being blended together over time. These interfaces allow us to set parameters that will automatically interpolate using either linear interpolation or a smoother, spline-based interpolation method, making them very useful for transitioning between animations. The surprising omission is that the interface to remove these keys is not provided. Once these interpolations are set in motion, they cannot be removed. This renders the `KeyTrack` functions useless unless we can be certain that we will not need to change these parameters once we have set them in motion.

REFERENCES

[Hoppe] Hoppe, H. "Progressive Meshes." *ACM SIGGRAPH 1996*, pp. 99–108 (available online at *http://research.microsoft.com/users/hhoppe*).

3

THE HIGH-LEVEL SHADER LANGUAGE

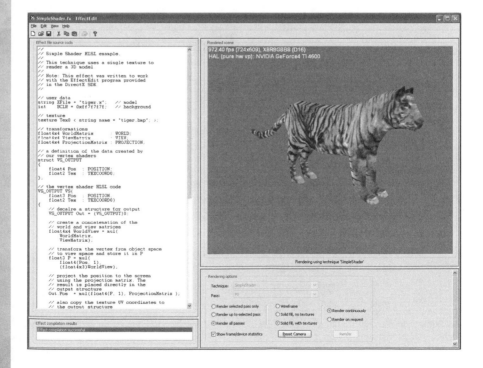

W ith the introduction of programmable vertex and pixel shaders in DirectX 8.0, graphics programmers were introduced to a whole new world of 3D rendering possibilities. No longer constrained by the rendering methods adopted by different hardware vendors, programmers and artists could now explore unconventional rendering techniques to make the appearance of their 3D environments unique.

In DirectX 9.0, further advancements have been made in programmable shader authoring. Not only have the specifications for vertex and pixel shaders increased in power, allowing more instructions and data to be used within each shader, but a new C-like language has been introduced to make shader programs more intuitive and readable. The High-Level Shading Language (HLSL), introduced with DirectX 9.0, is a giant leap forward for shader authors. Shaders can now be written in a more familiar language format and compiled for specific hardware platforms.

This compilation step ensures that well-written shaders can be used on future hardware, without requiring backward compatibility and outdated methods to run. Old shaders can be recompiled to use the latest additions to the vertex and pixel language specifications, increasing their lifecycle on future platforms. Alternative shader languages, such as the Cg language developed by NVIDIA, show the promise of cross platform-shader authoring. In short, graphics programming has evolved from a skill involving the use of operating system display routines to a bona-fide development language designed to run on its own set of unique hardware.

In this chapter, we take a close look at the HLSL language provided with the DirectX SDK. We will cover the structure, expressions, and data types unique to the HLSL, and introduce a few examples of common shaders that can be implemented using this language. We will also look at the runtime use of HLSL, and describe methods to allow your C++ application to communicate with the HLSL programs to guide their execution.

In addition to learning HLSL, readers are also urged to investigate the Cg programming language from NVIDIA. Both of the languages bear striking similarities, and are simply two methods to achieve the same goal: highly readable and reusable vertex and pixel shaders. For simplicity's sake, we will be focusing on HLSL for the shaders written in this book. However, all the shader methods explored are easily transferable to Cg. Appendix D, "Recommended Reading," contains links to sources of information on the Cg programming language for further reading.

THE HLSL SHADER FORMAT

Two types of shaders can be written using HLSL: vertex and pixel shaders. As their name suggests, vertex shaders modify vertex data, and pixel shaders produce the screen colors that are used to draw the object. Because they have different purposes, the structure of these shaders differs slightly. To understand both types of shaders, we will examine them one at a time, and then show how they can be used together inside a D3D effect file.

In their simplest form, a vertex shader is nothing more than a single function written in the HLSL language. This function is written to take certain types of input data from the application, namely the model vertices, and output the data needed to render the model on screen. This output data can later be sent to a pixel shader, which will interpret the data to produce the final appearance of the model.

Everything within the vertex shader is related to model geometry. Although the vertex shader can certainly compute color or light influences on a per-vertex basis, no textures are used at this point in the pipeline. The only data available to the vertex shader is a single vertex of the source model, and a set of read-only constant values that may be set by the application. The sample HLSL vertex shader in Listing 3.1 shows the basic structure of the vertex shader function.

LISTING 3.1   A sample HLSL vertex shader program.

```
// the object-to-screen
// transformation matrix
float4x4 WVPMatrix : WORLDVIEWPROJECTION;

// a definition of the data created by
// our vertex shader
struct VS_OUTPUT
{
    float4 Pos  : POSITION;
    float2 Tex  : TEXCOORD0;
};

// a vertex shader in HLSL code.
// this function takes a model vertex
// and transforms it to screen space
VS_OUTPUT VS(
    float3 Pos  : POSITION,
    float2 Tex  : TEXCOORD0)
{
```

```
    // declare a structure for output
    VS_OUTPUT Out = (VS_OUTPUT)0;

    // transform the vertex from object space
    // to screen space and store it in

                        // the output structure     Out.Pos = mul(
        float4(Pos, 1),
        WVPMatrix);

    // also copy the texture UV coordinates to
    // the output structure
    Out.Tex  = Tex;

    return Out;
}
```

Like the C programming language, HLSL shaders can contain three basic components: variable declarations, type definitions, and functions. Listing 3.1 contains a simple vertex shader designed to transform the vertices of a model from object space to screen space. It also allows the texture coordinates attached to each vertex to pass through to the pixel shader, where they will later be used to map a texture across the surface of each polygon. This shader contains a variable declaration, a structure definition, and a vertex shader function. Although the language appears very similar to C, there are some key differences. We will examine each component and explain them in turn.

VARIABLE AND DATA TYPES

HLSL provides a familiar set of data types for scalar values. Further data types are also provided to represent vectors, matrices, and shader-specific objects. As a convenience, HLSL also contains several `typedefs` to make the additional data types easier to use. Table 3.1 lists the entire set of scalar, vector and matrix types.

Unfortunately, the data types are not guaranteed to exist as stated on all hardware platforms. Due to the fact that different hardware vendors support different types of data on their products, one or more of these data types might actually be emulated rather than explicitly supported. For example, not all hardware vendors supply native support for the `int`, `half` or `double` data types. When native support is unavailable, these types are emulated using `float`. This can mean unexpected results if the

TABLE 3.1   Variable Types Available in HLSL Shaders

SCALAR DATA TYPES	DESCRIPTION
bool	Boolean values that can be set to true or false
int	32-bit signed integer
half	A half-precision, 16-bit floating-point value
float	A full-precision, 32-bit floating-point value
double	A double-precision, 64-bit floating-point value

VECTOR DATA TYPES	DESCRIPTION
vector	A vector of four float values
vector<t, num>	A vector containing *num* members of scalar *t* values

MATRIX DATA TYPES	DESCRIPTION
matrix	A matrix of 16 float values in a 4x4 grid
matrix <t, row, col>	A matrix of type *t* values in a grid of size *row* by *col*

OBJECT DATA TYPES	DESCRIPTION
string	An ASCII string
pixelshader	A Direct3D pixel shader object
vertexshader	A Direct3D vertex shader object
sampler	An object describing the use and filtering of a texture
texture	A Direct3D texture object

VECTOR TYPEDEFS	DESCRIPTION (# REPRESENTS VALUES BETWEEN 0 AND 4)
bool#x#	Defined as vector <bool, #>. Example: bool4
int#x#	Defined as vector <int, #>. Example: int4
float#x#	Defined as vector <float, #>. Example: loat4
half#x#	Defined as vector <half, #>. Example: half4
double#x#	Defined as vector <double, #>. Example: double4

MATRIX TYPEDEFS	DESCRIPTION (# REPRESENTS VALUES BETWEEN 0 AND 4)
bool#x#	Defined as matrix <bool, #, #>. Example: bool4x4
int#x#	Defined as matrix <int, #, #>. Example: int4x4
float#x#	Defined as matrix <float, #, #>. Example: float4x4
half#x#	Defined as matrix <half, #, #>. Example: half4x4
double#x#	Defined as matrix <double, #, #>. Example: double4x4
double#x#	Defined as matrix <double, #, #>. Example: double4x4

value stored as an `int` or `double` exceeds the value range that can be stored within a `float`. For this reason, it is recommended that the `float` value be used as the principal data type within shaders. The `int`, `double`, and `half` types should only be used if the range of values generated in known or a specific piece of target hardware is intended.

As in the C language, variables can also be labeled for scope with the `extern` keyword, or labeled as being `static`, `const` and `volatile`. HLSL contains some new keywords to further define the use of variables within shaders. Global variables or input parameters can be declared as `uniform`, which specifies that they do not change during the execution of the shaders (e.g., during a call to `DrawPrimitive`). For those familiar with shader assembly, this essentially identifies the values as being held within the table of shader constants. A second keyword, `shared`, is used as a hint that the variable exists in multiple HLSL shaders. Updating a shared variable within one HLSL object will set the corresponding variables in all shaders within the group.

Specific keywords are also used as hints for input parameters. All input variables are passed by value. HLSL does not allow for passing parameters by pointer or reference the way that C/C++ can. Instead, certain keywords can be used on input parameters to identify them as input or output data. The keyword `in` identifies a parameter as being input passed in by value. When no keyword is provided, the compiler will assume the `in` keyword was intended.

The `out` keyword makes a parameter behave somewhat like a reference being passed to a C++ function. When the function completes, the contents of the `out` parameter are copied back to the caller, just as if a non-const reference to a variable had been supplied. The final keyword, `inout`, is simply shorthand for a parameter that is input data and should have its final contents sent back to the caller.

Looking back at Listing 3.1, *semantics* are also used to further identify some of the data types listed. A semantic is an annotation that describes the intended use of the data. In vertex shaders, these semantics are identical to those used to describe the format of vertex buffers in DirectX 9.0. Semantics appear with a colon (:) and are placed immediately after the variable declaration with which they are associated. When semantics are used to identify the return value of a function, the semantic is placed after the function declaration, as in the following:

```
float4 VS(float3 Pos  : POSITION,
          float2 Tex  : TEXCOORDO) : POSITION
```

This function declaration contains three semantics. Each of the function's input parameters is identified with a semantic. The first parameter,

Pos, is identified to contain positional data. The second parameter, Tex, is labeled to contain texture coordinates. The texture coordinate semantic contains a numbering scheme that can be incremented to identify additional sets of texture coordinates as necessary. The function itself returns a four-unit floating-point vector. The trailing semantic appearing after the function identifies this return value to be positional data, a required output field for vertex shaders.

In Listing 3.1, you will notice that our vertex shader does not return a single position, but instead provides the caller with a small structure. This structure contains positional data along with an additional set of texture coordinates. In the definition of this structure, VS_OUTPUT, semantics are used to label each member of the structure. Labeling these members is required, and facilitates converting this output structure to pixel shader input parameters later in the pipeline.

User-defined semantics can also be used by the program to identify certain variables. For example, Listing 3.1 contains a variable declaration for a 4x4 matrix named WVPMatrix. This matrix is annotated with the semantic WORLDVIEWPROJECTION. This semantic is meaningless within the HLSL language, and appears only for the benefit of our program. The application has the ability to search for variables within the compiled HLSL shader by their data type, declared name, or semantic annotation. Locating the variable provides a handle through which the application can change the value held by the variable prior to executing the shader. By searching for the semantic WORLDVIEWPROJECTION, our program could locate the WVPMatrix and load in the desired matrix to transform a model into screen space.

EXPRESSIONS AND INTRINSIC FUNCTIONS

Working with HLSL is much the same as working with data in C or C++. Using a set of variables, arithmetic expressions can be performed to calculate new values. The expressions supported in HLSL mirror those of C and C++, including all math operators (+, −, *, \, etc.), logic operators, and comparison operators. A full list of these expressions is provided in Appendix C, "Programming Reference Sheets."

Because HLSL does not have the luxury of using standard C math libraries for more complex operations, a set of intrinsic functions are provided to perform these tasks. One such operation is the mul function, shown in Listing 3.1. Some of these functions, like mul, can map directly to vertex or pixel shader assembly instructions. For example, the use of mul in the sample listing can be mapped by the compiler directly to a low-level shader instruction that will transform our vertex by the provided matrix. Others, like `refract` function, expand to more complex routines. In this case, `refract` expands to the code required to calculate the refraction of a vector through a translucent media. When writing shaders using HLSL, a programmer must keep the underlying functionality in mind when using intrinsic functions, especially when working with older hardware that severely limits the instruction count that shaders can employ. The full list of intrinsic functions is also provided in Appendix C.

WORKING WITH TEXTURES AND SAMPLERS

Textures are accessed via HLSL pixel shaders through the use of texture *samplers*. A sampler is the encapsulation of a Direct3D texture stage, containing a reference to the texture used and all filtering information applied to the texture. An easy way to define a texture sampler is through the use of the sampler state definition supported in effect files. This includes the texture coordinate wrap modes and all mipmap filtering instructions. The sampler definition contains all the information usually set using `SetSamplerState` when using the fixed-function pipeline. Table 3.2 shows the sampler information that can be specified, and the values accepted (Table 3.2 is also provided in Appendix C).

TABLE 3.2   Texture Sampler Settings and Their Associated Values

SAMPLER STATE	TYPE	ACCEPTABLE VALUES
AddressU	dword	WRAP = 1, MIRROR = 2, CLAMP = 3, BORDER = 4, MIRRORONCE = 5
AddressV	dword	Same as AddressU
AddressW	dword	Same as AddressU
BorderColor	float4	A color value; the vector contains RGBA values from 0–1.
MagFilter	dword	NONE = 0, POINT = 1, LINEAR = 2, ANISOTROPIC = 3, PYRAMIDALQUAD = 6, GAUSSIANQUAD = 7

TABLE 3.2   *(Continued)*

SAMPLER STATE	TYPE	ACCEPTABLE VALUES
MinFilter	dword	Same as MagFilter.
MipFilter	dword	Same as MagFilter.
MaxAnisotropy	dword	Maximum anisotropy value; default value is 1.
MaxMipLevel	int	Maximum mipmap level to use from 0–n, where n is the number of mipmaps available. The largest texture is index 0. The smallest texture is index (n–1).
MipMapLodBias	float	A bias value applied to the mipmap level chosen. The default is 0.0.
SRGBTexture	bool	Set to true (nonzero value) when the texture being sampled is in sRGB format (gamma correction 2.2). See the DirectX SDK for more information on Gamma.
ElementIndex	dword	When a multi-element texture is assigned to the sampler, this indicates which element index to use. The default value is 0.

Listing 3.2 shows an example of a rudimentary HLSL pixel shader. In the global scope, a texture is declared, and a sampler object that will be used to access it. The application is responsible to assigning a D3DTexture9 object to the texture variable Tex0 prior to using the shader. The sampler specifies that the texture Tex0 will be accessed by our pixel shader, using linear interpolation for all mipmap filtering.

LISTING 3.2   A sample HLSL pixel shader program.

```
// declare a texture variable
// for the application to assign a
// D3DTexture9 object to
texture Tex0

// define a sampler.
// this tells DirectX how we intend
// to use our texture in the
// pixel shader.
sampler MySampler = sampler_state
{
    Texture   = (Tex0);
    MipFilter = LINEAR;
    MinFilter = LINEAR;
    MagFilter = LINEAR;
```

```
    // all unstated values
    // are left to their defaults
};

// the HLSL pixel shader.
// using the input texture coordinates,
// sample a texel using the sampler
// defined above and output the color
float4 PS(
    float2 TexCoords  : TEXCOORD0) : COLOR
{
    return tex2D(MySampler, TexCoords );
}
```

HLSL supports four types of samplers: `sampler1D`, `sampler2D`, `sampler3D`, and `samplerCUBE`. Each is designed to work with specific texture types. The HLSL compiler also accepts the generic term `sampler`, as used in Listing 3.2, which it will automatically map to one of the four true sampler types based on the texture and lookup method used.

The sampler object is then used in the pixel shader to perform the lookup of a texel from the mipmap chain provided. The actual lookup is performed using one of the intrinsic texture sampling functions provided by HLSL. In our example, a texel is sampled using the 2D lookup function `tex2D`. Additional texture sampling functions are provided for 1D, 3D, and projection sampling methods. The HLSL Intrinsic Function list shown in Appendix C contains the full list of these texture samplers.

The result of our example pixel shader is that the contents of the texture pointed to by `Tex0` are sampled using the texture coordinates supplied to the `PS` function. For each sample requested, a four-unit vector is returned containing the RGBA color of the texel sampled. The COLOR semantic applied to the pixel shader function allows this RGBA value to be returned within a `float4` object, signifying the final output of the pixel shader.

PROCEDURAL TEXTURE SHADERS

Pixel shaders are not restricted for supplying output intended for the render target. The same pixel shader functions can be used to create procedural textures that can then be loaded into future texture stages for use. This is done by compiling the pixel shader and supplying the compiled object to one of the D3DX texture rendering functions (`D3DXFillTextureTX`, `D3DXFillVolumeTextureTX`, and `D3DXFillCubeTextureTX`). These functions evoke the pixel shader once for each texel of the image, allowing the pixel shader to build the final texture.

The input parameters for these pixel shaders differ from those used to render model geometry. Procedural texture shaders must adhere to specific function definition templates that are compatible with the texture fill function being used. For example, `D3DXFillTextureTX` can only be evoked with a procedural texture shader built to take 2D texture coordinates as positional input data. The pixel shader must then use this data to produce a final color in the forms of a four-unit float vector that will be written to the texture.

CONSIDERATIONS FOR LEGACY HARDWARE

Writing HLSL shaders provides the programmer with a certain amount of freedom. Within reason, the shaders written in HLSL can be compiled to work on any hardware platform that supports programmable shaders through DirectX. However, the older video cards were designed to work with the original specifications for vertex and pixel shaders. These initial shader specifications are very limiting in terms of the operations that can be performed, the amount of temporary and constant register space provided, and the total number of operations that can be performed per shader.

Writing HLSL shaders for use on these components requires a bit more care, and some understanding of the low-level operations performed by the HLSL intrinsic functions. The HLSL compiler does a commendable job of creating shaders compatible with the older hardware specs, but the additional instructions needed to emulate the latest pixel and vertex shader methods often overflow the limits of the older specifications, or produce code that is much too slow to be useful in a real-time application.

While writing HLSL shaders for legacy hardware, the error codes generated by the compiler will alert you to instruction count limitations and attempts to use unsupported features. All of the D3DX functions that perform the compilation of shaders (`D3DXCreateEffect`, `D3DXCompileShader`, etc.) can fill a `D3DXBUFFER` with error strings if one is provided. When building HLSL shaders for legacy hardware, monitoring the output of these error messages can be a great aid in building shaders for older platforms.

Another useful tool is the command-line compiler included with the DirectX SDK. Located in the `\Bin\DXUtils` folder of the SDK, the fxc.exe program can compile HLSL shader files to produce effect object files. One of the most useful utilities of this stand-alone compiler is the ability to generate regular shader assembly instructions from the HLSL code. This is done using the using the /Fc compiler option. By compiling your HLSL shaders with this option and viewing the output, you can gain considerable insight into which HLSL intrinsic functions do not map well to the older shader specifications.

HLSL FUNCTIONS WITHIN EFFECT FILES

HLSL functions can be embedded directly into D3D effect files. This fully encapsulates the render method, making them easier to prototype and maintain. As shown in Chapter 1, the ability to include multiple techniques within an effect file means that we can now include multiple versions of our HLSL routines and use the validation method to find the best technique that will run on the target platform.

To associate pixel shaders and vertex shaders with a technique, they need only be assigned to a vertexshader or pixelshader object within the technique, along with the declaration of the language specification to be used when compiling the routines. The HLSL functions can be written directly into the technique itself, or by using references to external functions. Listing 3.3 shows our previous two shader examples embedded within a single effect file. The technique listed at the bottom of the file associates the pixel shaders with the technique for validation.

LISTING 3.3   A sample Direct3D effect file containing HLSL vertex and pixel shaders.

```
//
// Simple HLSL Shader example.
//
// This technique uses a single texture to
// render a 3D model.
//
// Note: This effect was written to work
// with the EffectEdit program provided
// in the DirectX SDK.
//

// user data
string XFile = "tiger.x";   // model
int    BCLR = 0xff202080;   // background

// texture
```

```
texture Tex0 < string name = "tiger.bmp"; >;

// transformations
float4x4 WorldMatrix      : WORLD;
float4x4 ViewMatrix       : VIEW;
float4x4 ProjectionMatrix : PROJECTION;

// a definition of the data created by
// our vertex shaders
struct VS_OUTPUT
{
    float4 Pos  : POSITION;
    float2 Tex  : TEXCOORD0;
};

// the vertex shader HLSL code
VS_OUTPUT VS(
    float3 Pos  : POSITION,
    float2 Tex  : TEXCOORD0)
{
    // declare a structure for output
    VS_OUTPUT Out = (VS_OUTPUT)0;

    // create a concatenation of the
    // world and view matrices
    float4x4 WorldView = mul(
        WorldMatrix,
        ViewMatrix);

    // transform the vertex from object space
    // to view space and store it in P
    float3 P = mul(
        float4(Pos, 1),
        (float4x3)WorldView);

    // project the position to the screen
    // using the projection matrix. The
    // result is placed directly in the
    // output structure
    Out.Pos  = mul(float4(P, 1), ProjectionMatrix );

    // also copy the texture UV coordinates to
    // the output structure
    Out.Tex  = Tex;
```

```
                return Out;
        }


        // define a sampler.
        // this tells DirectX how we intend
        // to use our texture in the
        // pixel shader.
        sampler Sampler = sampler_state
        {
            Texture   = (Tex0);
            MipFilter = LINEAR;
            MinFilter = LINEAR;
            MagFilter = LINEAR;
        };


        // the HLSL pixel shader.
        // using the input texture coordinates,
        // sample a texel using the sampler
        // defined above and output the color
        float4 PS(
            float2 Tex  : TEXCOORD0) : COLOR
        {
            return tex2D(Sampler, Tex);
        }


        // the final technique contains only our
        // vertex and pixel shaders. If we required
        // additional render states,
        // we could add them here
        technique SimpleShader
        {
            pass P0
            {
                // shaders
                VertexShader = compile vs_1_1 VS();
                PixelShader  = compile ps_1_1 PS();
            }
        }
```

The example shader also makes use of a few more user-defined annotations. These are added to make the shader compatible with the EffectEdit sample program included with the DirectX SDK. The EffectEdit program will parse these annotation strings to perform tasks such as loading our desired textures and setting the background color of the preview window. The EffectEdit program can then preview our shader for us, reporting any errors to its own output window. Figure 3.1 shows the EffectEdit program previewing the sample effect file contained in Listing 3.3.

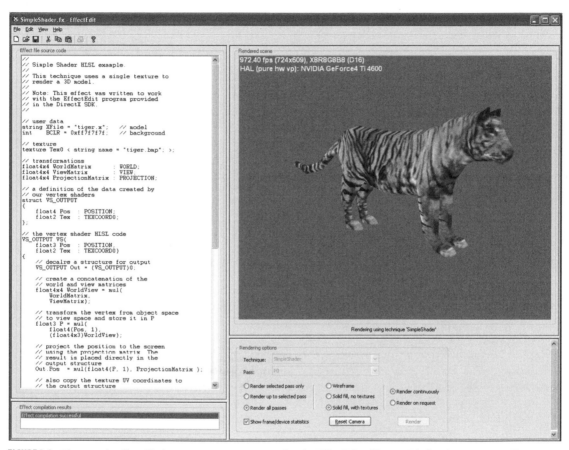

FIGURE 3.1   The sample effect file from Listing 3.3 running within the EffectEdit utility provided in the DirectX 9.0 SDK.

4

GAIA ENGINE OVERVIEW

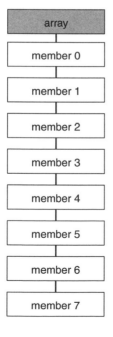

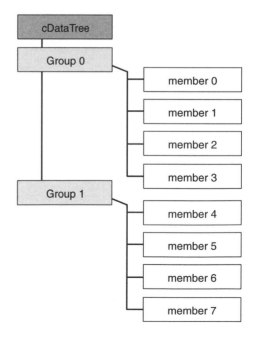

n the first three chapters, we introduced some of the DirectX components we will be relying on to facilitate the development of our engine: the Direct3D sample framework, the Direct3D extension library, and the new High-Level Shader Language (HLSL). In the final chapter of this part, we complete our introduction to the engine by explaining some of the key resource types used within it. As you read through the source code files, you will encounter these classes often, so we take a moment here to provide an overview of them and their functionality.

Don't worry if these earlier development tasks seem a little dull—they are. However, a little time spent in the trenches now will benefit us later as we get into the fun stuff. These simple classes and interfaces will save us a lot of time down the road, and help ensure that the portions of the game engine we write later in the book share a consistent framework. We will begin by introducing the engine and the coding practices used to build it, and then move on to some of the specific resource types we will be creating.

These resource types are best explained in detail by simply looking through the source code files provided. In this chapter, we present a brief introduction to each resource type and cover the highlights of their class design. For specific implementation details, refer to the source code files themselves.

MEET GAIA, THE 3D TERRAIN ENGINE

We will be referring to our 3D outdoor game engine as "Gaia," a name taken from the Greek goddess of the earth (it's a terrain engine after all). Naming the engine is useful for maintaining a logical separation between our source code and that of the D3DX support libraries, and can also provide a physical separation between our own type definitions and those of external libraries.

Many game engines make use of specialized third-party libraries to handle specific tasks such as managing 3D audio playback or physical simulations. To accommodate this, it is necessary to take steps to ensure that the engine code base does not clash with external source code or support libraries. The simplest approach is to wrap the entire engine code base in a namespace that will shield any class, type, or function declarations from the outside world. This might be a source of frustration for some programmers who are not used to namespaces, but using a namespace is far superior to appending some prefix to each function and type definition in the code to identify it.

While it might seem tempting to skip the use of namespaces, and instead name our engine functions with the prefix gaia, as in gaiaDrawBox() and gaiaPrintText(), this type of redundant naming gets cumbersome very quickly. To avoid any name collisions between the engine's type declarations and those of another author, the gaia prefix would be required on every class, data type, or function declared.

Instead of using prefixes, a single namespace can be used to insulate the entire engine code base. Each global function or class definition will be declared inside this space. This effectively emulates the gaia prefix while providing a few shortcuts that limit the amount it actually needs to be explicitly stated. This is because all classes and functions declared within the namespace gaia will naturally use that namespace by default, relieving the programmer from having to explicitly type the namespace on functions and types used within the class. In addition, the keyword phrase using namespace gaia can be declared at the top of all engine source code files to inform the compiler that the namespace gaia should be assumed as the default namespace, again eliminating the need to explicitly type the prefix.

For the seasoned C++ programmer, this use of a namespace to insulate library code is nothing new. The Standard Template Library (STL) does the same thing by wrapping all of its library templates in the namespace std. And if it's good enough for the STL, a set of thoroughly defined utility classes used by millions of programmers, it's good enough for us. For the remainder of this book, we'll assume the namespace gaia is in use. To make the code samples a little easier to read, the namespace might be left out of the listings that appear in the text.

THE APPLICATION HOST

To add our own layer of program control, we will be building our own class on top of the foundation provided by the Direct3D sample framework. The sample framework class CD3DApplication will serve as our base, allowing us to use it for initialization and enumeration of the video devices, display mode setup, and handling common window messages. Above this class, we will add our own resource and device managers, control the execution of our program, and render our world. We do this through the creation of our application hosting class, cGameHost.

The cGameHost class serves many purposes. First and foremost, it is the central object of our entire engine. We will employ a managerial approach to our class design, creating specific single-instance classes to manage key aspects of our engine. Examples of these manager classes would handle such things as the render pipeline, user input, and so forth. These self-contained managers will require a common thread, a means for the program to access and communicate with them. The `cGameHost` class will serve as a container for all manager objects and provide access methods to retrieve their interfaces.

To build this class, we will use the singleton declaration method to ensure that a single `cGameHost` class is created, and that the application has global access to its interface. The singleton base class is detailed in Appendix A, "Gaia Utility Classes." In the interest of flexibility, the singleton method also allows for class inheritance. If custom game-hosting functionality is needed, a specific game host object can be derived from `cGameHost` to perform the additional actions. The most beneficial aspect of the singleton declaration method is that from anywhere in the program, including within the managers themselves, the `cGameHost` object will provide access to the management objects used by the engine.

In addition to providing a communication switchboard for the device managers, the `cGameHost` class also serves as the core of the application. This class represents the main program shell, where all interaction with the host operating system is contained. In our case, this means that the desktop window containing the game is held within the `cGameHost` object, and all messages sent to the window are processed within this class. We gain these facilities easily by deriving our class from the `CD3DApplication` class provided by the Direct3D sample framework. However, deriving our own class on top of this base allows us to take control of certain aspects of the program.

To begin with, we will be handling the updating of our game world a little differently than the DirectX samples do. The DirectX samples maintain a one-to-one relationship between the update of their world state and the rendering of each frame. On each pass, the entire application state is updated and a new frame is rendered. These update passes happen without any type of governance, so real-time values must be used during each update to determine how much an object should move or animate.

We take the more game-centric approach and divide time into discreet steps which we call *ticks*. Each tick represents a fixed interval of time. Therefore, each time we execute a tick, we know exactly how much time has passed. This fixed time step approach frees us from needing to monitor a real-time clock and perform more complicated variable-time updates on our world state.

The immediate criticism of the fixed-time approach is that it does not allow animation to run as smoothly as the unbridled variable-time approach. This is a valid concern. If we only update our game world at a certain time interval, then our animations will never appear smoother than the time interval will allow. However, the fixed-time method does not dictate that only one time step must be used. We leave ourselves open to the prospect of having more than one type of update tick.

For example, we could update game state at one frequency and update animation at a higher frequency. This allows us to simplify any state machines or logic operations we must perform to update our game world, while still providing smooth, detailed animation. For our sample engine, we limit our ticks to 1/30th of a second each, or about 33 milliseconds each. We also update animation at the same rate, but leave the door open to move to higher animation rates if we so choose.

Our time-step approach is handled in our overload of the CD3D Application member function FrameMove, shown in Listing 4.1. We also add a few thread management functions to co-exist peacefully with other Windows applications. Our application will be idle until a full tick's worth of real time has passed. When this amount of time has elapsed, we update our game state and then go back to being idle. If we assume our update does not consume more than a tick of real time processing the world, our application will spend a fair amount of time idle. By decreasing our thread priority and relinquishing the remainder of our time slice after executing each tick, we allow other threads the chance to update.

Without these thread checks in place, our application would consume 100 percent of the available CPU all the time. This can cause other threads that are waiting to execute to pile up, and puts an unnecessary burden on the operating system to keep all threads running smoothly. Adding these measures helps facilitate efficiency thread management by the operating system and ensures that we will get the execution priority we desire at the time we need it most.

LISTING 4.1   Time and thread priority management within the cGameHost class.

```
HRESULT cGameHost::FrameMove()
{
  static HANDLE hThread = GetCurrentThread();

  // add the real time elapsed to our
  // internal delay counter
  m_updateTimeCount += m_fElapsedTime;

  // is there an update ready to happen?
  if (m_updateTimeCount > k_millisecondsPerTick)
  {
    // bump up our priority for thread activation
```

```cpp
      // while we are executing a game tick
      SetThreadPriority(
        hThread,
        THREAD_PRIORITY_TIME_CRITICAL);

      // perform the proper number of updates
      while(m_updateTimeCount > k_millisecondsPerTick)
      {
        HRESULT result;

        // update the scene
        if(FAILED( result = updateScene()))
          return result;

        // subtract the time interval
        // emulated with each tick
        m_updateTimeCount -= k_millisecondsPerTick;
      }

      // return to normal priority
      // while we wait for the next tick
      SetThreadPriority(
        hThread,
        THREAD_PRIORITY_NORMAL);

      // we know our next logic execution will not occur
      // until a full tick worth of time has elapsed,
      // so we forfeit the rest of the time slice
      // allotted to us by Windows and let any waiting
      // threads execute. This prevents us from consuming
      // 100% of the CPU waiting for time to pass.
      Sleep(0);
  }

  return S_OK;
}
```

One of the key management objects contained by cGameHost is the re-source manager. Our application host will also use its own resource management system for the device objects we will be creating. The root of this resource system, the cResourcePoolManager class, is built from a set of data pool support classes provided as part of our engine. Before we discuss the resource objects themselves, we take a moment to understand the data pools that are being used and the resource management scheme being put in place.

CREATING POOLS OF DATA

One of the keys to efficient memory management is to limit the total number of allocations made. The simplest way to do so is to group similar objects together into larger allocations. We'll call these *data pools*, and use them as containers for multiple objects. The contained objects are considered members of the pool, and are provided to callers on demand through the use of handles. Members can be requested and released by clients, growing the pool in fixed increments to accommodate more members as needed.

This is where the code can get a little convoluted. We want these pools to be somewhat type safe, so they are constructed as template classes—using a specific data type to represent the members of the pool. However, it is also necessary to communicate with all pools using a common interface. When we later build the resource manager to maintain pools of textures, vertices, and animation, communication with the various data pools through a common interface will be vital to constructing and destructing these resources. Therefore, while the data pools themselves are individual instantiations of a template class, they must also inherit from a common interface that external managers can use to construct and release members.

While it would be perfectly reasonable to simply allocate a large array of objects and reference them by their array index, this approach is woefully inflexible. The size of the array must be known prior to requesting the first member, and it cannot grow beyond that original allocation size, thereby limiting the total number of objects that can be used within the game. The rigid array provides optimal memory use, at the cost of limiting the number of objects it can hold. This is an ideal approach to add to an application when all object counts are known and can indeed be pre-allocated, but for our development cycle, we want a bit more flexibility.

The solution used within the engine to house the data pools, the `cDataPool` template class, does not actually contain an array of member objects. Instead, it contains a linked list of member object arrays, called `cPoolGroups`, These groups contain a fixed number of member objects each, and can be added or removed from the data pool as needed. This creates a compromise between efficient memory use and flexible object amounts. While the pool can grow as needed, it can only do so in predefined chunks, each allocating a block of new member objects.

The greatest asset of this design is that it can be converted to a regular array without affecting the rest of the game. The nested tree of objects created within the pool still creates a unique index for each member. If the objects held inside the data pool tree were collapsed into a regular array, these index values would remain unchanged. Figure 4.1 shows the two data structures side-by-side, and compares the indexing methods to show their similarity. This property of the data pool allows us to work with it in its flexible, albeit less efficient form, knowing that we can later replace it with an efficient, regular array allocation once our total memory needs are known. To the game, the index values used as handles to the objects within the pool will remain unchanged.

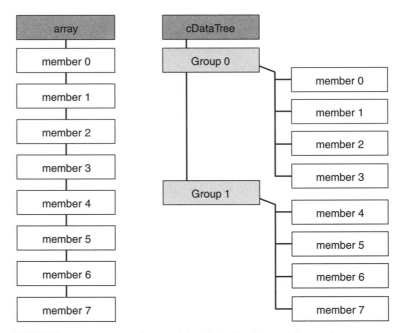

FIGURE 4.1   Comparing the layout of the cDataPool tree with a regular array.

Using either the tree storage method of cDataPool or a regular array implies that individual memory locations will be reused. As members of the pool are released, they become available for future callers to use. Therefore, we need to track which members are available for use, so that open slots within the pool can be located quickly as callers request them. Within each cPoolGroup, a linked list of open members is maintained. This is a simple array of word values equal to the number of members in the group. Each value in this array denotes whether its corresponding pool member is in use or available.

Each member that is in use has a constant value (INVALID_INDEX) stored in this array to signal it as being unavailable. Those members that are available form a linked list of indexes. Each member contains the index of the next open member in the list. Our `cDataPool` class stores the index to the first open entry, and the last open entry contains its own index to mark the end of the chain. We can return an open member to a caller by simply returning the first open index and moving our internal handle to the next open index (if any). As callers release members back into the pool, we simply set our internal handle to point directly to the returned member, which in turn is set to point to the former head of the open list.

This process is far easier to understand when looking at the source code. The complete source code for the data pool objects can be found in the file `source_code\core\data_pool.h` on the accompanying CD-ROM. The complete functionality of these objects is too involved to provide a full listing within the book, but the functions responsible for adding and removing members to the pool can be found in Listing 4.2. These examples show the basic operations necessary to locate an available `cPoolGroup` within the pool, retrieve an open index from it, and build a `cPoolHandle` for the caller containing the index value. To release the member, the member is located within the pool and placed at the head of the open list of nodes.

LISTING 4.2   Functions responsible for adding and removing members from the data pool.

```
#define INVALID_INDEX 0xffff
#define CLEAR_HANDLE(h) (h=INVALID_INDEX)

//
// retrieve a new handle from the pool,
// increasing the pool size if needed
//
template <class T>
inline cPoolHandle cDataPool<T>::nextHandle()
{
  debug_assert(isInitialized(),
    "the cDataPool is not initialized");

  // find or create a group with an available slot
  unsigned groupNumber=0;
  cPoolGroup<T>* openGroup =
    findOpenGroup(&groupNumber);

  // find the first open slot within the group
  int index = openGroup->nextMember();
  --m_totalOpen;
```

```cpp
    // build a handle to return
    return buildHandle(groupNumber, index);
}

//
// return a member to the pool
//
template <class T>
inline void cDataPool<T>::release(cPoolHandle* pHandle)
{
  debug_assert(isInitialized(),
    "the cDataPool is not initialized");
  debug_assert(pHandle,
    "A valid handle must be provided");

  if (isHandleValid(*pHandle))
  {
    debug_assert(m_groupList.size(),
      "The cDataPool has not been properly created");

    // dissect the handle into it's
    // group and index values
    int groupIndex = getGroupNumber(*pHandle);
    int itemIndex = getItemIndex(*pHandle);

    cPoolGroup<T>* group = getGroup(groupIndex);

    // tell the group to release the member
    group->release(itemIndex);

    // clear the caller's handle
    CLEAR_HANDLE(*pHandle);

    // try and see if we can remove the last group
    cPoolGroup<T>* pGroup=m_groupList.back();
    if (pGroup->totalOpen() == m_groupCount)
    {
      pGroup->destroy();
      delete pGroup;
      m_groupList.pop_back();
    }

    ++m_totalOpen;
  }
}
```

```
template <class T>
inline cPoolGroup<T>*
cDataPool<T>::findOpenGroup(unsigned* groupNumber)
{
  // find and return the first group with an open slot
  *groupNumber = 0;
  for (MemberGroupList::iterator iter =
      m_groupList.begin();
      iter != m_groupList.end();
      ++iter)
  {
    cPoolGroup<T>* pGroup = *iter;
    if (pGroup->totalOpen())
    {
      // an open slot has been found
      return(pGroup);
    }
    ++(*groupNumber);
  }

  // there are no open slots,
  // so we need to add a new cPoolGroup
  // before we make a new group, make sure
  // we have not reached our max
  // of MAX_UINT16 members
  debug_assert(m_groupList.size()*(m_groupCount+1)
      < (uint16)MAX_UINT16,
      "the cDataPool is full!!!!");

  // create the new group
  return(addGroup());
}

template <class T>
inline cPoolGroup<T>* cDataPool<T>::addGroup()
{
  // append a new group to the list to start things off
  cPoolGroup<T>* pNewGroup =
    new cPoolGroup<T>(m_groupCount);
  m_groupList.insert(m_groupList.end(), pNewGroup);

  // gain access to the new group and innitialize it
  cPoolGroup<T>* pGroup = m_groupList.back();
  pGroup->create();
```

```cpp
    // increment our internal counters
    m_totalMembers += m_groupCount;
    m_totalOpen += m_groupCount;

    // return the new group pointer
    return(pGroup);
}

template <class T>
inline uint16 cPoolGroup<T>::nextMember()
{
    debug_assert(m_memberList && m_nextOpenList,
      "Group has not been created");
    debug_assert(m_totalOpen, "no open slots");

    // return the first member of our
    // open list, and move our internal
    // handle to the next member
    uint16 slot = m_firstOpen;
    m_firstOpen = m_nextOpenList[slot];
    --m_totalOpen;

    debug_assert(m_firstOpen != INVALID_INDEX,
      "Invalid Open Index");

    debug_assert(isOpen(slot), "invalid index");

    // signal this member as being is use
    m_nextOpenList[slot] = INVALID_INDEX;

    return(slot);
}
```

MANAGING SHARED DATA RESOURCES

The engine contains several varieties of shared resources. These resources represent data that multiple game objects will access and share. Examples include textures, vertex buffers, index buffers, and render methods. In fact, many of the shared resources are dependent on video hardware, as they might use hardware-resident memory for a portion of their storage. Managers of these devices will need access to all dependent resources. For example, the display manager will need access to all textures, vertex and index buffers so it can handle cases where the interface to the video device is lost and regained.

This requires a few key classes. First, we define a base class for all shared resources, `cResourcePoolItem`, which provides a common interface that external callers can use. This includes basic interface functions to create and destroy the resource, enable and disable it, and stream it to and from files on disk. These member functions are provided as pure virtual functions within the base class, forcing all classes derived from `cResourcePoolItem` to provide the actual implementation for these members based on the actual data held. This virtual interface allows an external caller such as a device manager to influence a set of `cResourcePoolItem`-based objects without knowing the specific data type they represent.

With the same idea in mind, we also add a class called `cResourcePool`. This class is an extension of the `cDataPool` class, designed to hold `cResourcePoolItem`-based objects and provide additional methods to operate on these resources. Like the `cResourcePoolItem` class, `cResourcePool` employs a common base interface that callers can use. Given that all `cResourcePoolItem` objects also contain a standard set of interface methods, the `cResourcePool` adds member functions to iterate through all the members of the pool and pass data to these functions. For external callers, this provides bulk processing of shared resource types. The manager of the display card, for example, can use this type of interface to quickly enable or disable all texture objects within a `cResourcePool`.

Shared resources are often identified by a text string. With textures, for example, this string might be the actual path name of the source image on disk. In addition to providing the bulk processing operations, `cResourcePool` also stores a lookup table of these resource name strings. This provides callers with a method to search for shared resource objects by name. The map container class of the Standard Template Library (STL) is used to build this phonebook of resource names and provide accelerated searching methods to locate individual members of the pool.

Finally, the `cResourcePoolManager` singleton class provides the central repository for all shared resource pools. Individual `cResourcePool` objects can be created and registered with the `cResourcePoolManager` class, along with index values identifying the resource type held within the pool and the family to which it belongs. These index values are held in global enumerations found within the `cResourcePoolManager` header file. One enumeration identifies all possible resource families (audio, video, etc.). Additional enumerations identify the individual resource types held within each family.

```
// resource families
    enum RESOURCE_FAMILY
    {
```

```
    k_nVideoResource=0,
    k_nAudioResource,
    k_nGameResource,

    //...etc

    k_nTotalResourceFamilies
};

// members of the video family..
enum VIDEO_RESOURCES
{
    k_nTextureResource=0,
    k_nVBufferResource,
    k_nIBufferResource,
    k_nRenderResource,

    //...etc

    k_nTotalVideoResources
};
```

The combined family and type indexes are held as 16 bits each inside a single 32-bit value. This value, called a cResourceCode, is used to uniquely identify all classes of resource objects held within the manager. As new resource pools are created, they register themselves with the manager, providing a cResourceCode to identify themselves. External callers can then gain access to the cResourcePool interfaces by requesting them from the manager using the proper cResourceCode.

The functionality of the resource classes will become more apparent as we build the actual engine resources and the managers that use them. For now, refer to the resource-related source code files on the accompanying CD-ROM to further explore their functionality. The resource source files are listed at the top of this chapter. Listing 4.3 shows an example of how these resource objects can be created and used.

ON THE CD

LISTING 4.3   Example code showing the use of resource-related classes.

```
// imagine a texture resource class
class cTexture : public cResourcePoolItem
{
...
};
```

```
// and a resource pool used to hold them
typedef cResourcePool<cTexture> cTexturePool;

//
// the following code shows an
// example of how they might be used
//

void resource_setup()
{
    // create a pool for textures
    cTexturePool* myTexturePool = new cTexturePool;

    // and register it with the resource
    // manager singleton along with a
    // family and resource type value
    ResourceManager.registerResourcePool(
        cResourceCode(k_nVideoResource,
        k_nTextureResource),
        cResourcePoolInterface*) myTexturePool);

    // now we can create a few sample textures
    myTexturePool.createResource("texture 0");
    myTexturePool.createResource("texture 1");
    myTexturePool.createResource("texture 2");
}

void resource_cleanup()
{
    // tell the resource manager to destroy
    // all video display resources
    ResourceManager.destroyResourceFamily(
        k_nVideoResource);

    // unregister the texture resource pool
    cResourcePoolInterface* pTexturePool =
        ResourceManager.unregisterResourcePool(
            cResourceCode(k_nVideoResource,
                        k_nTextureResource));

    // and destroy it
    delete pTexturePool;
}

void resource_sample
```

```
{
    resource_setup ();

    // find a resource given its code and name
    cTexture* myTexture = ResourceManager.findResource(
        cResourceCode(k_nVideoResource,
        k_nTextureResource),
        "texture 0"

    // do something with the resource
    if (myTexture)
    {
        myTexture->restoreResource();
        // .. etc
    }

    resource_cleanup ();
}
```

THE RESOURCE BASE CLASS

All engine resource objects are derived from the base class cResource
PoolItem. This class provides a common set of functions used by the cResourcePoolManager classes to create and destroy the resources, and save
and load them from the hard drive. cResourcePoolItem objects also maintain a core set of data for each resource object, including the resource
code that identifies the resource type, an interface to the resource's manager, and a cPoolHandle index for the resource. A bit field of flags is also
maintained, recording the current state of the resource object.

The cResourcePoolItem provides a set of common member functions
for retrieving the resource's name, querying the state of the resource, and
retrieving the resource's pool handle. The most important member functions, however, are a set of pure virtual functions used to maintain the
resource itself. Engine resources derived from the cResourcePoolItem base
class are responsible for providing instantiations of these pure virtual interface functions defined by cResourcePoolItem. These functions create
the interface used by the manager objects to manipulate the resource.
Listing 4.4 shows the member functions.

LISTING 4.4   The cResourcePoolItem base class virtual interface functions.

```
// innitialize the resource (called once)
virtual bool createResource()=0;

// destroy the resource
virtual bool destroyResource()=0;

// purge the resource from volatile memory
virtual bool disableResource()=0;

// restore the resource to volatile memory
virtual bool restoreResource()=0;

// load the resource from a file
// (or NULL to use the resource name)
virtual bool loadResource(const tchar* filename=0)=0;

// save the resource to a file
// (or NULL to use the resource name)
virtual bool saveResource(const tchar* filename=0)=0;
```

With this simple set of interface methods, a manager can fully maintain a set of resource objects. Most notably, the interface functions disableResource and restoreResource allow the manager to purge or restore the resource to volatile memory. An example of this would be textures residing in video card memory. If the video device interface is lost, the resource manager can be notified to disable all of the dependent resources. When the video device is restored, these child resources can easily be restored by calling the appropriate member function on each.

With D3DX, we have the luxury of using the built-in resource manager provided by Microsoft. For most of our video-dependent resources, we will take advantage of this automated management for restoring video-resident resources after a temporary loss of the device. Setting up resources in this manner requires the simple addition of the D3DPOOL_MANAGED flag during creation of Direct3D resources that support automated management. We also benefit from the automated memory management this flag provides, ensuring that textures are uploaded and removed from video memory as necessary when memory space is limited.

This does not apply to dynamic resources, such as textures or geometry we might need to recalculate often. These resources are better off being hand-managed by us rather than Direct3D, since we understand when and how they will be replaced with new data. Our resource interface affords us the opportunity to use both methods, depending on how we choose to overload the virtual functions for each resource type we define.

TEXTURE RESOURCES AND SURFACE MATERIALS

Our simplest resource is the `cTexture` object. This class is essentially a wrapper object to contain an `IDirect3DTexture9` object in a format compatible with our resource management scheme. We mention the class here simply because we will be using it quite often while rendering models. Apart from our management wrapper, the `cTexture` class also contains functions to load texture files from disk using the methods provided by the D3DX library.

Surface materials, however, are our own creation and need a bit of explaining. D3DX suffers from a backward-compatibility fetish that still standardizes on a single texture per surface material. This is evidenced by the primary structure used to store these objects, `D3DXMATERIAL`, which allows for only a single texture to be specified. Years ago, this would have been adequate, but for current top-end video hardware it is horribly outdated.

For our rendering needs, we provide an updated surface material class, `cSurfaceMaterial`, which contains up to 16 textures in addition to the standard diffuse, secular, and emissive lighting hues. Although 16 textures might seem like overkill for today's video cards that can still only use four to eight textures per pass, providing this extra space affords us the space to supply textures for multiple render passes within the same surface material.

For example, we might create a surface material that is designed to render in two passes, with each pass using four unique textures. The eight textures fit well within our limits, and provide unique texture indices for our HLSL shaders to use. We could also use the storage space to store multiple versions of the surface material, like summer and winter versions of each texture. Shaders could be written with initialization code that chooses the proper set to use. With all these possibilities, perhaps even a 16-texture limit is too limiting!

`cSurfaceMaterials` also contain a set of bit flags, one for each texture slot. These 16 flags signify whether a texture has been loaded into the corresponding slot. As we will see in a moment, this bit field allows us to validate surface materials with the render methods that will use them.

RENDER METHOD RESOURCES

The `cEffectFile` class is our container for the `ID3DXEffect` object. In addition to providing our usual set of resource management and file I/O functions, `cEffectFile` parses the compiled effect for variables and constants the engine knows how to set. As we discussed in Chapter 2, "Fundamental 3D Objects," Direct3D effect files can contain variables in the global scope with annotations or semantics that can be sought out by the application. The application can then set these variables using the interface functions provided by `ID3DXEffect` by way of its base class `ID3DXEffectBase`.

These functions, described within the documentation of the DirectX SDK, accept either a string literal or a handle to identify the variable being set. Accessing effect variables by handle is far more efficient because it does not involve the costly string comparisons associated with searching by variable name. The `cEffectFile` class takes advantage of this by pre-parsing the effect file at the time it is loaded to build a list of handles to known variable types. Table 4.1 lists some of the variables recognized by the `cEffectFile` class.

TABLE 4.1   Some of the User-Defined Variables Recognized by the `cEffectFile` Class

SEMANTIC	DATA TYPE	DESCRIPTION
World	Matrix	The object-to-world transform matrix
View	Matrix	The world-to-view transform matrix
Projection	Matrix	The view-to-screen transform matrix
WorldView	Matrix	World * View
ViewProjection	Matrix	View * Projection
WorldViewProjection	Matrix	World * View * Projection
WorldMatrixArray	Matrix	An array of world matrices
MaterialAmbient	Color	The ambient material color
MaterialDiffuse	Color	The diffuse material color
MaterialEmissive	Color	The emissive material color
MaterialSpecular	Color	The specular material color
MaterialPower	Float	The specular material power
CurNumBones	Int	The number of bone influences used per vertex for skeletal animation
<name>X	Texture	A Texture object having some name followed by a number between 0 and 16; e.g., Tex0, Texture7, etc.

Pre-parsing these semantics for handles also allows us to set some bit fields internally to identify which variables are present within an effect. For example, we set a bit for each numbered texture slot found within the effect file. By comparing these texture flag bits against those of a `cSurfaceMaterial` resource using a logical AND operation, we can quickly validate surface materials to determine if they contain the proper number of textures required by a given render method.

The parent resource of the `cEffectFile` object is the `cRenderMethod`. Our final engine will render the scene in multiple, distinct stages. Two examples of these stages would include lighting and the application of bump maps. To render the scene, we allow objects to contain multiple effect files—one for each stage of the render process. The `cRenderMethod` object is used to store these `cEffectFiles`. `cRenderMethod` is nothing more than a collection of links to `cEffectFile` object files, one for each stage of the render process. `cRenderMethod` also has the ability to store a unique `cSurfaceMaterial` for each stage, allowing it to represent an entire rendering process.

For now, we'll simplify things by using a single `cEffectFile` object per model. This will allow us to get our engine up and running quickly without getting bogged down in bump maps and other render effects. We will revisit this subject in the third part of the book, when we begin using multiple shaders per object for greater effect. For now, even though our models will contain a `cRenderMethod`, the set will contain only one `cEffectFile` object in the "default" slot.

INDEX AND VERTEX BUFFERS

Index and vertex buffer resources are used frequently in the example engine, and are useful as stand-alone resources. For a majority of our engine data, the complete model resource we cover in a moment suits our basic needs, reserving index and vertex buffers for those cases where a traditional model does not apply. Index and vertex buffers are especially useful for dynamic data, which must be handled with care when using device-resident resources such as these. Using dynamic vertex and index buffers allows us to build geometry on-the-fly, or animate existing geometry on the CPU. We will use both methods as we construct the terrain engine.

To clarify, we use the term *dynamic* to mean *completely replaced*. Locking a vertex or index buffer to change a few random values yields staggeringly poor performance on most video cards. We will therefore not support this action within our interface for these resources. Within our engine, we completely replace the contents of dynamic buffers each time they are updated. This allows the driver to maintain a one-way path for dynamic data. Once data has been delivered to the video card; no attempt is ever made to read it back into system memory to update a few specific values.

The class objects `cVertexBuffer` and `cIndexBuffer` provide the basic operations we require for our buffers. These objects house both our regular and dynamic buffers. To support *dynamic* (read "replaced") buffer data, we employ a method endorsed by NVIDIA and Microsoft as the best means to update dynamic data.

The method uses an oversized buffer to hold the dynamic data. For example, if your dynamic data consisted of 10 vertices, you would create a dynamic buffer large enough to hold 100. Of this larger space, you continue to use only 10 vertices at a time. In the first frame, you use vertices 0 through 9. Indexes 10 through 19 are used in the second frame, and so on. When you run out of room in the buffer, the entire contents of the buffer are discarded and the process starts over at vertex 0. This sliding window scheme is considered the friendliest method to use because it results in the least number of Direct Memory Access (DMA) operations being interrupted. Listing 4.5 shows the algorithm pseudo code, based on the method outlined in the Microsoft DirectX 9 Developer FAQ [D9Faq].

LISTING 4.5 **The recommended method for updating dynamic index or vertex buffers.**

```
Create a DirectX buffer object (vertex or index)
using the D3DUSAGE_DYNAMIC and D3DUSAGE_WRITEONLY
usage flags and the D3DPOOL_DEFAULT pool flag.
This buffer should be larger than the size
of the data you intend to use by at least 2x.

// init an index value
I = 0;

for each frame
{
  // Given a buffer size of M
  // and a desired amount of new data N...
  if (I+N < M)
  {
    I += N;
    Lock the buffer using the D3DLOCK_NOOVERWRITE flag.
    Write N units of data starting at index I
    Unlock the buffer
```

```
    // This tells Direct3D and the driver that
    // you will be adding new data and won't be
    // modifying any data that you previously wrote.
    // Therefore, if a DMA operation was in progress,
    // it isn't interrupted.
}
else
{
  I = 0
  Lock the buffer using the D3DLOCK_DISCARD flag
  Write N units of data starting at index I
  Unlock the buffer

  // This tells Direct3D and the driver that
  // you are resetting the buffer contents.
  // All previous data is flagged as disposable.
  // If a DMA operation in progress for the old data,
  // the driver is free to supply the caller with
  // a completely new buffer and discard
  // the old one at its leisure
}

render the frame using N units of data,
beginning at index I
}
```

MODEL RESOURCES

The cModelResource class is perhaps the most important resource object we will use; it is certainly the resource class we will interface with the most often. This resource class is a container for a complete D3DXFRAME-based hierarchy tree. Because multiple nodes can be contained within these objects, cModelResource can actually represent more than one physical object within the game. For example, a human gladiator character might contain a complete skeleton of animated nodes, skinned meshes for flesh and clothing, and individual static models for each weapon or piece of armor. Each mesh in turn maintains links to cRenderMethods and cSurfaceMaterial objects, making the cModelResource into a representation for an entire *entity* within our engine, not just a specific piece of geometry.

As mentioned previously, we perform this storage feat using a D3DXFRAME hierarchy. These objects were described in Chapter 2, "Fundamental 3D Objects," as the ideal storage method for skeletal animation and skinned meshes. A great feature of the D3DX implementation of these structures is that they are user-extendable. By deriving our own structures from D3DXFRAME and D3DXMESHCONTAINER, we can add our own platform-specific data on top of the data provided in the base classes.

This is important, because it allows us to hook in links to our custom resources, `cEffectFile` and `cSurfaceMaterial`. This transforms the simple tree of single-texture-mapped meshes provided by D3DX into an HLSL shaded, multitextured database. Using these extended classes requires the creation of a D3DX interface for managing nodes within the frame hierarchy. However, the first step is declaring our new data types. Listing 4.6 shows our extensions to D3DXFRAME and D3DXMESHCONTAINER.

LISTING 4.6   The model hierarchy classes derived from `D3DXFRAME` and `D3DXMESHCONTAINER`.

```
//-------------------------------------------------
// Name: struct D3DXFRAME_DERIVED
// Desc: Structure derived from D3DXFRAME
//       so we can add some app-specific
//       info that will be stored with
//       each frame
//-------------------------------------------------
struct D3DXFRAME_DERIVED:
public D3DXFRAME
{
    uint16  frameIndex;
    uint16  parentIndex;
};


//-------------------------------------------------
// Name: struct D3DXMESHCONTAINER_DERIVED
// Desc: Structure derived from D3DXMESHCONTAINER
//       so we can add some app-specific
//       info that will be stored with each mesh
//-------------------------------------------------
struct D3DXMESHCONTAINER_DERIVED:
public D3DXMESHCONTAINER
{
    // SkinMesh info
    D3DXMESHDATA          RenderMeshData;
    uint32                NumAttributeGroups;
    LPD3DXATTRIBUTERANGE  pAttributeTable;
    DWORD                 NumBoneInfluences;
    uint8*                pBoneIndexList;
```

```
        LPD3DXBUFFER          pBoneCombinationBuf;
        uint32                NumBoneMatrices;
        cSIMDMatrix*          pBoneOffsetMatrices;
        cRenderMethod**       ppRenderMethods;
};
```

Our additions to the D3DXFRAME base class are minimal. The
D3DXFRAME_DERIVED objects used to build the tree are allocated into a
fixed array. Therefore, even though we use a tree structure to use the
data, we can still identify each node of the tree using its unique index in
the linear array. We can do this because we are able to assume our
D3DXFRAME_DERIVED trees to not dynamically change size or order.
One a hierarchy is loaded, it remains in the same configuration for the remainder of its life.

To maintain more family information than the base D3DXFRAME
structure provides, we can use index values into the array they are stored
within to identify any potential parent and root objects. The frameIndex is
the root node of the entire tree. The parentIndex refers to the immediate
parent of the node. A value of –1 (0xffff for word values) is used to signify
unused index values.

Why not use pointers? This data is intended as a reference object.
Multiple instances of this model can be placed in the world, each with its
own set of D3DXFRAME_DERIVED structures. These unique structures
would contain the transform matrices for each particular instance of the
frame nodes. By storing our family information as index values rather
than pointers, it becomes easier to create new instances of this model by
simply allocating a new array of frame objects and copying the data.
There are no fix-ups to apply, since the indices are all relative from the
root of the array used to hold the data.

The D3DXMESHCONTAINER_DERIVED structure is a little more involved. On top of the D3DXMESHCONTAINER base class, we add all the
data that is unique to our engine. This includes a list of cRenderMethods
and cSurfaceMaterials used by the mesh, skinning information for the
mesh, and the mesh itself. We store our own D3DMESHDATA structure
apart from the one contained in the base class to maintain a separation
between the system memory version of the model and the one optimized
and loaded into video memory for our render method to use.

In addition to allowing us to extend the base classes, the D3DX functions used to provide file I/O for the frame tree can also be extended to
include our custom data. This creates an interface with which we can extend the original Direct3D X file format to suit our needs. This requires us
to build three key interface classes: one to manage the allocation and de-

struction of our data structures, one to manage the saving of these structures within the X file, and one to load the data from the x file.

These three interfaces are provided by the D3DX classes ID3DXAllocateHierarchy, ID3DXLoadUserData, and ID3DXSaveUserData. To add our user data, we simply derive our own classes from the interfaces and provide the functionality behind each pure virtual member function defined in the base class. The d3dx_frame_manager source code files located on the accompanying CD-ROM show these functions at work. These files show the allocation, cleanup, and file I/O routines in better detail than we could hope to provide within the book text.

ON THE CD

SCENE NODES AND OBJECTS

Two virtual base classes within the engine serve as the basis for almost every item in our world: cSceneNode and cSceneObject. A cSceneNode defines a specific coordinate system in the 3D environment. These nodes can be linked together in a parent-child hierarchy to create an entire scene graph for the environment. All objects within our scene are ultimately derived from the cSceneNode base class, including the cSceneObject.

While the cSceneNode class maintains a transformation matrix and parent-child link information to define the overall scene graph, the cSceneNode class does not contain any volumetric data. This is where the cSceneObject becomes useful. Based on the cSceneNode, cSceneObject adds a local and world-space bounding box to define a volume of space around each node. Whether the cSceneObject represents a game model or a portion of our terrain, this bounding box will provide a rough estimate of the space occupied by the underlying geometry.

Having a base class that contains the matrix transformation and axis-aligned bounding box for an object provides us with a consistent interface upon which any game-specific item can be built. Whether it is a patch of grass, a tree, or the sun, all objects will maintain a common set of properties provided by the cSceneObject class. In Chapter 5, "World Management," we will exploit this foundation class further as we construct a quadtree to manage the spatial relationship between cSceneObject-derived classes. cSceneObject is also used as the basis for our render pipeline, providing a common interface that we can use to process objects during each stage of rendering.

THE RENDER QUEUE

One of the most important aspects of maintaining a render pipeline such as ours is to control the number of costly state changes requested by the program. A state change is anything that instructs the video card to alter its processing of our models and textures. These time-consuming state changes include activating vertex and pixel shaders, as well as changing D3D render states and texture samplers. Using effect files through D3DX makes this problem a little more difficult, since effect files can contain a myriad of render state changes. These render states might be set redundantly in multiple effect files, causing the same render state values to be set over and over again.

We place a little faith in the video card driver to manage these redundant state changes, since their direct management is out of our control. However, we can take direct control over the activation of the techniques within the effect files to ensure that the entire set of render states, including the vertex and pixel shader, are not used more than once in a given scene. Moreover, we can extend our management to include models, vertex buffer, index buffer, and texture activation as well. If we prioritize these state changes by cost, we can control the order in which they are given to the video hardware for rendering.

This is done with a render queue, found within our code base as `cRenderQueue`. This queue is little more than an execution list of objects we want to render. Rather than render objects directly to the screen, we submit them to the render queue. Once all of the objects are placed in the queue, we can sort the queue entries in terms of cost and then render the entire scene. The trick is devising a way to represent an entry within the queue as a compact piece of data that is easily sorted.

The basic ingredients of rendering are geometry, material, and rendering method. These three things, along with a few basic parameters such as transformation matrices, are all that are required to display an object. As luck would have it, we already have a concise representation for each of these objects in the form of our resource objects `cModelResource`, `cSurfaceMaterial`, and `cEffectFile`. In fact, our resource manager already assigns each of these objects a 16-bit index that represents their location within an allocated pool of objects. Using these indices, we can represent the basic members of a render queue entry as three-word values.

Suppose we enforce an order to the word values. Knowing that activating an effect file (which consists of a vertex and pixel shader) is a very costly operation, we place the index for the `cEffectFile` as the highest word in our three-word set. Geometry changes are the next largest expense, since they consist of index buffers and potentially multiple vertex streams. With that in mind, we place the `cModelResource` index as the second word value and round out the set with the `cSurfaceMaterial` index as the lowest word.

This construction of the three-word values in terms of priority creates a 48-bit sorting index for the render queue. If we sort these entries in terms of their 48-bit values, we will ensure that all objects being rendered with the same `cEffectFile` are grouped together in the list. Within each of these groups, all objects using the same `cModelResource` geometry resources are grouped together. Finally, all objects within a geometry group using the same surface materials are grouped together. The ordered list now represents a more efficient number of resource state changes required to render the entire scene.

The `cRenderEntry` code expands on this idea to represent each submission to the render queue as a 20-byte value. This is much larger than our 48-bit example, but provides far more information with which we can sort our rendering operations. `cRenderEntry` provides 12 bytes of data used to sort the entry, plus an additional 8 bytes containing a callback pointer and user-defined parameter. This allows a caller to submit an entry to the render queue and provide a callback function that will be triggered when the actual rendering needs to take place. The `cRenderQueue` collects all the entries, sorts them by priority, and then renders them one by one by triggering the callback functions provided.

The 12 bytes of data used to sort the `cRenderEntry` objects within the queue contain the same basic information as our example: geometry, material, and render method. The `cRenderEntry` expands on each of these to include additional parameters that are needed to identify specific usage of each resource. For example, the rendering method is represented in the queue entry as not only the word index of the `cEffectFile` resource, but an additional parameter describing which pass of the effect is being used. Armed with this data, we can sort our list by effect file, and by individual passes within the effect file.

Looking over the `cRenderQueue` and `cRenderEntry` class definitions is the best way to gain familiarity with the prioritized queue we will use for our render pipeline. One highlight to note is the flags set to each callback to perform the final rendering of each queue entry. As the render queue processes the list, it keeps track of which resources are currently in use. When it encounters a new resource in the list, the callback is sent with a flag informing the user to activate the new resource. Listing 4.7 shows highlights of the `cRenderEntry` and `cRenderQueue` classes. Following this, Listing 4.8 shows how one of our objects, the `cSceneModel`, uses the render queue to submit itself for rendering, and then handles the callback to perform the actual rasterization of the model at the proper time.

LISTING 4.7 Class definitions and highlights of cRenderEntry and cRenderQueue.

```
/*  cRenderEntry
-----------------------------------------

  A Render Entry is a 20 byte piece
  of data used to represent
  a desired render operation in the queue.
  The top 12 bytes represent a numerical
  value which allows us to sort these
  objects into an optimal render order.

  Render Entries are sorted in the
  queue by the following data...

  cPoolHandle hEffectFile;
  uint8 renderPass;
  uint8 renderParam :6;
  uint8 modelType   :2;
  cPoolHandle hModel;
  uint16 modelParamA;
  uint16 modelParamB;
  cPoolHandle hSurfaceMaterial;

  modelType describes whether
  the hModel, modelParamA and
  modelParamB values contain
  actual model data or raw
  vertex and index buffer indices.
  The modelType value itself
  is taken from the eTypeFlags
  enum in cRenderEntry.

-----------------------------------------
*/

// these flags are passed to the
// render callbacks to let the
// object know which of it's render
// components need to be activated
enum eActivationFlagBits
{
```

```
    k_activateRenderMethod = 0,
    k_activateRenderMethodPass,
    k_activateRenderMethodParam,
    k_activateModel,
    k_activateModelParamA,
    k_activateModelParamB,
    k_activateSurfaceMaterial,

    k_totalActivationFlags
};

class cRenderEntry
{
public:

// we turn on byte packing
to ensure a tight fit
#pragma pack(1)

    // FIELDS USED TO SORT ENTRY (12 bytes)
    union
    {
        // this union allows us to sort our
        // render parameters as 3 dword values
        struct
        {
            uint32 sortValueA;
            uint32 sortValueB;
            uint32 sortValueC;
        };

        struct
        {
            // The following members map to
            // sortValueA (first 32 bits)
            // (listed in reverse priority)

            // user-defined render parameter
            // packed together with the
            // model type (1 byte total)
            uint8 modelType   : 2;
            uint8 renderParam : 6;
            // which render pass to use
            uint8 renderPass;
            // which effect file to use
```

```
        cPoolHandle hEffectFile;

        // The following members map to
        // sortValueB (second 32 bits)
        // (listed in reverse priority)

        // secondary vertex buffer or model frame
        uint16 modelParamA;
        // primary vertex buffer or model index
        cPoolHandle hModel;

        // The following members map to
        // sortValueC (third 32 bits)
        // (listed in reverse priority)

        // the surface material used
        cPoolHandle hSurfaceMaterial;
        // index buffer or model subset
        uint16 modelParamB;
      };
    };

    // ADDITIONAL UNSORTED FIELDS (8 bytes)

    cSceneNode* object;
    uint32   userData;

// we can go back to default packing now
#pragma pack()

    // these enum values are used to set
    // the modelType value above. This
    // tells the queue if the model
    // data represents a model resource
    // or a set of vertex and index buffers
    enum eTypeFlags
    {
      k_bufferEntry = 0,
      k_modelEntry,
    };

    cRenderEntry(){};
    ~cRenderEntry(){};

    // clear the entry to default values
```

```cpp
    void clear()
    {
      sortValueA = 0;
      sortValueB = 0;
      sortValueC = 0;
    }
};

// cRenderEntry sorting functor
// used within a QuickSort
// algorithm to sort the queue
typedef cRenderEntry* LPRenderEntry;
struct sort_less
{
  bool operator()(
    const LPRenderEntry& a,
    const LPRenderEntry& b)const
  {
    if (a->sortValueA
      > b->sortValueA)
    {
      return false;
    }
    else if (a->sortValueA
      < b->sortValueA)
    {
      return true;
    }

    if (a->sortValueB
      > b->sortValueB)
    {
      return false;
    }
    else if (a->sortValueB
      < b->sortValueB)
    {
      return true;
    }

    if (a->sortValueC
      > b->sortValueC)
    {
      return false;
    }
```

```
      else if (a->sortValueC
        < b->sortValueC)
      {
        return true;
      }

      return false;
  };
};

void cRenderQueue::sortEntryList()
{
  //
  // Perform a standard quick-sort using the
  // sort_less functor above
  //
  profile_scope(cRenderQueue_sortEntryList);

  // see "core\quick_sort.h" for
  // implementation details
  QuickSort(
    m_entryList,
    m_activeEntries,
    sort_less());
}

void cRenderQueue::reset()
{
  m_activeEntries = 0;
}

//
// This function is responsible for
// executing the render queue
//
void cRenderQueue::execute()
{
  profile_scope(cRenderQueue_execute);

  if (m_activeEntries)
  {
    cDisplayManager& displayManager =
      TheGameHost.displayManager();
    LPDIRECT3DDEVICE9 d3dDevice =
      TheGameHost.d3dDevice();
```

```
// sort the entry list
sortEntryList();

// issue the callback to render
// the first item in the queue with all
// activation flags set
u32Flags activationFlags(0xffffffff);
m_entryList[0]->object->renderCallback(
  m_entryList[0],
  activationFlags);

// render any additional items,
// sending only the flags for resources
// which must be activated
for (int i=1; i<m_activeEntries; ++i)
{
  cRenderEntry* currentEntry = m_entryList[i];
  cRenderEntry* previousEntry = m_entryList[i-1];

  activationFlags.value=0;

  //
  // check for effect changes
  //
  if (previousEntry->hEffectFile
      != currentEntry->hEffectFile)
  {
    // end the last render method
    cEffectFile* pLastMethod =
      displayManager.effectFilePool().
      getResource(previousEntry->hEffectFile);
    if (pLastMethod)
    {
      pLastMethod->end();
      safe_release(pLastMethod);
    }

    SET_BIT(activationFlags,
      k_activateRenderMethod);
    SET_BIT(activationFlags,
      k_activateRenderMethodPass);
    SET_BIT(activationFlags,
      k_activateRenderMethodParam);
  }
  else if (previousEntry->renderPass
```

```cpp
            != currentEntry->renderPass)
{
  SET_BIT(activationFlags,
    k_activateRenderMethodPass);
  SET_BIT(activationFlags,
    k_activateRenderMethodParam);
}
else
{
  if (previousEntry->renderParam
    != currentEntry->renderParam)
  {
    SET_BIT(activationFlags,
      k_activateRenderMethodParam);
  }
}

//
// check for model changes
//
if (previousEntry->hModel
    != currentEntry->hModel
  ||
  previousEntry->modelType
    != currentEntry->modelType)
{
  SET_BIT(activationFlags, k_activateModel);
  SET_BIT(activationFlags, k_activateModelParamA);
  SET_BIT(activationFlags, k_activateModelParamB);
}
else
{
  if (previousEntry->modelParamA
    != currentEntry->modelParamA)
  {
    SET_BIT(activationFlags, k_activateModelParamA);
  }
  if (previousEntry->modelParamB
      != currentEntry->modelParamB)
  {
    SET_BIT(activationFlags, k_activateModelParamB);
  }
}

//
```

```
      // Check for surface material changes
      //
      if (previousEntry->hSurfaceMaterial
          != currentEntry->hSurfaceMaterial)
      {
        SET_BIT(activationFlags, k_activateSurfaceMaterial);
      }

      //
      // issue the callback to render
      //
      currentEntry->object->renderCallback(
        currentEntry,
        activationFlags);
    }

    // end the last render method
    cRenderEntry* lastEntry =
      m_entryList[m_activeEntries-1];
    cEffectFile* pLastMethod =
      DisplayManager.effectFilePool().
      getResource((cPoolHandle)lastEntry->hEffectFile);

    if (pLastMethod)
    {
      pLastMethod->end();
      safe_release(pLastMethod);
    }
  }

  // reset for the next frame
  reset();
}
```

LISTING 4.8   A sample pair of functions showing the use of cRenderEntry and cRenderQueue.

```
// a simplified version of the cSceneModel
// render function used to add the contained
// model to the render queue
void cSceneModel::render()
{
  const D3DXMESHCONTAINER_DERIVED*
    pMeshContainer = meshContainer();

  if (pMeshContainer != NULL
```

```cpp
                    && pMeshContainer->ppRenderMethodList)
        {
          for (UINT iMaterial = 0;
               iMaterial < pMeshContainer->NumMaterials;
               iMaterial++)
          {
            cRenderMethod* pMethod =
              pMeshContainer->ppRenderMethodList[iMaterial];

            if (pMethod)
            {
              cEffectFile* pEffect =
                pMethod->getEffect(
                TheGameHost.currentRenderStage());
              cSurfaceMaterial* pMaterial =
                pMethod->getMaterial(
                TheGameHost.currentRenderStage());

              if (pEffect && pMaterial)
              {
                uint16 numPasses = pEffect->totalPasses();

                for(uint16 iPass = 0;
                    iPass < numPasses;
                    iPass++ )
                {
                  cRenderEntry* pRenderEntry =
                    DisplayManager.openRenderQueue();

                  pRenderEntry->hEffectFile =
                    (uint8)pEffect->resourceHandle();
                  pRenderEntry->hSurfaceMaterial =
                    pMaterial->resourceHandle();
                  pRenderEntry->detailLevel =
                    m_lod;
                  pRenderEntry->modelType =
                    cRenderEntry::k_modelEntry;
                  pRenderEntry->hModel =
                    m_pModelResource->resourceHandle();
                  pRenderEntry->modelParamA =
                    m_modelFrameIndex;
                  pRenderEntry->modelParamB =
                    iMaterial;
                  pRenderEntry->renderPass =
                    (uint8)iPass;
```

```
              pRenderEntry->object =
                (cSceneNode*)this;
              pRenderEntry->userData =
                iMaterial;

              DisplayManager.closeRenderQueue(
                pRenderEntry);
          }
        }
      }
    }
  }
}

// this function is called by the render queue
// to perform the actual rendering of the model.
void cSceneModel::renderCallback(
  cRenderEntry* entry,
  u32Flags activationFlags)
{
  LPDIRECT3DDEVICE9 d3dDevice =
    TheGameHost.d3dDevice();
  const D3DXMESHCONTAINER_DERIVED* pMeshContainer =
    meshContainer();
  bool skinModel=
    pMeshContainer->pSkinInfo != NULL;

  UINT iMaterial = entry->userData;
  cRenderMethod* pMethod =
    pMeshContainer->ppRenderMethodList[iMaterial];
  cEffectFile* pEffect =
    pMethod->getEffect(
      TheGameHost.currentRenderStage());
  cSurfaceMaterial* pMaterial =
    pMethod->getMaterial(
      TheGameHost.currentRenderStage());

  if (pEffect && pMaterial)
  {
    // do we need to activate the render method?
    if (TEST_BIT(
          activationFlags,
          k_activateRenderMethod))
    {
      pEffect->begin();
```

```
        }

        // do we need to activate the render pass?
        if (TEST_BIT(
              activationFlags,
              k_activateRenderMethodPass)
          || TEST_BIT(
              activationFlags,
              k_activateRenderMethodParam)
          || TEST_BIT(
              activationFlags,
              k_activateRenderMethodLOD))
        {
          m_pModelResource->setLOD(m_lod);
          if (skinModel)
          {
            int numBoneInfluences =
              pMeshContainer->NumBoneInfluences-1;
            pEffect->setParameter(
              cEffectFile::k_boneInfluenceCount,
              &numBoneInfluences);
          }
          pEffect->activatePass(entry->renderPass);
        }

        // do we need to activate the surface material
        if (TEST_BIT(
              activationFlags,
              k_activateSurfaceMaterial))
        {
          pEffect->applySurfaceMaterial(pMaterial);
        }

        const cCamera* pCamera =
          TheGameHost.activeCamera();

        D3DXMATRIX matWorldViewProj =
          (D3DXMATRIX)worldMatrix() *
          (D3DXMATRIX)pCamera->viewProjMatrix();

        // set the view matrix
        pEffect->setMatrix(
          cEffectFile::k_worldViewProjMatrix,
            &matWorldViewProj);
```

```
    pEffect->setMatrix(
      cEffectFile::k_worldMatrix,
      &worldMatrix());

    // draw the mesh subset
    m_pModelResource->renderModelSubset(
      entry->modelParamA,
      entry->modelParamB );
  }
}
```

THE MODEL EDITOR

ON THE CD

Also located on the accompanying CD-ROM is `shader_edit_debug_exe`. This simple test of the resource system and file I/O functions allows users to load models from Direct3D X files, add textures and define render methods, and then view the output in a sample window. Animation playback is also provided, along with the ability to load and append new animations to the file. Once edited, models can be saved back out as new Gaia-extended X files, retaining file references to all the texture and shader information supplied. This application also shows the application of our engine to the Microsoft Foundation Class library (MFC), which is useful for making these types of tools.

REFERENCES

[FAQ] *Microsoft DirectX 9.0 Developer FAQ* (available online at *http://msdn. microsoft.com/library/en-us/dndxgen/html/directx9devfaq.asp*).

II
INTRODUCTION TO TERRAIN SYSTEMS

Now that the introductory part of the book is behind us, we can move forward using our basic display engine and D3DX foundation to explore terrain rendering methods. In this section, we will cover the two main components of any good landscape engine: the ground geometry and textures. These two elements create the backdrop for our world, and the surface we will later populate with water, grass, flowers, and trees.

Being the two most important aspects of the engine also means that we have many potential methods to discuss. We will present each of the most popular methods in detail, and discuss the implementation of each. However, our demo engine will focus on a few key methods to use for our next demo program.

We begin this part of the book by laying down a little more foundation for our engine. We will discuss world management and the quadtree approach to dividing space into more manageable subareas. This type of spatial management structure is crucial to have in place before we can begin devising our terrain geometry storage methods. It will also be a valuable aid in reducing the number of objects we attempt to render, allowing us to quickly find only those objects most likely to be visible on screen.

The next three chapters deal with the ground itself. We begin in Chapter 6, "Basic Terrain Geometry," by discussing the input mechanism for terrain information: the venerable height map. Methods are described to create this data in paint packages or by using procedural, random methods. With the data source defined, we can convert the height map to actual vertex information and perform a brute-force rendering method to see our data on screen.

The next two chapters, Chapter 7, "The ROAM Terrain System," and Chapter 8, "Tiled Geometry Techniques," introduce terrain geometry management. Now that our data is in vertex form, we find that such a large set of vertices is unlikely to render with any great speed. To alleviate this problem, we look at some popular management schemes that provide level-of-detail (LOD) modes. By rendering more geometry close to the camera, and less geometry in the distance, we can reduce the overall amount of data processed for rendering and create a more efficient engine.

In Chapter 9, "Texturing Techniques," we add texture maps to the terrain geometry to create a reasonable landscape. As our first foray into HLSL shader coding, this chapter will introduce the setup and application of texture blending techniques along with simple lighting methods. While far from eye-catching, this first pass at rendering will show our terrain textured to represent real-world surfaces such as grass, rock, and sand. The result is a barren, textured landscape with efficient LOD management; the perfect stage on which to begin the third and final section of this book.

5

WORLD MANAGEMENT

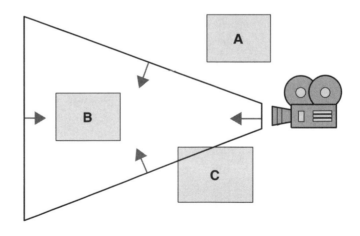

Before we can start building our 3D terrain, we have one final chapter of foundation-related issues with which to contend. Keep in mind that our intent is to build a complete terrain engine as we explore these topics. To do so, we have some fundamental tasks to discuss before our world can take shape.

First, we need to deal with the scale of the task before us. Planets are big, and the most interesting sections are comprised of rolling hills or mountainous regions. As you might expect, these areas are the most challenging and data intensive to represent in 3D. One of the key considerations when working with such a large data set is how to ensure that the engine can focus on the areas that need the most attention and neglect the others. This is traditionally done with some type of *space partitioning*.

Partitioning space is a matter of dividing the world into sections, allowing the engine to determine which sections need rendering and which do not. The engine is also given the opportunity to decide how much detail is required when rendering each section of the world, elevating the processing required for less important areas. The most efficient methods store these sections in a nested tree structure of some kind, allowing multiple sections to be discarded or classified with a single test. Four our engine, we will discuss the quadtree technique and methods to enhance it for even greater efficiency.

For the purposes of this book, we are focusing on a small section of terrain to show our methods. Later, we will convert this small patch of land into an island and surround it with water. The quadtree allows us to determine which sections of the island are visible, but its potential scales far above our limited environment. Using a quadtree (albeit of a larger size) a terrain engine could manage many "islands" of terrain, using the quadtree to determine which are within the vicinity of the camera. This would allow a program to load this data dynamically from the hard drive as the camera ventures into new areas. The result would be a seemingly endless landscape, with only the necessary portions consuming precious memory resources. Areas of the environment outside the camera view could be purged from memory, awaiting the time when they are needed again.

THE MOTIVATION BEHIND SCENE ORGANIZATION

The first step in any render pipeline is determining which objects need to be rendered. This is our primary motivation behind partitioning the space. Determining visibility is a simple matter of determining which objects are within the camera's view, or *frustum*. The frustum is a six-sided shape that describes the volume of space that can be seen by the camera. Figure 5.1 shows a simple representation of a few world objects and a sample camera frustum.

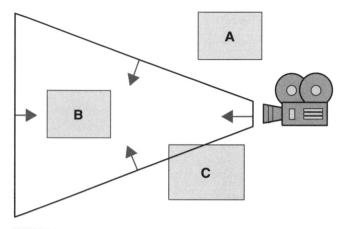

FIGURE 5.1   The planes of a 2D camera frustum. Objects B and C contain points in the positive half-space of all planes, and are therefore inside the frustum.

To determine if an object is visible, we need to determine if any part of it lies inside the frustum. This can be done in a variety of ways. Assuming the object can be summarized with some type of bounding shape, such as a sphere or box, frustum testing becomes a series of six tests, one for each side of the frustum.

Each side of the frustum is considered a plane in 3D space. Each plane contains a normal vector pointing into the frustum. This normal defines the positive half-space of the plane. Given these six planes, six tests are performed with each object to see if any portion of the object exists in the positive half-space of each plane. If a portion of the shape is in the positive half-space of all six planes, it lies inside the frustum and is visible. Figure 5.1 shows a representation of this in 2D using a four-sided frustum.

As you might expect, these tests are rather costly in terms of performance. Even if we represented each object with a bounding box shape, we would still have eight vertices to test per object (the box corners). Multiply the vertex count by the frustum sides and you find a potential for 48 plane half-space tests per object. This is far too many to be considered efficient for a fully populated landscape, which might contain thousands of objects that must be tested for visibility each frame.

The task is greatly reduced by using a scene organization method. Suppose we could break up the space into smaller areas, each represented by a rectangular volume called a *sector*. As objects move about the world, they move from sector to sector, and we keep track of which objects belong to each sector. When it comes time to determine which objects need to be rendered, we simply determine which of these rectangular sectors are visible. All objects contained within those sectors are thereby also deemed visible and sent through the render pipeline.

What we gain in efficiency, we lose in precision. Not all of the objects within a sector might actually be visible, since a portion of the sector itself might lie outside the camera frustum. However, if we know that a given sector rectangle straddles the edge of the frustum, we can go one step further and test each object within the sector individually. By doing this, we regain our precision while still reducing the overall number of tests performed, since nodes that were either fully inside or fully outside the frustum did not need any further testing. Figure 5.2 summarizes the efficiency gained by using the sector approach.

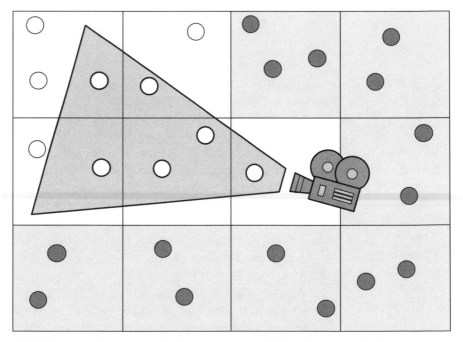

FIGURE 5.2   The efficiency gained using sector divisions. Without the sectors, the brute-force approach would require individual tests for all 24 circle objects. In this example, the sector approach would require testing of the five populated sectors shown in white, reducing the test count to 10 objects.

There is a flaw in this simple use of sectors. Even when using a sector-based approach, there is still the problem of having to test the bounds of all the populated sectors for visibility. If our game objects are dispersed evenly enough, we might not actually gain any efficiency with this approach. However, we have shown that grouping objects into sectors has the potential to become more efficient. Therefore, if we grouped the sectors into even larger volumes, we could gain further efficiency by limiting the number of populated sectors we need to test.

Nesting these sectors creates a hierarchy tree. Each sector contains a set of smaller child sectors, which together fill the space defined by their parent. If the parent is not visible, neither are the children. If the parent is completely visible, the children are, too. Should the parent straddle the visibility test volume, we step down into each child, testing it as a new parent. This recursive testing continues until all visible sectors are found, or we run out of tree levels to test.

THE BASIC QUADTREE

The quadtree and the oct-tree best represent the concept of nesting these sectors into a tree hierarchy. Each is a regimented tree hierarchy in which each node contains an equal number of subnodes. Quadtrees are essentially 2D spatial organization. Each 2D rectangle of a quadtree is divided equally into four child nodes arranged in a 2x2 grid. Each child node can be divided into four smaller children, and so on. The oct-tree is a quadtree extended into three dimensions, with each sector having eight child nodes in a 2x2x2 grid.

For our landscape engine, a full 3D representation is not needed. Proportionally, our environment is very flat. The landscape can extend along the x- and y-axes for great distances, with very little vertical space to worry about by comparison. Therefore, we can use the quadtree and use the simple four-child 2D layout rather than the more robust oct-tree method. As we will see later, we can still add some height, or z-axis related information to extend our quadtree into a pseudo-3D hierarchy, but for now we will focus on the 2D approach.

Traditionally, quadtrees are created to contain a minimal amount of nodes within the tree. When a branch of the tree can be identified as empty (there are no objects appearing in the tree below the branch), then all nodes within the branch can be discarded. This allows for a minimal amount of storage space for the tree, since empty nodes consume no memory, but can cause a lot of dynamic allocation and destruction of memory when mobile objects are introduced.

To make our development process easier, and keep the quadtree more manageable, we will use what is known as a fully expanded tree representation. That is, all nodes within the tree exist even if they are empty. This way, as objects move around our world, we have no dynamic node creation or destruction to worry about, and our memory consumption for the tree remains large, but constant.

Therefore, the problem becomes this: how do we assign objects to nodes within the tree? Look at Figure 5.3. We will use these images as a guide to show the process of placing an object in the tree. In the first drawing, we begin with the topmost node of the tree. This node encompasses the entire world, as well as the test object shown. Placing the object in the proper subnode is a recursive problem. Given that the object currently belongs to the root node, we perform the following recursive process until the final node is found.

1. Check the object against all child nodes of the current node. If no child nodes exist, jump directly to step 3.
2. If the object is fully contained in a child node, set the child node as the current node and repeat step 1.
3. The object is a member of this node. Add it to the list of members for the current node and exit.

In Figure 5.3, these steps are run three times. Each time, a child node is found that contains the node and the process is repeated. In the final drawing, we see that the object spans more than one child node (the dotted lines), and cannot become a member of any of them. Instead, it becomes a member of the parent node—the smallest node that contains it. Figure 5.4 shows the tree hierarchy created from this process and the object listed below the node chosen to contain it.

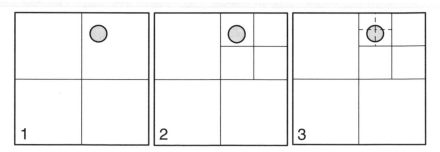

FIGURE 5.3   A series of quadtree recursions needed to assign an object to a particular node within the quadtree.

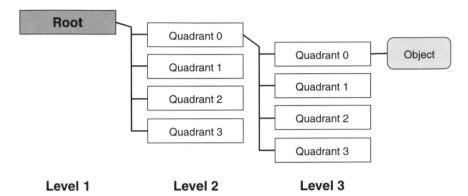

FIGURE 5.4   The quadtree hierarchy built from the process shown in Figure 5.3.

ENHANCING THE QUADTREE

Now that we understand the purpose and structure of a quadtree, and how to insert objects into it, we can look at some implementation details that extend the usefulness and efficiency of the tree. As stated earlier, we will use a fully expanded tree because of the simplicity and fixed-memory use it provides. It also allows for an interesting management scheme that provides direct sorting of objects into the tree without the recursive steps shown previously.

We borrow this concept from Matt Pritchard, who defined a direct-access method for quadtrees in his *Game Programming Gems 2* article [Pritchard]. We will provide a brief synopsis of the method here. Further exploration into the details can be found within Pritchard's article, or by exploring the source code on the accompanying CD-ROM for our implementation of the method.

ON THE CD

In short, the method uses the nature of the Logical XOR operation and the fact that each quadtree node is divided along the center point of each axis. If the quad tree sectors are stored in power-of-two integer values, computing the XOR of any object bounds creates a bit pattern that can be interrogated to find the proper tree level to place the object within. As with most computer graphics algorithms, this sounds complicated, but is really quite simple to use.

In Figure 5.5, we see a quadtree with an overall size of 256x256—power-of-two dimensions that require 8 bits of data per axis (one unsigned byte per axis). We know that quadtree nodes divide evenly, so the first-level splits will occur at position 128 on each axis, defining the four children of this node, as shown by the dotted lines. In binary terms, we can see that each level of our tree can be identified by the highest bit used by the splitting plane. See Table 5.1 for examples.

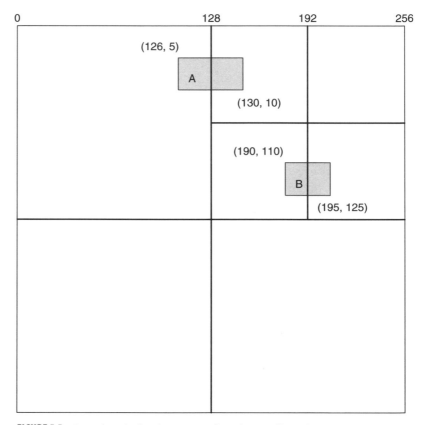

FIGURE 5.5   A quadtree built using power-of-two integer dimensions.

To determine which level of the tree our objects need to be inserted into, we examine their span along each axis. Taking the logical XOR of the axis extents will produce a bit pattern. The highest bit set in that pattern tells us which splitting plane the object crosses, and therefore which level of the tree it should become a member of. For example, two objects appear in Figure 5.5. Looking at Object A, we see that it spans the x-axis from 126 to 130. Taking the XOR of these values reveals the following:

```
126 (binary 01111110)
XOR   130 (binary 10000010)
--------------------------
      252 (binary 11111100)
```

In the result bit pattern, we see that the highest bit set is bit 7. Subtracting this value from our maximum value, also 7, yields 0. This tells us that Object A resides in level 0 of the tree (the root level). Looking at Table 5.1, we see that bit 7 in the XOR result does indeed match with the bit pattern for splitting on an interval of 128, a split that is performed at level 0 of our tree.

TABLE 5.1   The Bit Patterns Used to Identify Levels of the Power-of-Two Quadtree

LEVEL	SPLITTING PLANE INTERVAL	BINARY VALUE OF INTERVAL	HIGHEST BIT
0	128	10000000	7
1	64	01000000	6
2	32	00100000	5
3	16	00010000	4
4	8	00001000	3
5	4	00000100	2
6	2	00000010	1
7	1	00000001	0

The second Object, B, spans the *x*-axis from 190 to 195. Computing the XOR of these values yields 125 (binary 1111101). The highest bit set in this result is position 6. According to Table 5.1, position 6 signals tree level number 1. We could also deduce this as our maximum bit position, 7, minus the highest bit set, 6. Again, mentally walking the tree confirms that Object B would be placed one level down from the root, since it straddles the next splitting line at 192.

Of course, what we have not mentioned is that the level should also be determined using the span along the *y*-axis. The final tree level chosen would be the lesser of the two. For example, if the *x*-axis span of an object resolved to tree level 5, and the *y*-axis span resolved to tree level 3, we would place the object in tree level 3. Placing the object in a deeper part of the tree would violate our construction rules for the quadtree, because the object in question crossed a splitting plane in level 3 and should be placed no deeper.

To find the highest bit position set in our XOR results, we use the assembler instruction BSR, or Bit Scan Reverse. This simple x86 instruction will return the index of the highest bit set in a number much faster than we could do ourselves in C/C++. In the numeric tools provided with our sample engine (outlined in Appendix A, "Gaia Utility Classes"), we provide a function called `highestBitSet` to perform this task.

Once the proper tree level is known, the final step is to determine which node within that level is the parent to the object being tested. Again, the power-of-two dimensionality of our tree makes this a simple task. If all sectors of a given tree level are stored in a two-dimensional array, the proper sector can be found by taking the coordinates of the object being tested and converting them to the scale of the node grid at the tree level. For example, we calculated that Object B in Figure 5.5 would be placed at tree level 1. Tree level one contains a 2x2 grid of nodes. Therefore, the coordinates of Object B need to be scaled into the range [0, 1] on each axis to figure out the column and row index in which to place the object.

A simple shift operation does the trick. Coordinates of our world are in the range [0,255], 8 bit values. To get them to the range [0,1], we need to convert them to 1-bit values. Shifting the coordinate values to the right by 7 places will perform the conversion (8-bit value to 1-bit value is a right-shift of 7). For Object B, we take the coordinates (190, 20) and shift them right seven places to get the index values (1,0). These index values tell us exactly which node in the level 1 grid is the parent of Object B.

You should note that the entire functionality behind this method hinges on a quadtree with a dimension of 256x256 units. Our world is not stated in integer values, nor will it likely conform to this scale. To use this fast, direct-access method for the quadtree we will have to take our real-world coordinates and convert them to table-space. This implies scaling the values from their natural range to the range [0,255] and converting them from floating-point to integer values.

Adding Another Dimension to the Quadtree

As stated at the beginning of our quadtree discussion, quadtrees are a 2D spatial sorting technique. Extending the technique to three dimensions creates an oct-tree, where each node has eight children arranged in a 2x2x2 grid. This implies that we will also extend all of our math and fast-lookup routines to include the z-axis span of each object. While this is perfectly reasonable, it does increase the complexity and storage demands of our simple direct-access quadtree.

Instead of using a full-blown oct-tree, we can take a half step into the third dimension by adding a 32-bit field to each object. In this field, we set one bit for each region of z-axis space containing an object. To explain this idea, imagine that we divided the world into 32 equal layers along the z-axis. For every object in the world, we could build a 32-bit number by setting a bit for each layer in which the object exists. See Figure 5.6 for an example using eight layers.

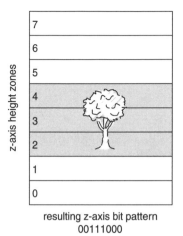

z-axis height zones

7
6
5
4
3
2
1
0

resulting z-axis bit pattern
00111000

FIGURE 5.6   In a world divided into eight layers, we can build an 8-bit value
to describe the layers an object occupies. In this figure, the object resides in
layers 2, 3, and 4—which equates to the binary pattern 00011100, or 28
decimal.

As objects are added to nodes within our quad tree, we OR their *z*-axis
bit fields together. This creates a *z*-axis bit field describing the contents of
the node. When we search the quadtree for objects, we can provide a 2D
shape to search with as well as a *z*-axis bit field of the height layers we
want to search. A simple AND operation for the corresponding bit field of
each node will tell us quickly if any members of that node reside in the
layers being tested. If the result of this logical AND produces a nonzero result, then we know that members exist in the desired levels, and we
should test each member individually to find them.

Using this method, we get all the benefits of a fast, small quadtree
representation while still enabling a testing mechanism for the third dimension. While the partitioning of the *z*-axis is crude, having only 32
possible layers, the testing mechanism provided by performing logical operations on 32-bit values is incredibly fast. Therefore, we gain some additional precision for our spatial partitioning without much overhead.

FAST QUADTREE SEARCHES

Searching the quadtree begins with the same operations as with sorting
an object into the quadtree. Given a 3D search volume, we create a 2D
search volume and a 32-bit value representing the span of the original 3D
shape in *z*. To begin our search, we must determine the tree node that

fully contains the 2D search volume. This is exactly the same procedure as if we were sorting the search volume into our tree.

The node found as the search volume's parent is the topmost level of the tree we need to search. We first test the z-axis bits for the node against the bits representing our search layers. If a match is found, we know there are members of this node that might be in our search space. We test all members of this node against the search volume to find intersecting objects, and then step down into its children to repeat the process. As we find objects in these nodes that intersect our search volume, we add them to a linked list that will serve as our search result. When the entire process is complete, this linked list will contain all quadtree members that intersect the search volume.

Maintaining the z-masks of our quadtree require some maintenance whenever objects are added, removed, or relocated within the tree. As objects are added or removed from nodes, the parent nodes must be notified up the chain. This allows them the opportunity to readjust their own combined z-masks so they are up to date. The quadtree node class, cQuadTreeNode, contains a pair of member functions to handle these notifications. Listing 5.1 shows these two functions, descendantMemberAdded and descendantMemberRemoved.

LISTING 5.1   Notification functions that keep the quadtree node *z* masks up to date.

```
void cQuadTreeNode::rebuildZMask()
{
  // reset our overall z mask to the mask
  // defined by our local members only
  m_zMask = m_zLocalMask;

  // sum up the masks of our children
  for (int i=0;i<4;++i)
  {
    if (m_pChildNode[i])
    {
      m_zMask.setFlags(m_pChildNode[i]->zMask());
    }
  }
}

void cQuadTreeNode::descendantMemberAdded(u32Flags zMask)
{
  // update our zMask
  m_zMask.setFlags(zMask);
```

```
  // notify our parent of the addition
  if (m_pParentNode)
  {
    m_pParentNode->descendantMemberAdded(zMask);
  }
}


void cQuadTreeNode::descendantMemberRemoved()
{
  // update our zMask
  rebuildZMask();

  // notify our parent of the removal
  if (m_pParentNode)
  {
    m_pParentNode->descendantMemberRemoved();
  }
}
```

SLOW QUADTREE SEARCHES

While a slow quadtree search is never desirable, there are times when we want to perform more testing operations than simple bounding-box intersection tests. The most notable example of this is when the quadtree is used to find a set of objects present in the camera frustum. As discussed earlier in this chapter, the frustum is a set of six planes that denote camera space.

Camera frustums do not map well to axis-aligned boxes. Their pyramidal nature creates a box that has much more volume than the original frustum. When this box is used alone to search the quadtree, many more objects will be added to the search results than are truly necessary. This is fine when fast searching is desired, but when false-positive results will impede our performance, we must do true frustum testing to minimize the set of results. In these cases, the only alternative is to incorporate the actual shape of the camera frustum into the quadtree search, preventing objects that lie outside the frustum bounds from being added to the search result.

We leave this as an option because frustum testing is not always required. For example, when using simple rendering methods, it is often more efficient to use a faster quadtree search and allow some off-screen objects to flow through the render pipeline. Even though we will be rendering these objects needlessly, their render speed is far superior to the frustum search time. For more advanced rendering, the opposite will be true. When rendering using complex shaders, we will be better served to spend more time doing a thorough search and reducing the number of items rendered.

To facilitate this, we must first create a data object to represent the camera frustum. The `cFrustum` class satisfies this need by maintaining a set of six planes. These planes represent the sides of the camera frustum. A `cPlane3d` class is used to hold each the six planes as a member of the `cFrustum`. `cPlane3d` maintains the data for each plane as a standard four-unit plane equation. This object can then be used as an optional parameter for our quadtree searches. See the geometry source code folder on the accompanying CD-ROM for implementation details on the `cPlane3d` class.

`cFrustum` contains a handy member function that can extract the frustum planes from the current camera projection matrix. This straightforward operation makes building a `cFrustum` object simple and easy. Credit for the plane extraction method goes to Gil Gribb and Klaus Hartmann, who documented the process for both DirectX and OpenGL [Gribb]. In their document, Gribb and Hartmann show that the frustum planes can be extracted from any camera matrix using the simple process shown in Listing 5.2.

Note that the coordinate space for the extracted planes is identical to the coordinate space defined by the camera matrix. For example, if the camera matrix maps from world space to camera space, the extracted frustum planes will be in world space. If a series of matrices are concatenated to produce a model-space to camera-space transform matrix, the frustum planes extracted will be in model space. This property makes the Gribb\Hartmann method a very powerful tool.

LISTING 5.2   Extracting 3D planes from an arbitrary camera matrix.

```
inline void cFrustum::extractFromMatrix(
  const cMatrix4x4& matrix,
  bool normalizePlanes)
{
  // Left clipping plane
  leftPlane.normal.x = matrix._14 + matrix._11;
  leftPlane.normal.y = matrix._24 + matrix._21;
  leftPlane.normal.z = matrix._34 + matrix._31;
  leftPlane.distance = matrix._44 + matrix._41;

  // Right clipping plane
  rightPlane.normal.x = matrix._14 - matrix._11;
```

```
rightPlane.normal.y = matrix._24 - matrix._21;
rightPlane.normal.z = matrix._34 - matrix._31;
rightPlane.distance = matrix._44 - matrix._41;

// Top clipping plane
topPlane.normal.x = matrix._14 - matrix._12;
topPlane.normal.y = matrix._24 - matrix._22;
topPlane.normal.z = matrix._34 - matrix._32;
topPlane.distance = matrix._44 - matrix._42;

// Bottom clipping plane
bottomPlane.normal.x = matrix._14 + matrix._12;
bottomPlane.normal.y = matrix._24 + matrix._22;
bottomPlane.normal.z = matrix._34 + matrix._32;
bottomPlane.distance = matrix._44 + matrix._42;

// Near clipping plane
nearPlane.normal.x = matrix._13;
nearPlane.normal.y = matrix._23;
nearPlane.normal.z = matrix._33;
nearPlane.distance = matrix._43;

// Far clipping plane
farPlane.normal.x = matrix._14 - matrix._13;
farPlane.normal.y = matrix._24 - matrix._23;
farPlane.normal.z = matrix._34 - matrix._33;
farPlane.distance = matrix._44 - matrix._43;

// it is not always nessesary to normalize
// the planes of the frustum. Non-normalized
// planes can still be used for basic
// intersection tests.
if (normalizePlanes)
{
  leftPlane.normalize();
  rightPlane.normalize();
  topPlane.normalize();
  bottomPlane.normalize();
  nearPlane.normalize();
  farPlane.normalize();
}
}
```

To determine if objects are visible in the camera frustum, we use a set of six plane-rectangle tests. These tests classify an axis-aligned rectangle

as either being in one of the half-spaces separated by the plane, or intersecting the plane itself. All of the planes extracted using the source code
shown in Listing 5.2 will contain surface normals that point into the frustum interior. This means that the camera frustum is defined as the volume created by the union of the positive half-spaces defined by each
plane. Therefore, if a rectangle lies in the negative half-space of any frustum plane, we know that the object is outside the frustum.

To perform the frustum-rectangle test, we first define a test to find in
which half-space the rectangle lies in relation to a plane. This test can
then be used with the frustum sides to determine a result. Listing 5.3
shows the plane-rectangle test and the combined frustum-rectangle test
code.

LISTING 5.3   The plane-rectangle test and the frustum-rectangle test.

```
enum ePlaneClassifications
{
  k_plane_front = 0,
  k_plane_back,
  k_plane_intersect
};

/*  signedDistance
---------------------------------------------

  Returns the signed distance between
  the plane and the provided 3D point.
  Negative distances are "behind" the
  plane, i.e. in the opposite direction
  of the plane normal.

---------------------------------------------
*/
inline float cPlane3d::signedDistance(
  const cVector3& Point) const
{
    // the plane is stored as a normal
    // vector and a distance from the
    // origin along the vector.
    return(normal.dotProduct(Point) + distance);
}

inline int planeClassify(
  const cRect3d& rect,
```

```
    const cPlane3d& plane)
{
  cVector3 minPoint, maxPoint;

  // build two points based on the direction
  // of the plane vector. minPoint
  // and maxPoint are the two points
  // on the rectangle furthest away from
  // each other along the plane normal

  if (plane.normal.x > 0.0f)
  {
    minPoint.x = (float)rect.x0;
    maxPoint.x = (float)rect.x1;
  }
  else
  {
    minPoint.x = (float)rect.x1;
    maxPoint.x = (float)rect.x0;
  }

  if (plane.normal.y > 0.0f)
  {
    minPoint.y = (float)rect.y0;
    maxPoint.y = (float)rect.y1;
  }
  else
  {
    minPoint.y = (float)rect.y1;
    maxPoint.y = (float)rect.y0;
  }

  if (plane.normal.z > 0.0f)
  {
    minPoint.z = (float)rect.z0;
    maxPoint.z = (float)rect.z1;
  }
  else
  {
    minPoint.z = (float)rect.z1;
    maxPoint.z = (float)rect.z0;
  }

  // compute the signed distance from
  // the plane to both points
```

```cpp
      float dmin = plane.signedDistance(minPoint);
      float dmax = plane.signedDistance(minPoint);

      // the rectangle intersects the plane if
      // one value is positive and
      // the other is negative
      if (dmin * dmax < 0.0f)
      {
        return k_plane_intersect;
      }
      else if (dmin)
      {
        return k_plane_front;
      }

      return k_plane_back;
    }

    inline bool cFrustum::testRect(
      const cRect3d& rect) const
    {

      if ((planeClassify(rect, leftPlane)
          == k_plane_back)
        || (planeClassify(rect, rightPlane)
          == k_plane_back)
        || (planeClassify(rect, topPlane)
          == k_plane_back)
        || (planeClassify(rect, bottomPlane)
          == k_plane_back)
        || (planeClassify(rect, nearPlane)
          == k_plane_back)
        || (planeClassify(rect, farPlane)
          == k_plane_back))
      {
        return false;
      }

      return true;
    }
```

With these test cases in place, we can now perform a more rigorous quadtree search using not only an axis aligned box, but an additional camera frustum. This is a far slower search when used, but provides a more accurate result. In later chapters, when our rendering workload increases, we will use the optional frustum-culling method provided by the quadtree to reduce the number of objects we need to process.

ON THE CD

The quadtree search process is best explained by looking through the example source code provided on the accompanying CD-ROM. Two classes are provided in the `source/gaia` folder, `cQuadTree` and `cQuadTreeNode`, which contain the search methods described in this chapter. The source code itself is too lengthy to include here as a listing, so readers are encouraged to look over the commented source code on the CD-ROM for implementation details of the quad tree.

REFERENCES

[Gribb] Gribb, G., and K. Hartmann. "Fast Extraction of Viewing Frustum Planes from the World-View-Projection Matrix," (available online at *www2.ravensoft.com/users/ggribb/plane%20extraction.pdf*).

[Pritchard] Pritchard, M. "Direct Access Quadtree Lookup." *Game Programming Gems 2*. Charles River Media, Inc., 2001, pp. 394–401.

BASIC TERRAIN GEOMETRY

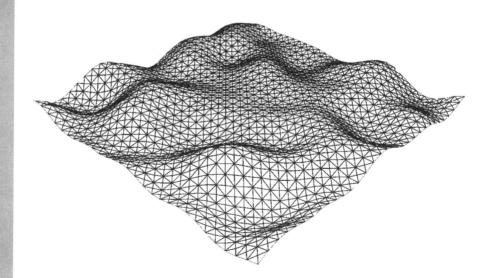

W ith the basic concepts of world-space partitioning behind us, we are ready to begin defining the landscape geometry from our world. In this chapter, we look at the data set used to define our 3D landscape, and various methods to generate it.

From this data, we will build the polygonal landscape and view it using a very rudimentary approach. In the next chapter, we will examine alternatives to this brute-force approach that provide greater scalability and overall efficiency. Obviously, before these systems can be explored, we need to define and create the data.

HEIGHT MAPS AS TERRAIN INPUT DATA

The height map is the simplest and most common data input scheme for terrain geometry. A height map is a 2D array of height values arranged in a regular grid. For each (x, y) location on the grid, a value for z is stored. This value for z is the height of the terrain at the (x, y) position. To enable a smaller data size for the overall table, the z information is usually stored as an unsigned byte, where 0 is the lowest terrain height and 255 is the highest. This creates a grid of terrain data in the range [0,255].

Another useful aspect of this approach is that a 2D array of byte values is identical to a grayscale bitmap. For each pixel of the bitmap, a value between 0 and 255 is stored for the black-to-white color range. This is identical to the [0,255] height value range we want to store for terrain height information. Using grayscale bitmaps as the storage method for our terrain data means that we can easily visualize the terrain as a bitmap. Figure 6.1 shows a sample height map in grayscale form. Dark areas of the image are low sections of the terrain, and light areas are higher sections.

Using bitmaps as input data allows us to use paint programs as terrain construction tools. We can simply paint the elevations of our terrain as shades of gray, and then save the bitmap out for our engine to load. We can also take advantage of real-world sources for terrain data such as the United States Geological Survey (USGS) terrain through the use of a free conversion program.

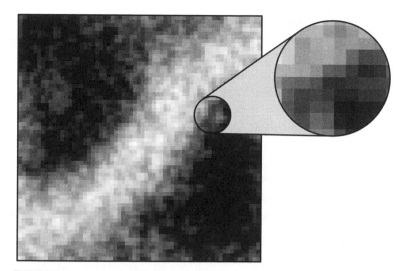

FIGURE 6.1   A sample terrain height map. The bitmap provides a view of the terrain from above. Low areas are shown as dark pixels, and higher elevations as bright pixels.

The USGS provides terrain information for the United States in a format known as a Digital Elevation Model (DEM) file. DEM files come in a variety of formats, and can range in detail from 10 meters per sample to 90 meters. For low-elevation terrain visualization, like ours, the higher resolution of 10 meters per sample is preferred. Either way, the DEM file format itself is beyond the scope of this book. Instead, we provide a utility program on the CD-ROM that can convert the DEM file, as well as other real-world terrain sources, into height map images.

ON THE CD

The program, 3DEM by Visualization Software LLC, is a free utility that can load data files from the USGS, NASA mars orbiter and earth satellites, and the global terrain data provided by the National Oceanic and Atmospheric Administration (NOAA). The elevation data within these files can easily be extracted and converted to a grayscale image for use within our engine. A link to the Visualization Software LLC home page is also provided in the recommended reading list of Appendix D, "Recommended Reading." More information on real-world source data and DEM files can be found there. Links are also provided in Appendix D for free access to USGS terrain data files.

PROCEDURAL HEIGHT MAPS

If a height field is little more then a grayscale bitmap, it would stand to reason that we could create one using source code rather than a paint program or real-world data source. The first strategy that comes to mind is to simply generate a random set of height field values. This would work, but the resulting terrain is an unrealistic, chaotic mixture of disconnected height values. Instead, what we require is a method to build random height values using a few simple rules to guide the overall appearance of the terrain.

Many methods for generating random height maps have been documented over the years, and most boil down to one simple premise: generate a random set of values, and then filter those values until the terrain becomes reasonably smooth. "Reasonably smooth" is a relative term that generally equates to making sure adjacent values in the height map contain values within some delta range. When a height map value is too different from its neighbors, the resulting terrain will contain a sharp pit or spike, which looks unrealistic for most applications.

The idea of generating random height values, and then filtering the results to lessen the delta between neighboring values is akin to giving a monkey a paintbrush along with some black and white paint, and then blurring his painting until it looks like a mountain range. The idea might work, but it is not likely to produce a decent mountain landscape each time. There are easier methods to use that generate random values while maintaining a realistic appearance for terrain. The results of these "guided" methods are much more likely to produce an appealing result than the monkey-painter approach will.

MIDPOINT DISPLACEMENT

The first procedural method we will look at is a recursive process called *midpoint displacement*. In this method, we begin with a flat height map and begin raising and lowering values to create a random terrain. Rather than assigning a random value to each pixel of the height map without rhyme or reason, we start by dividing the image into four quadrants and adjusting each corner. We then treat each quadrant as a new image and repeat the process, dividing each quadrant into four smaller areas and adjusting the height at each corner. As we step lower and lower in detail, we decrease the range in which we raise or lower corners.

This is better explained with images. Figure 6.2 shows the process in stages. We will be using floating-point values for the construction process between 0 and 255. We use floating-point numbers for greater precision during construction, and the range [0, 255] so we can convert the final result back to 8-bit grayscale values. In each stage of our process, we will generate random values in a fixed range and use them to offset points on the height map. In the first stage, the range covers the complete set of values from −128 to 128. We will call the current range extents *delta*, making the total range [*−delta, delta*].

In the left panel of Figure 6.2, the four corners of the height map are set to random values. The image is then divided into four quadrants as shown by the dotted lines. This creates five new locations, shown as numbered points on the image. For each point, we compute a base value by averaging the values of the corners to which it is linked. For example, the base value for point number 1 is set to the average of the values stored at corner points *A* and *B*.

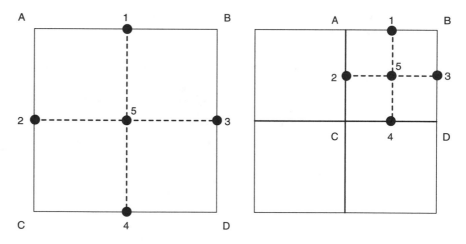

FIGURE 6.2   The two stages of the midpoint displacement method.

Continuing with point number 1, we displace the point using a random value generated in the range [*−delta, delta*], writing the new value back to the position of point number 1. We continue by generating random offset values in the same range for points 2, 3, and 4. Position 5 is slightly different because its base value is calculated as the average of all four corners. The rest of the process is the same; calculating a random value in the range [*−delta, delta*] and using it to offset the base value at this position. Once all five points are offset, we move on to the next stage.

In the next stage, we step into one of the quadrants built by the previous stage and repeat the entire process. A set of new quadrants is built, as shown in the right panel in Figure 6.2. We generate base values for these points using the quadrant corners, and offset using random values. However, to guide the creation of the terrain, we multiply the range value *delta* by a scale value. This scale value, let's call it *roughness*, is a value between 0 and 1 that will reduce our random range each time *delta* is multiplied against it. This is shown as Formula 6.1.

$$\text{delta} = \text{delta} * \text{roughness} \tag{6.1}$$

The ideal *roughness* value is 0.5, which will reduce the random range by half with each stage. Tuning the *roughness* value controls how the terrain heights fluctuate as we get further and further into the recursion process. A higher roughness values creates a more chaotic terrain, with the terrain growing smoother as the *roughness* value approaches zero.

The process is complete when all values in the height map have been set; at this point, we can transfer the values to our terrain geometry, or convert them to integer values for storage as a grayscale bitmap. Figure 6.3 shows three sample height maps created with this technique and a variety of *roughness* values.

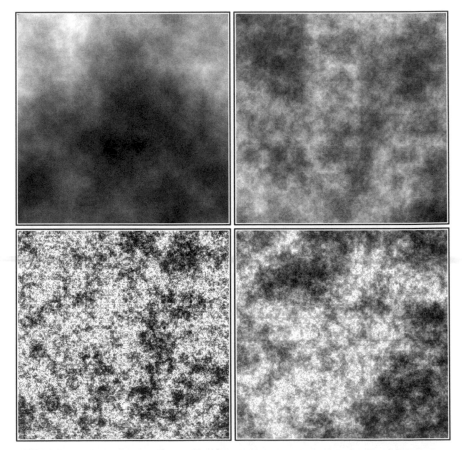

FIGURE 6.3   Four sample height maps created with the midpoint displacement method. Clockwise from the top left, these images were created with falloff values of 0.65, 0.75, 0.85, and 0.95.

PERLIN NOISE

No discussion of procedural terrain generation would be complete without discussing noise functions. The king of all noise functions was created in 1983 by Ken Perlin [Perlin1]. Perlin created a function for the creation of random values that at is the root of almost all marble, wood, and noise creation filters found in 3D rendering packages and paint programs. In fact, Perlin won an Oscar for his work in 1997 based on the impact his procedural texture work has had on the motion picture industry since his papers were first published in the mid 1980s.

Perlin noise can be calculated in n dimensions, but for our discussion, we will focus on the 2D implementation of the technique. In addition, we provide a slightly simplified version of the original Perlin noise function. At its heart, 2D Perlin noise is really an interpolation between normal vectors arraigned on a grid, so we will focus on this portion of the technique. In Figure 6.4, we see a height map cut into grid squares.

The entire image, regardless of its pixel dimensions, is overlaid with a grid representing a floating-point range of numbers. For example, we are generating noise in Figure 6.4 on a grid representing the values from 0 to 4 across the entire image. Each whole number creates a grid line, so each grid square is a single unit long on all sides. The scale used controls the complexity of the noise. More grid squares per image create a tighter-packed noise, like the white noise of a badly tuned TV set. Fewer grid squares create more billowy, cloud-like noise patterns.

On each grid point, a random normal vector is placed. These are simply 2D vectors of unit length pointing in some random direction at each grid square. A common way to compute them is to build a lookup table of 256 vectors sweeping a full circle, and then randomly pick one from the set for each grid point. This ensures a random distribution of vectors that have an equal chance of pointing in any direction.

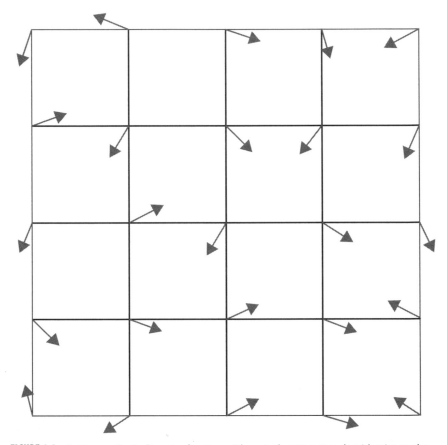

FIGURE 6.4 Setting up the Perlin noise function with normal vectors at each grid point on the image.

For each pixel location of the image, we find the grid cell that contains it. We will be generating a value based on the data of this cell alone. The next step is to build four directional vectors connecting the corners of the cell with the location being calculated, as shown in Figure 6.5.

Each corner of the grid cell is now the base for two vectors, one random unit vector and one directional vector pointing to the pixel we are trying to generate. For each of these vector pairs, we compute the dot product. This produces a scalar height value for each corner of the grid. We can then combine these four values to determine the height at the pixel we want to solve. This can be done in a variety of ways to produce different results, the most common being a weighted interpolation of the four values based on the proximity of the sample position to each corner of the grid cell.

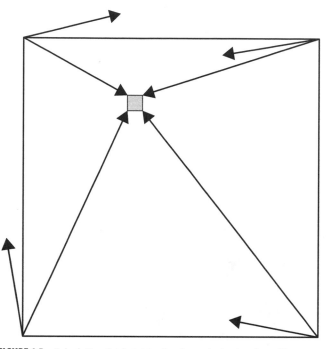

FIGURE 6.5   Calculating the height value for a pixel using the grid normal vectors and vectors connecting the grid points to the position being calculated.

Given four values, one associated with each corner, we combine them by performing three total blending operations. To begin, we must compute the blending weights based on our position within the unit square. To compute these weight values, we use Equation 6.1, substituting our x and y grid-relative coordinates for t.

$$w = 6t^5 - 15t^4 + 10t^3 \qquad (6.1)$$

This equation might differ from other explanations of Perlin noise. Perlin originally documented his method using the equation shown in Equation 6.2. While faster to compute, this original method was prone to producing artifacts in the final result. In a follow-up to his original publication [Perlin2], Perlin describes the reasons behind the artifacts and presents Equation 6.1 to help reduce their appearance. Because of the discrepancy, many sources can be found in print and on the Web that use either equation. In our source code, both are provided for experimentation.

$$w = 3t^2 - 2t^3 \qquad (6.2)$$

With the *x*-axis weight value, we blend the top pair or corner values using Equation 6.3. In this equation, the result (*v*) is computed using the weight value from Equation 6.1 and two corner values c_a and c_b. The same procedure is then repeated for the bottom two corner values. Finally, a third blend is performed using the same equation between the results of the first two blends and the *y*-axis blend weight. The final result is a height value between 0 and 1 for the pixel in question. We then scale this to our desired grayscale range and write it to the bitmap. Figure 6.6 shows sample Perlin noise results.

$$v = c_a(w) + c_b(1 - w) \qquad (6.3)$$

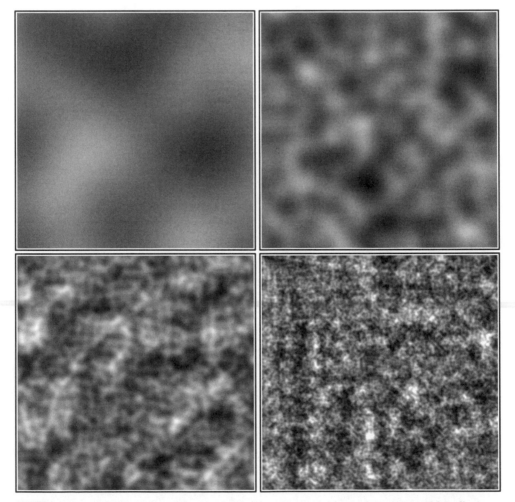

FIGURE 6.6 Sample Perlin noise images generated with various grid sizes, octave counts, and fall-off values.

To code our Perlin noise function, we compartmentalize it into a single routine we can call for each pixel of the height map. Rather than creating a set of vertex normals on the grid as a first step, we define a function that will pick a pseudo-random vector from our vector table based on an (x, y) grid corner. This way, we do not need to generate and store the grid point normals. Each time we need to reference a normal, we can regenerate it from the grid location and be guaranteed to get the same one each time.

A common method used to do this is to define a set of 256 normals, as mentioned earlier, as our set of potential vectors. We then create a second lookup table containing 256 random entries in the range [0,255]. This is our secondary index table. Given the pre-generated set of 256 vectors (**V**), our secondary lookup table (**T**) and an (x, y) grid location, we use the following function to choose a normal vector:

```
cVector2 RandomGridNormal(
        unsigned char x,
        unsigned char y)
    {
        return V[ (T[x] + T[y]) % 255 ];

    };
```

This function uses the x and y grid coordinates as indexes into the secondary lookup table **T**. From this table, two random values are read and added together. The result is modulated with 255 to bring it back to the [0, 255] range. This new value is used as an index into the vector pool **V** to read the normal vector. The result is a normal vector that appears random, but will be calculated identically whenever the same values for x and y are provided. This removes the need to store a big set of grid normals for our image, since we can quickly recompute the vectors as we need them.

Now we can write the noise function. Given an (x, y) image location, and a scale for the overall noise pattern, the noise function computes the four surrounding grid point normals and then computes the resulting value of their interpolation. We define the entire process within the cPerlinNoise class, shown in Listing 6.1.

LISTING 6.1   The Perlin noise class.

```cpp
class cPerlinNoise
{
public:

  enum
  {
    k_tableSize = 256,
    k_tableMask = k_tableSize-1,
  };

    cPerlinNoise();
    ~cPerlinNoise();

  float noise(int x, int y, float scale);

private:

  cVector2 m_vecTable[k_tableSize];
  unsigned char m_lut[k_tableSize];

  // Private Functions...
  void setup();
  const cVector2& getVec(int x, int y)const;
};

void cPerlinNoise::setup()
{
  float step = 6.24f / k_tableSize;
  float val=0.0f;

  srand(timeGetTime());

  for (int i=0; i<k_tableSize; ++i)
  {
    m_vecTable[i].x = sin(val);
    m_vecTable[i].y = cos(val);
    val += step;

    m_lut[i] = rand() & k_tableMask;
  }
}

const cVector2& cPerlinNoise::getVec(
  int x,
```

```
    int y)const
{
  unsigned char a = m_lut[x&k_tableMask];
  unsigned char b = m_lut[y&k_tableMask];
  unsigned char val = m_lut[(a+b)&k_tableMask];
  return m_vecTable[val];
}

float cPerlinNoise::noise(
  int x,
  int y,
  float scale)
{
  cVector2 pos(x*scale, y*scale);

  float X0 = floor(pos.x);
  float X1 = X0 + 1.0f;
  float Y0 = floor(pos.y);
  float Y1 = Y0 + 1.0f;

  const cVector2& v0 =
    getVec((int)X0, (int)Y0);
  const cVector2& v1 =
    getVec((int)X0, (int)Y1);
  const cVector2& v2 =
    getVec((int)X1, (int)Y0);
  const cVector2& v3 =
    getVec((int)X1, (int)Y1);

  cVector2 d0(pos.x-X0, pos.y-Y0);
  cVector2 d1(pos.x-X0, pos.y-Y1);
  cVector2 d2(pos.x-X1, pos.y-Y0);
  cVector2 d3(pos.x-X1, pos.y-Y1);

  float h0 = dotProduct(d0, v0);
  float h1 = dotProduct(d1, v1);
  float h2 = dotProduct(d2, v2);
  float h3 = dotProduct(d3, v3);

  float Sx,Sy;

/*
  Perlin's original equation was faster,
  but produced artifacts in some situations
  Sx = (3*powf(d0.x,2.0f))
```

```
    -(2*powf(d0.x,3.0f));

  Sy = (3*powf(d0.y,2.0f))
    -(2*powf(d0.y,3.0f));
*/

  // the revised blend equation is
  // considered more ideal, but is
  // slower to compute
  Sx = (6*powf(d0.x,5.0f))
    -(15*powf(d0.x,4.0f))
    +(10*powf(d0.x,3.0f));

  Sy = (6*powf(d0.y,5.0f))
    -(15*powf(d0.y,4.0f))
    +(10*powf(d0.y,3.0f));

  float avgX0 = h0 + (Sx*(h2 - h0));
  float avgX1 = h1 + (Sx*(h3 - h1));
  float result = avgX0 + (Sy*(avgX1 - avgX0));

  return result;
}
```

The benefits of Perlin noise become more apparent when multiple results are combined to create a final image. The process of combining multiple noise functions is called fractional Brownian Motion (fBM), but the application is far simpler than the name suggests. Imagine two Perlin noise functions run at different scales. For example, we could create two Perlin noise maps, one at twice the scale of the other. By simply adding the results together, we allow one noise result to displace the other, creating a wholly new noise result.

Figure 6.7 shows the results of adding two noise maps together. The individual noise maps are referred to as *octaves*, since one is twice the scale of the other. By combining octaves using addition, multiplication, or other factors, new noise patterns emerge. In Figure 6.7, the finer noise pattern within octave number 2 adds detail to the first octave when added to the result. To create a robust terrain, we would normally add many octaves to the result to enhance the large hills formed by the large-scale octaves with fine-detail elements.

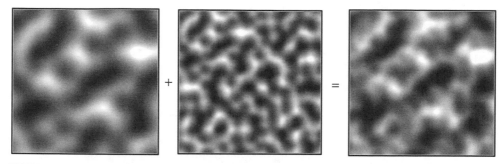

FIGURE 6.7   A sample Perlin noise image generated by adding two octaves together.

PROCESSING HEIGHT MAP DATA

Before the terrain can be used, it must be converted from the grayscale height map information to a polygonal mesh. To visualize this, picture the height map image as a grid of height values. This grid will translate directly to the vertex mesh we will be creating. The x and y position of each pixel on the height map translates to an x and y vertex position. The color value stored at each pixel location translates to the z position of each vertex. We will need to scale these values to the size and height of the terrain we desire, but apart from that, the process is straightforward. As we read the grayscale values from the range [0,255], we simply scale these to the maximum height extents of the terrain we desire. The same is true for (x, y) vertex positions, where we scale the integer pixel position values to real-world coordinates for our terrain.

Each 2x2 set of pixels creates a matching 2x2 set of vertices, forming two triangles. We record the data for each vertex as a simple list of (x, y, z) positional information. Triangle data is recorded as a set of three indices into the vertex list, describing which vertices are used to form each triangle. These two lists of data will later become our vertex and index buffers. In addition to the vertex positions, we also compute a surface normal for the triangle by taking the cross product of two normalized edge vectors, as shown in Figure 6.8.

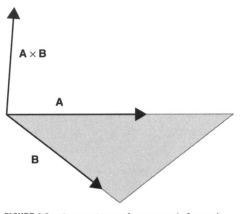

FIGURE 6.8   Computing surface normals for each face of the mesh.

Once all of the face normals are computed, we can combine them into vertex normals. If we attempted to render using the face normals, our terrain would be lit very coarsely. To create a smoother lighting model, we need to compute normals for each vertex that are the average of the adjoining face normals. For each vertex, the normals of the faces to which the vertex belongs are averaged, and then renormalized. This creates a normal for each vertex that is ready for use in lighting calculations. We now have position and surface normal information for each vertex, which together comprise the bare essentials for rendering our terrain. The remaining step is to load the data into a Direct3D vertex buffer and use it for rendering. Listing 6.2 shows this process.

You will notice in the `buildHeightAndNormalTables` function within Listing 6.2 that we take a substantial shortcut in calculating the vertex normals of our terrain. Rather than performing the cross-product calculations ourselves and averaging the results, we allow the D3DX support library to do the work for us. D3DX provides a function named `D3DXComputeNormalMap` that can covert a texture containing grayscale height information to a corresponding normal map. The axis values for each surface normal are encoded into the red, green, and blue color channels of the resulting texture. To save some work, we use this function to convert a texture containing our height data to a texture containing the calculated normals, and then simply extract the results.

Our wrapper class for DirectX textures, `cTexture`, provides this functionality behind the member function `generateNormalMap`. In Listing 6.2, this function is used to generate a texture containing surface normals from the original height map data. The normal vectors are extracted by reading each pixel of the resulting texture and remapping the color channel values from their native [0,255] range to unit vector space [−1,1].

LISTING 6.2   Building tables of elevation and surface normals from the height map.

```
// Here we convert the height map data into
// floating point height and surface normals.
// each is stored within a table of values
// within the terrain system class
//
void cTerrain ::buildHeightAndNormalTables(cTexture* pTexture)
{
  safe_delete_array(m_heightTable);
  safe_delete_array(m_normalTable);

  int maxY = m_tableHeight;
  int maxX = m_tableWidth;
  int x,y;

  m_heightTable = new float[maxX*maxY];
  m_normalTable = new cVector3[maxX*maxY];

  // first, build a table of heights
  D3DLOCKED_RECT lockedRect;
  if(SUCCEEDED(
    pTexture->getTexture()->
    LockRect(0, &lockedRect,
      0, D3DLOCK_READONLY)))
  {
    uint8* pHeightMap = (uint8*)lockedRect.pBits;

    for(y=0; y<maxY; ++y)
    {
      for(x=0; x<maxX; ++x)
      {
        int iHeight =
          pHeightMap[(y*lockedRect.Pitch)+(x*4)];
        float fHeight =
          (iHeight * m_mapScale.z)
          + m_worldExtents.z0;

        m_heightTable[(y*maxX)+x] =
          fHeight;
      }
    }
```

```
      pTexture->getTexture()->UnlockRect(0);
}

// create a normal map texture
cTexture temp;
temp.createTexture(
  m_tableWidth,
  m_tableHeight,
  1, 0,
  D3DFMT_A8R8G8B8,
  D3DPOOL_SCRATCH);

// how much to scale the normals?
float scale =
  (m_tableWidth * m_worldExtents.sizeZ())
  /m_worldExtents.sizeX();

// Use D3DX to convert our height map into a
// texture of surface normals
temp.generateNormalMap(
  pTexture->getTexture(),
  D3DX_CHANNEL_RED, 0, scale);

// now read out the normals and
// store them in our intenal structure
if(SUCCEEDED(temp.getTexture()->LockRect(
  0, &lockedRect, 0, D3DLOCK_READONLY)))
{
  uint8* pNormalMap =
    (uint8*)lockedRect.pBits;

  for(y=0; y<maxY; ++y)
  {
    for(x=0; x<maxX; ++x)
    {
      int index =
        (y*lockedRect.Pitch)+(x*4);
      cVector3 normal;

      normal.z = pNormalMap[index+0] - 127.5f;
      normal.y = pNormalMap[index+1] - 127.5f;
      normal.x = pNormalMap[index+2] - 127.5f;

      normal.normalize();
      m_normalTable[(y*maxX)+x] = normal;
```

```
        }
     }

     temp.getTexture()->UnlockRect(0);
   }

   temp.releaseTexture();
}
```

TERRAIN GEOMETRY BASE CLASSES

To maintain and display the basic terrain, we use two classes. One class, cTerrain, represents the entire terrain. To aid in culling portions of the terrain for display, the entire terrain is subdivided into grid-aligned sections. These sections are represented by the second class, cTerrainSection. These two classes represent the foundation we will use for all future terrain methods.

As shown in Listing 6.2, cTerrain stores the height and surface normal information for the entire terrain in a set of tables. This turns the cTerrain object into the central repository for terrain-related data. Functions are provided to access these tables directly, or interpolate between table entries when data is needed at a higher resolution than the table can store. These functions will prove useful in Chapter 9, "Texturing Techniques," when we begin to texture the terrain.

Rendering the entire terrain as one gigantic set of triangles would be inefficient, considering that the terrain might extend far out of the camera range in all directions. To work within our display system, we divide the terrain into manageable sections, which are represented by the cTerrainSection class. For example, to represent a terrain of 256x256 vertices, we would create a cTerrain to store the entire data set. The cTerrain object would further subdivide the terrain into 32x32 vertex sections, creating a total of 64 cTerrainSection objects to represent each.

The cTerrainSection class is derived from the cSceneObject class we described in Chapter 4, "Gaia Engine Overview." This allows each cTerrainSection object to be added to the quadtree and flow through our render pipeline as if it were an individual model. However, unlike cSceneObjects, we do not want to store a complete set of geometry for each cTerrainSection. In fact, using vertex and index buffers, we find that a great deal of information can be stored once in the cTerrain and used in rendering each cTerrainSection.

TERRAIN GEOMETRY INDEX BUFFERS

The most obvious of these sharing opportunities is the index buffer. Given that all cTerrainSections are of equal size and contain the same number of vertices, we can create a single index buffer object and use it to render any section of the terrain. cTerrain contains a single cIndexBuffer object for just this purpose. To make things even easier, we provide a member function in the cIndexBuffer class to create an index buffer optimized for vertex grids such as our terrain section. Listing 6.3 shows this function. Given a set of parameters describing a regular grid of vertex data, the cIndexBuffer member function createSingleStripGrid will create an index buffer containing a single triangle strip that covers the entire grid. See the DirectX SDK for more information on triangle strips and the rendering efficiency they can provide.

The process is simple. First, the number of horizontal strips required to cover the grid is calculated. Then, each strip is created in order. The ends of each strip are connected to the beginning of the next strip using a degenerate triangle, which indexes the same vertex more than once, producing a triangle with zero surface area. Because these triangles have no surface area, they do not equate to pixels on screen when rendered. This allows us to use these triangles to connect our individual horizontal strips into a single unified strip—knowing that the connecting triangles will never be visible on screen.

LISTING 6.3   Creating a triangle strip index buffer for vertices arranged in a grid pattern.

```
bool cIndexBuffer::createSingleStripGrid(
  uint16 xVerts,  // width of grid
  uint16 yVerts,  // height of grid
  uint16 xStep, // horz vertex count per cell
  uint16 yStep, // vert vertex count per cell
  uint16 stride,  // horz vertex count in vbuffer
  uint16 flags)
{
  int total_strips =
    yVerts-1;
  int total_indexes_per_strip =
    xVerts<<1;

  // the total number of indices is equal
  // to the number of strips times the
  // indices used per strip plus one
  // degenerate triangle between each strip
```

```
int total_indexes =
  (total_indexes_per_strip * total_strips)
  + (total_strips<<1) - 2;

unsigned short* pIndexValues =
  new unsigned short[total_indexes];

unsigned short* index = pIndexValues;
unsigned short start_vert = 0;
unsigned short lineStep = yStep*stride;

for (int j=0;j<total_strips;++j)
{
  int k=0;
  unsigned short vert=start_vert;

  // create a strip for this row
  for (k=0;k<xVerts;++k)
  {
    *(index++) = vert;
    *(index++) = vert + lineStep;
    vert += xStep;
  }
  start_vert += lineStep;

  if (j+1<total_strips)
  {
    // add a degenerate to attach to
    // the next row
    *(index++) = (vert-xStep)+lineStep;
    *(index++) = start_vert;
  }
}

// finally, use the indices we created above
// to fill the Direct3D index buffer
bool result=
  create(D3DPT_TRIANGLESTRIP, total_indexes, flags,
pIndexValues);

// destroy our local data and return
delete [] pIndexValues;
return result;
}
```

One oddity in Listing 6.3 is the use of a step value for vertices in the *x* and *y* direction. Two parameters are provided to the function, (xStep and yStep), which are used to step over vertices when creating triangles for the vertex grid. While this added functionality is not much use to us now, we will find this flexibility useful later when we create levels of detail for our terrain. While the xStep and yStep values would normally be 1, we can increase the values later to create an index buffer that uses fewer triangles to cover a cTerrainSection by referencing every other or every third vertex in the grid. More of this will be covered in Chapter 7, "The ROAM Terrain System."

TERRAIN GEOMETRY VERTEX BUFFERS

Terrain vertex data can be an overwhelming amount of information to store. At first glance, it appears that each terrain section will contain unique vertex data. The probability of finding two sections of our terrain with identical topography is extremely low, providing us with no means to compact the amount of data we need to maintain. However, if we consider each terrain section as an individual model, we find the opportunity to share much of the vertex information. This will allow us to store the vertex data much more efficiently while still creating a nonrepeating terrain.

Consider an example terrain where each cTerrainObject represents a 32x32 vertex subset of the overall terrain. In this example, each vertex contains position, surface normal, and texture coordinates. If this data is copied directly from the terrain, it will all be unique world-relative data. However, if we consider each section as a 32x32 vertex model that will be translated to its world position, we find that much of the model-space data is identical throughout all the terrain sections.

Put more simply, instead of giving each cTerrainSection real-world vertex position and texture coordinates, we give them *x*- and *y*-axis values in the range 0 to 1 for both position and texture addressing. When rendering the terrain section, we scale the [0,1] coordinate range to the size we want, and then offset it to the proper world-relative location in the vertex shader. Because each terrain tile will use an identical set of *xy* position and *uv* texture data, we can store it once in the cTerrain object and reference it to render any cTerrainSection.

This still leaves some unique data for each cTerrainSection to maintain, such as vertex height (*z*-axis position) and the surface normal, but removing the 2D plane location and texture coordinates from each section greatly reduces the overall storage required for the terrain. The implication is that two vertex streams must be used to render each terrain section: the shared vertex data stored in the `cTerrain`, and the unique vertex data stored in each `cTerrainSection`.

Looking back at the `cRenderEntry` class described in Chapter 4, we see that we have already equipped our render queue to handle rendering with multiple vertex streams. While it might have seemed unnecessary at the time, it's certainly going to prove useful now. When submitting the `cTerrainSection` objects into the render queue, we add both of the vertex streams to the `cRenderEntry` object. When the time comes to perform the actual rendering, these two streams will be activated for the vertex shader to access as if they were one interleaved vertex buffer. This facet of Direct3D helps make the use of multiple vertex streams transparent to the vertex shaders.

Listing 6.4 shows the entire process of setting up our `cTerrain` and `cTerrainSection` classes for a given terrain. At the top of the listing, the vertex description is shown specifying the two streams of vertex data that will be used to render the terrain. The listing then shows the `cTerrain::create` function, which is the starting point for the entire process. This function will convert the height map provided into vertex data using the code shown in Listing 6.2, and then create the individual sectors and shared data.

LISTING 6.4   The setup process for `cTerrain` and `cTerrainSection` objects.

```
// vertex definitions for the basic terrain.
// we use two vertex streams. The first is a
// single vertex buffer shared by all the
// sectors of the terrain. The second is a
// vertex buffer created by each sector of the
// terrain to store local height and normal
// data
static D3DVERTEXELEMENT9 vertex_description[]=
{
  // local data (stream 0)
  { 0, 0, D3DDECLTYPE_FLOAT2,
    D3DDECLMETHOD_DEFAULT,
    D3DDECLUSAGE_POSITION, 0 },
  { 0, 8, D3DDECLTYPE_FLOAT2,
    D3DDECLMETHOD_DEFAULT,
    D3DDECLUSAGE_TEXCOORD, 0 },

  // sector data (stream 1)
  { 1, 0, D3DDECLTYPE_FLOAT1,
```

```
          D3DDECLMETHOD_DEFAULT,
          D3DDECLUSAGE_POSITION, 1 },
        { 1, 4, D3DDECLTYPE_FLOAT3,
          D3DDECLMETHOD_DEFAULT,
          D3DDECLUSAGE_NORMAL,   0 },
      D3DDECL_END()
    };

    //
    // This function is the starting point
    // for converting a height map into
    // vertex data
    //
    bool cTerrain ::create(
      cSceneNode* pRootNode,
      cTexture* heightMap,
      const cRect3d& worldExtents,
      uint8 shift)
    {
      bool result = false;

      m_sectorShift = shift;
      m_sectorUnits = 1<<shift;
      m_sectorVerts = m_sectorUnits+1;

      m_pRootNode = pRootNode;
      m_worldExtents = worldExtents;
      m_worldSize = worldExtents.size();

      m_tableWidth = heightMap->width();
      m_tableHeight = heightMap->height();

      m_mapScale.x = m_worldSize.x/m_tableWidth;
      m_mapScale.y = m_worldSize.y/m_tableHeight;
      m_mapScale.z = m_worldSize.z/255.0f;

      // convert the height map to
      // data stored in local tables
      buildHeightAndNormalTables(heightMap);

      m_sectorCountX =
        m_tableWidth>m_sectorShift;
      m_sectorCountY =
        m_tableHeight>m_sectorShift;
```

```
    m_sectorSize.set(
      m_worldSize.x/m_sectorCountX,
      m_worldSize.y/m_sectorCountY);

    // create the vertex and index buffer
    // objects which are shared by the sectors
    if (buildVertexBuffer())
    {
      if (setVertexDescription())
      {
        if (buildIndexBuffer())
        {
          // now go build each sector of the terrain
          result = allocateSectors();
        }
      }
    }

    if(!result)
    {
      destroy();
    }

    return result;
}

//
// This function creates the individual
// sectors of the terrain
//
bool cTerrain ::allocateSectors()
{
  m_pSectorArray =
    new cTerrainSection[
      m_sectorCountX*m_sectorCountY];

  // create the sector objects themselves
  for (int y=0; y<m_sectorCountY; ++y)
  {
    for (int x=0; x<m_sectorCountX; ++x)
    {
      cVector2 sectorPos(
        m_worldExtents.x0+(x*m_sectorSize.x),
        m_worldExtents.y0+(y*m_sectorSize.y));
```

```
      cRect2d sectorRect(
        sectorPos.x, sectorPos.x+m_sectorSize.x,
        sectorPos.y, sectorPos.y+m_sectorSize.y);

      uint16 xPixel = x<<m_sectorShift;
      uint16 yPixel = y<<m_sectorShift;

      uint16 index = (y*m_sectorCountX)+x;

      if (!m_pSectorArray[index].create(
        m_pRootNode,
        this,
        x, y,
        xPixel, yPixel,
        m_sectorVerts,
        m_sectorVerts,
        sectorRect))
      {
        return false;
      }
    }
  }

  return true;
}

bool cTerrain ::buildVertexBuffer()
{
  cString tempName;
  tempName.format("terrain_system_%i", this);

  // create the vertex buffer
  // shared by the sectors
  m_pVertexGrid =
    DisplayManager.vertexBufferPool().
    createResource(tempName);

  cVector2 cellSize(
    m_sectorSize.x/m_sectorUnits,
    m_sectorSize.y/m_sectorUnits);

  cVector2 vert(0.0f,0.0f);
  sLocalVertex* pVerts =
    new sLocalVertex[m_sectorVerts*m_sectorVerts];
```

```
  // fill the vertex stream with x,y positions and
  // uv coordinates. All other data (height and
  // surface normals) are stored in the vertex
  // buffers of each terrain section
  for (int y=0; y<m_sectorVerts; ++y)
  {
    vert.set(0.0f, y*cellSize.y);

    for (int x=0; x<m_sectorVerts; ++x)
    {
      pVerts[(y*m_sectorVerts)+x].xyPosition = vert;
      pVerts[(y*m_sectorVerts)+x].localUV.set(
        (float)x/(float)(m_sectorVerts-1),
        (float)y/(float)(m_sectorVerts-1));

      vert.x += cellSize.x;
    }
  }

  // now that we have built the data,
  // create one of our vertex buffer
  // resource objects with it
  bool result = SUCCEEDED(
    m_pVertexGrid->create(
    m_sectorVerts*m_sectorVerts,
    sizeof(sLocalVertex),
    0, pVerts));

  safe_delete_array(pVerts);

  // if the vertex buffer creation was
  // a success, create the vertex declaration
  // and add it to the class data
  // setup the vertex declaration
  if (result)
  {
    m_pVertexGrid->setVertexDescription(
      sizeof(vertex_description)/sizeof(D3DVERTEXELEMENT9),
      vertex_description);
  }

  return result;
}

bool cTerrain::setVertexDescription()
```

```
{
  // create the vertex declaration
  // and add it to the vertex
  // buffer containing our basic grid
  bool success =
  m_pVertexGrid->setVertexDescription(
    sizeof(vertex_description)/
     sizeof(D3DVERTEXELEMENT9),
    vertex_description);

  return success;
}

bool cTerrain ::buildIndexBuffer()
{
  cString tempName;
  tempName.format("terrain_system_%i", this);

  m_pTriangles =
    DisplayManager.indexBufferPool().
    createResource(tempName);

  // create the index buffer which
  // all terrain sections can share
  return SUCCEEDED(
    m_pTriangles->createSingleStripGrid(
    m_sectorVerts,  // width of grid
    m_sectorVerts,  // height of grid
    1,  // horz vertex count per cell
    1,  // vert vertex count per cell
    m_sectorVerts,  // horz vertex count in vbuffer
    0));
}
```

RENDERING THE TERRAIN SECTIONS

As alluded to earlier, the render pipeline we built in Chapter 4 is already prepared for multiple vertex streams. All that remains is for us to submit the individual cTerrainSection objects for rendering, and then handle the sorted drawing requests as they arrive. As you'll recall, we built a system in which individual cSceneObjects are submitted to the cRenderQueue, sorted for optimal rendering, and then processed via callback functions. Our cTerrainSection objects, being derived from the cSceneObject base class, fit into this system perfectly. As cTerrainSection objects are found in the quadtree, they use overloads of the standard cSceneObject rendering functions to add themselves to the queue and perform the final draw when requested.

Listing 6.5 shows the member functions responsible for rendering cTerrainSection objects. Note that while all render calls are routed to the cTerrainSection objects, they forward the drawing request back to the parent cTerrain. This allows the cTerrain to apply the data resources shared by all cTerrainSections. Within the cTerrain render function, all necessary drawing resources are activated, including the two vertex streams that make up the terrain geometry, prior to performing the actual draw primitive call.

LISTING 6.5   The setup process for cTerrain and cTerrainSection objects.

```
void cTerrainSection::render()
{
  // ask our parent to complete the submission
  m_pTerrainSystem->submitSection(this);
}

void cTerrainSection::renderCallback(
  cRenderEntry* entry,
  u32Flags activationFlags)
{
  // ask our parent to complete the render
  m_pTerrainSystem->renderSection(
    this, activationFlags, entry);
}

void cTerrain ::submitSection(
  cTerrainSection* pSection)const
{
  cEffectFile* pEffectFile =
    m_pRenderMethod->getActiveEffect();
  cSurfaceMaterial* pSurfaceMaterial =
    m_pRenderMethod->getActiveMaterial();

  if (pEffectFile)
  {
    profile_scope(cTerrain _submitSection);
    int total_passes = pEffectFile->totalPasses();

    // check the neighbor sectors for connection needs
```

```cpp
        uint16 sX = pSection->sectorX();
        uint16 sY = pSection->sectorY();

        int index = (sY*m_sectorCountX)+sX;

        for (int iPass=0; iPass<total_passes; ++iPass)
        {
          cRenderEntry* pRenderEntry =
            DisplayManager.openRenderQueue();

          pRenderEntry->hRenderMethod =
            (uint8)pEffectFile->resourceHandle();
          pRenderEntry->hSurfaceMaterial =
            pSurfaceMaterial->resourceHandle();
          pRenderEntry->modelType =
            cRenderEntry::k_bufferEntry;
          pRenderEntry->hModel =
            m_pVertexGrid->resourceHandle();
          pRenderEntry->modelParamA =
            pSection->sectorVertices()->resourceHandle();
          pRenderEntry->modelParamB =
            m_pTriangles->resourceHandle();
          pRenderEntry->renderPass =
            iPass;
          pRenderEntry->object =
            (cSceneNode*)pSection;
          pRenderEntry->userData =
            0;

          DisplayManager.closeRenderQueue(pRenderEntry);
        }
      }
    }

    void cTerrain ::renderSection(
      cTerrainSection* pSection,
      u32Flags activationFlags,
      const cRenderEntry* pEntry)const
    {
      cEffectFile* pEffectFile =
        m_pRenderMethod->getActiveEffect();
      cSurfaceMaterial* pSurfaceMaterial =
        m_pRenderMethod->getActiveMaterial();

      if (pEffectFile)
```

```
{
  profile_scope(cTerrain _renderSection);
  LPDIRECT3DDEVICE9 d3dDevice =
    TheGameHost.d3dDevice();

  // do we need to activate the render method?
  if (TEST_BIT(activationFlags,
    k_activateRenderMethod))
  {
    pEffectFile->begin();
  }

  // do we need to activate the render pass?
  if (TEST_BIT(activationFlags,
    k_activateRenderMethodPass))
  {
    pEffectFile->activatePass(pEntry->renderPass);
  }

  // do we need to activate the primary vertex buffer
  if (TEST_BIT(activationFlags,
    k_activateModel))
  {
    m_pVertexGrid->activate(0,0, true);
  }

  // do we need to activate the secondary vertex buffer
  if (TEST_BIT(activationFlags,
    k_activateModelParamA))
  {
    pSection->sectorVertices()->activate(
      1,0, false);
  }

  // do we need to activate the index buffer
  if (TEST_BIT(activationFlags,
    k_activateModelParamB))
  {
    m_pTriangles->activate();
  }

  // do we need to activate the surface material
  if (TEST_BIT(activationFlags,
    k_activateSurfaceMaterial))
  {
```

```
            pEffectFile->applySurfaceMaterial(
               pSurfaceMaterial);
        }

        // apply our render settings to the method
        int sectorX = pSection->sectorX();
        int sectorY = pSection->sectorY();

        cVector4 sectorOffset(
           1.0f,
           1.0f,
           m_worldExtents.x0+(m_sectorSize.x*sectorX),
           m_worldExtents.y0+(m_sectorSize.y*sectorY));

        cVector4 uvScaleOffset(
           (float)1.0f/(m_sectorCountX+1),
           (float)1.0f/(m_sectorCountY+1),
           (float)sectorX,
           (float)sectorY);

        pEffectFile->setParameter(
           cEffectFile::k_posScaleOffset,
           (D3DXVECTOR4*)&sectorOffset);

        pEffectFile->setParameter(
           cEffectFile::k_uvScaleOffset,
           (D3DXVECTOR4*)&uvScaleOffset);

        // render!!!
        HRESULT hr = d3dDevice->DrawIndexedPrimitive(
           m_pTriangles->primitiveType(),
           0,
           0,
           m_sectorVerts*m_sectorVerts,
           0,
           m_pTriangles->primitiveCount());
    }
}
```

THE BASIC TERRAIN DEMONSTRATION

In this chapter, we showed how to create a simple height map image using a variety of techniques, and then convert the image to vertex information suitable for rendering. In the next chapter, we will examine more efficient ways to store and manage the vertex and triangle index data, but for now, we take a moment to visualize our results. The demonstration program `chapter6_demo0` showcases the techniques we have discussed so far. This program (along with source code) can be found on the accompanying CD-ROM. Figure 6.9 shows a sample wireframe mesh generated using the techniques described.

ON THE CD

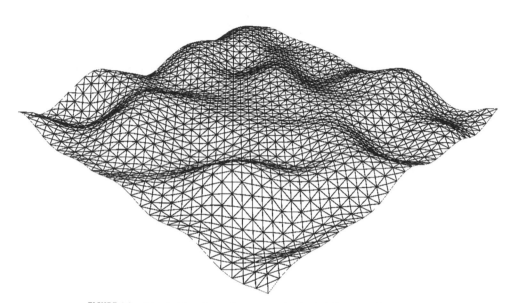

FIGURE 6.9   A basic triangle mesh generated using height map information.

For simplicity, no realistic texture maps are created for the terrain at this point. We will address texture mapping techniques in Chapter 9. For the time being, the height map itself is mapped across the terrain by the sample program to show the relationship between the image pixels and the resulting geometry. This first demo can be considered a brute-force approach to terrain rendering. No level-of-detail (LOD) management is applied, only quadtree visibility culling. While this might seem impractical, many of the current high-end video cards can use this method with remarkably high frame rates.

In the next chapter, we will examine methods to lessen the amount of geometry drawn. This will help facilitate more efficient rendering on more limited video cards, but might actually prove unnecessary in the near future. As advances in 3D hardware acceleration continue to progress, we find that the unremarkable brute-force approach can still have considerable appeal. The lack of any setup or LOD management work required on the CPU might actually make this the preferred method on video hardware that can handle a high level of geometry throughput. As always, some experimentation is required to find the method best suited to the target hardware platform.

REFERENCES

[Perlin1] Perlin, K. "Making Noise: Tutorial and History of the Noise Function," (available online at *www.noisemachine.com*).

[Perlin2] Perlin, K. "Improving Noise." *Computer Graphics* Vol. 35 No. 3, (available online at *http://mrl.nyu.edu/~perlin/paper445.pdf*).

CHAPTER

7

THE ROAM TERRAIN SYSTEM

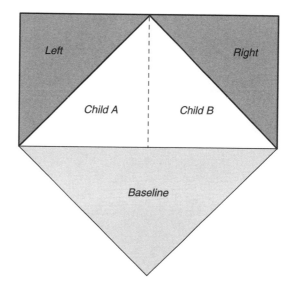

n the previous chapter, we examined basic terrain construction using height map data, and a few basic ways we can generate the height map data. In this chapter, we look at more robust methods for terrain geometry management. Until now, we have dealt with the terrain geometry at a uniform resolution. In a sense, we have been drawing our highest level of detail (LOD) for the entire terrain. This approach will quickly become impractical on limited video cards as the terrain grows larger and our rendering methods become more complex. This chapter introduces methods to store the terrain in modular units, and provide LOD control to reduce the rendering burden as much as possible.

We will present several popular methods for geometry management. Each method has strengths and weaknesses, leaving the programmer with a difficult choice of which method to use in his application. Small example programs are provided on the CD-ROM to demonstrate each method, but the final terrain engine provided with this book will focus on just one technique. However, we base all the techniques on the foundation class objects `cTerrain` and `cTerrainSection`, created in the previous chapter. By sharing a common set of interface functions, we allow the different terrain methods to be largely interchangeable.

ON THE CD

All of the techniques presented have the same basic goal in mind: more terrain triangles where you need them, and less where you don't. In essence, each approach maintains a higher triangle count in areas near the camera, while reducing the triangle count in more distant areas. The underlying assumption relies on the fact that these distant areas represent less actual screen pixels when rendered, and can therefore have their triangle count reduced will little visual effect on the screen. Of course, we would also take the complexity of the terrain into account, making sure that areas with little variation (flat lands, etc.) use a minimal triangle count, while more complex areas retain their triangles regardless of camera distance.

REAL-TIME OPTIMAL ADAPTING MESHES

The first system we will examine is the Real-Time Optimal Adapting Mesh algorithm, better known as ROAM. ROAM was first introduced in a paper by Mark Duchaineau et al [Duchaineau] as an algorithm designed to facilitate the rendering of large areas of terrain. While the method described in the paper was revolutionary, many game authors have found the need to further develop the idea for hardware compatibility. In our discussion of the technique, we will cover the basic principles behind ROAM, but our implementation will differ somewhat from the one described in the original paper.

ROAM relies on a property of the right isosceles triangle. As shown in Figure 7.1, a right isosceles triangle can be subdivided into two equal right isosceles triangles by splitting the original triangle along the line connecting the apex vertex to the center of the baseline. This splitting process can be repeated infinitely, doubling the number of triangles with each split. This creates a binary tree hierarchy, since each triangle is the potential parent of two smaller triangles. The ROAM method is basically a method of managing which triangles are split and which are collapsed into their parent. This allows us to raise or lower the detail of the terrain geometry on a triangle-by-triangle basis.

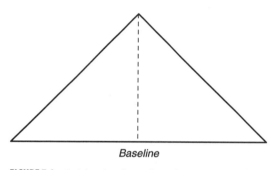

Baseline

FIGURE 7.1   A right triangle can be split into two smaller right triangles.

Each time a triangle is split, it creates a new vertex in the middle of its baseline. The position of this vertex can be interpolated as the average of the two baseline endpoints. However, this new vertex would inherit its *z*-axis position from the height mesh, raising or lowering it to match with the underlying terrain data. We will call the amount this new vertex would be moved in *z* the *displacement* value, and store it as an absolute value (see Figure 7.2).

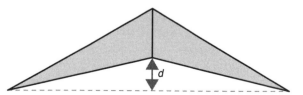

FIGURE 7.2   The displacement value for a triangle is the difference between the interpolated vertex position and the true vertex position as dictated by the underlying height map.

On its own, this displacement value is not very useful; it only tells us how much a single vertex will be moved when a triangle is split. To determine if a triangle should be split, we need to know whether it accurately describes the height data it covers. We need more than a single vertex height delta to tell us that. Luckily, as we traverse down the binary triangle tree, the triangles grow smaller and smaller, with each set of triangle vertices covering a smaller and smaller area of the height map. This means that the ratio of triangle area to height map area is approaching 1:1 as we go further down the tree. Therefore, if we examine all the displacement values of a triangle's children, we can get a more accurate description of whether the triangle being examined accurately described the height map data it represents.

We do this by recursively walking down through the children and locating the largest error delta between triangle vertices and actual height data. We already store this error per triangle as the displacement value, so our task is to find the largest displacement value and store this in the parent triangle. We'll call this maximum of the underlying displacement values the *error metric* for the triangle. This value will serve as a measurement of how well a triangle represents the underlying height data. An error metric of zero is a perfect triangle that exactly matches the underlying height information. Higher error metric values denote triangles that are a poor representation of the area they cover.

The error metric, which is precomputed for each triangle in the tree, can then be compared with a runtime value based on camera distance to decide whether a triangle should be split. Because the error metric is actually the maximum displacement value of all child nodes, we are assured to split triangles recursively until the triangle that generated the error value is found. Credit for this error metric calculation goes to Seumas McNally, who used this technique with great success in the Longbow Digital Arts® game TreadMarks™. McNally's insights into binary triangle trees and the ROAM technique were instrumental in TreadMarks winning three awards, including top honors, in the second annual Independent Games Festival. McNally's enhancements were documented by Brian Turner in his Gamasutra article, "Real-Time Dynamic Level of Detail Terrain Rendering with ROAM" [Turner].

The runtime value used to test each triangles error metric is an application-specific value. The purpose is to define a value that is the maximum error metric tolerated. Triangles that contain an error metric smaller than this value are left intact; those with a greater error metric are divided. Each time a triangle is split, the test is repeated among the two children. To add view-dependence to the test, the maximum tolerance value should increase as we move further away from the camera.

This ensures that triangles closer to the camera are split with more scrutiny than those further away.

SPLIT DECISIONS

In practice, we use three values to control the triangle split: *distance, scale,* and *limit*. Distance is a simple measure of the space between the point in question and the viewer. When coupled with the error metric, a ratio can be created of error over distance. If this ratio value exceeds the limit value provided, a split must be performed. The use of an additional scale value allows us to exaggerate or diminish the error metric to further control the LODs chosen. A higher scale value will increase the error ratio and make splits more likely to occur. Fractional scale values approaching zero have the opposite effect. The final calculation is shown as Equation 7.1.

$$Split\,? = \frac{ES}{D} > L \qquad (7.1)$$

E = error metric
S = error scale
D = distance to viewer
L = ratio limit

As Equation 7.1 shows, when the ratio between the scaled error and distance value exceeds our imposed limit, we must split the triangle. This simple equation allows us to take view distance and terrain topography into account when testing for splitting situations. Areas of the terrain closer to the camera are more likely to be split, as are areas that have high error values such as rocky or mountainous regions. Areas that require very few triangles, such as flat lands, will have very low error values—helping to ensure that we do not waste additional triangles in these areas.

The scale value helps us to control the priority between distance and terrain roughness. Large scale values weight the equation toward terrain topography, making rough terrain more likely to split than terrain that is close to the camera. A small scale value has the opposite effect, making distance far more important to the calculation than terrain roughness. Some experimentation is necessary to arrive at the scale and limit values best suited for a given terrain.

In performing the triangle splits, we take one more step to maintain the validity of our triangle mesh. Notice in Figure 7.3 that if one triangle is split, and has its new vertex displaced, a gap will appear in the terrain. This is called a T-junction, and it is a problem that all terrain tessellation methods must account for. To fix this, we must ensure that when one triangle splits, the triangle that shares the hypotenuse edge is also split.

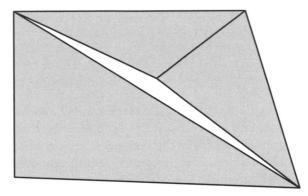

FIGURE 7.3 Splitting one triangle without adjusting the triangle that shares the split edge can result in a gap.

This creates a cascading problem within the mesh. As triangles are split, they might force neighboring triangles to split. To use the binary triangle tree effectively, we must ensure that each split or merge operation we perform updates the neighboring triangles as well. Each triangle must not only be aware of the child nodes below it, but also the three neighboring triangles that share the triangle's edges. The triangle links are shown in Figure 7.4.

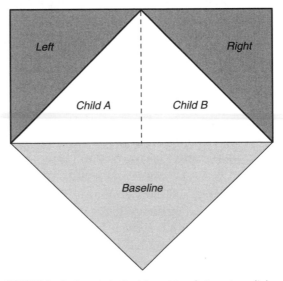

FIGURE 7.4 Each node in the binary triangle tree stores links to the child nodes and the three neighboring triangles.

When a triangle is split, one of two cases can result. If the base neighbor (as shown in Figure 7.4) shares a hypotenuse with the triangle being split, then it alone needs to be split in order to prevent gaps. If the base neighbor does not share a hypotenuse with the triangle being split, it must be recursively split until a triangle is created that does share a hypotenuse edge with the splitting triangle. This recursive process is shown in Figure 7.5.

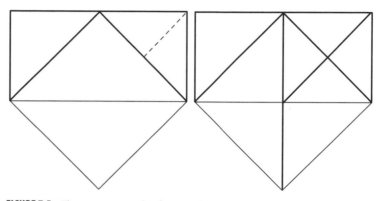

FIGURE 7.5   The steps required to force a split in an adjacent triangle. On the left, the desired split is shown as a dotted line. On the right, the total number of forced split operations is shown.

IMPLEMENTING ROAM

In Chapter 6, "Basic Terrain Geometry," we introduced the cTerrain and cTerrainSection classes for managing a basic set of static terrain geometry. For our implementation of ROAM, we will derive new classes from these base objects. This is a recurring theme that we will use for each of the terrain geometry methods we will cover. While the implementations change, the interfaces remain largely the same between all methods.

Just as we subdivided the original terrain into a grid of cTerrain Section objects, we will divide our ROAM terrain into similar pieces. While the ROAM method relies strongly on the binary triangle tree, we find in practice that building a single tree for the entire terrain is impractical. Building such a tree from a single root triangle would cause us to perform many needless split operations simply to reach a minimum LOD for our terrain. Instead, we continue to divide the terrain into grid sections, each of which contains a pair of binary triangle trees. These grid squares become the minimum resolution for the terrain, since our least-detailed version of the terrain would simply be to draw the root triangles of each grid section.

Two classes are derived to house the ROAM-enabled terrain: cRoamTerrain and cRoamTerrainSection. These maintain the same relationship as the cTerrain and cTerrainSection pair of classes. cRoamTerrain is the central repository for all terrain data, and cRoamTerrainSection objects represent discrete areas of the terrain arranged in a grid. While each class inherits the bulk of their functionality from the original terrain base classes, some additions must be made to contend with the dynamic nature of a ROAM terrain.

For each frame, we will subdivide the terrain using our error metric test found in Equation 7.1 to build a list of triangles that best represent the terrain. To facilitate this dynamic list of triangles, we need to add some memory management to our cRoamTerrain class. We will begin by defining the data structure required per triangle, and then examine ways to manage the allocation and release of these structures efficiently.

As shown in Figure 7.4, each triangle in the ROAM system maintains linkage information to five neighboring and child triangles. We represent this with the simple structure shown in Listing 7.1, cTriTreeNode. This structure represents a single node in our binary triangle tree and the five links maintained to neighboring and child nodes. cRoamTerrain contains a fixed pool of these structures, allowing cRoamTerrainSection objects to request node structures rather than perform any type of runtime memory allocation. This is a fixed size pool, meaning that not all requests for new nodes will be honored. When the pool is empty, all further node requests will fail and triangle splitting must cease. Listing 7.1 also contains the requestTriNode member function of the cRoamTerrain class used to manage cTriTreeNode structure requests.

LISTING 7.1   Managing cTriTreeNode requests within the cRoamTerrain class.

```
/*  cTriTreeNode
-----------------------------------------------

    This is a single node within the ROAM
    binrary triangle tree. A pool of these
    structures are stored within the
    cRoamTerrain class for allocation.


-----------------------------------------------
*/
```

```
struct cTriTreeNode
{
  cTriTreeNode *baseNeighbor;
  cTriTreeNode *leftNeighbor;
  cTriTreeNode *rightNeighbor;
  cTriTreeNode *leftChild;
  cTriTreeNode *rightChild;
};


// this function handles client requests for
// cTriTreeNode objects from our local pool.
// we use m_nextTriNode to store the next
// available index in the pool. When this
// index reaches the end of the pool, all
// nodes are in use.
cTriTreeNode* cRoamTerrain::requestTriNode()
{
  cTriTreeNode* pNode = 0;

  if (m_nextTriNode < k_maxTriTreeNodes)
  {
    // pull a node from the pool
    // and erase any old data in it
    pNode = &m_pTriangleNodePool[m_nextTriNode];
    memset(pNode, 0 ,sizeof(cTriTreeNode));
    ++m_nextTriNode;
  }

  // this may be zero. Callers must
  // handle this possibility
  return pNode;
}
```

You might notice in Listing 7.1 that no mechanism is provided to re-lease cTriTreeNode objects that are requested from the pool. This is by de-sign. We will be building a new binary triangle tree from scratch each frame, so no individual nodes are ever returned to the pool. Instead, the entire pool is reset at the start of each frame by simply resetting the m_nextTriNode counter back to zero. Within each cRoamTerrainSection, we also clear the child links of the root triangles, thereby completely de-stroying the tree built in the previous frame.

Using the fixed-size pool of cTriTreeNode structures and performing the reset operation each frame completely removes the need for any type of runtime memory allocation to maintain the ROAM system. This is far more efficient than dynamic allocation, but imposes a substantial drawback. The pool has a limited quantity, which will force us to stop splitting triangles once the well runs dry. When this occurs, we must draw whatever triangles we have split thus far and continue on to the next frame. Each `cRoamTerrainSection` contains two base `cTriTreeNode` structures as members of the class, so we are guaranteed a minimum of two triangles per terrain section. While this will prevent any holes from appearing in the terrain, running out of triangles to split might force sections of the terrain to use lower LOD representation than we desire.

We contend with this case by prioritizing the tessellation of `cRoam TerrainSection` objects. Knowing that we might run out of `cTriTreeNode` structures at some point, we need to ensure that `cRoamTerrainSection` objects closest to the camera perform their triangle split operations first. If we run out of `cTriTreeNode` structures, the `cRoamTerrainSection` objects forced to use lower LODs will most likely be those at the end of the queue, furthest away from the camera.

To maintain this priority list, `cRoamTerrainSection` objects that are found to be within the camera frustum compute their distance to the camera, and then submit themselves to a tessellation queue within the `cRoamTerrain` parent class. Within this class, a fixed-size queue of pointers to `cRoamTerrainSection` objects is used to maintain a list of sections that require tessellation in the next frame. Once all terrain sections are submitted to the queue, a quick-sort algorithm is run to sort the list by proximity to the viewer. This re-ordered list is then used to schedule each `cRoamTerrainSection` for tessellation, ensuring that sections closest to the camera get first pick from the `cTriTreeNode` pool.

Complex? Yes. However, it does the trick without the need for runtime allocation. The last remaining caveat is that the tessellation queue itself is a fixed size, and must therefore be large enough to hold all `cRoamTerrainSection` objects that require tessellation. Exceeding the limits of the tessellation queue would return us to the original problem of having to abort the tessellation process early, resulting in poor triangle subdivision in some locations. The good news is that our tessellation queue entries are merely pointers, so we can afford to pre-allocate a tessellation queue that can hold as many `cRoamTerrainSection` pointers as we feel we will ever encounter. Assertions placed in the code will alert us to situations where we overrun the end of the tessellation queue. Should this situation arise, we will need to increase the size of the tessellation queue. Listing 7.2 shows some of the member functions found within `cRoamTerrain` that are responsible for maintaining and processing the tessellation priority queue.

It should also be noted that the original ROAM implementation presented by Duchaineau et al [Duchaineau] also introduced a method of storing split and merge operations in a pair of priority queues. These queues were used to prioritize split and merge operations across the mesh, using frame-to-frame coherency of the mesh to begin each process. In our implementation of ROAM, we take a simpler approach and recursively split the triangles in a top-down manner, creating a new mesh for each frame. While less ideal, our brute-force is easier to code and manage as a way of introducing the ROAM algorithm and binary triangle tree. Successful implementations of the ROAM algorithm in popular games such as Longbow Digital Arts game TreadMarks have shown that the priority queues are not necessary to sustain a playable frame rate. Therefore, adding the priority queues described by the original paper is left as an exercise for the reader.

LISTING 7.2   Highlights of the cRoamTerrain class member functions used to manage the tessellation queue for cRoamTerrainSections.

```
//
// reset is called at the start of each frame
// to return all counters to zero, preparing
// both the triangle node pool and the
// tessellation queue for new entries
//
void cRoamTerrain::reset()
{
  // reset internal counters
  m_tessellationQueueCount = 0;
  m_nextTriNode=0;

  // reset each section
  int total = m_sectorCountY*m_sectorCountX;
  for (int i=0; i<total; ++i)
  {
    m_pRoamSectionArray[i].reset();
  }

}

//
// As sections are pulled from the quad tree,
// they add themselves to the tessellation queue
//
bool cRoamTerrain::addToTessellationQueue(
```

```cpp
                   cRoamTerrainSection* pSection)
{
  if (m_tessellationQueueCount
    < k_tessellationQueueSize)
  {
    m_tessellationQueue[m_tessellationQueueCount] =
      pSection;
    ++m_tessellationQueueCount;
    return true;
  }

  // while we handle this failure gracefully
  // in release builds, we alert ourselves
  // to the situation with an assert in debug
  // builds so we can increase the queue size
  debug_assert(
    0,
    "increase the size of the ROAM tessellation queue");
  return false;
}

// local sorting functor used
// by the quick sort algorithm
typedef cRoamTerrainSection* LPRoamSection;
struct sort_less
{
  bool operator()(
    const cRoamTerrainSection*& a,
    const cRoamTerrainSection*& b)const
  {
    return a->queueSortValue()
      < b->queueSortValue();
  }
};

//
// This function is called to sort the queue and
// allow each section to tessellate in order
//
void cRoamTerrain::processTessellationQueue()
{
  // sort the tessellation list
  // see "core\quick_sort.h"
  // for details
  QuickSort(m_tessellationQueue,
```

```
      m_tessellationQueueCount,
      sort_less());

  // tessellate each section
  uint32 i;
  for (i=0; i<m_tessellationQueueCount; ++i)
  {
    // split triangles based on the
    // scale and limit values
    m_tessellationQueue[i]->tessellate(
      m_vScale, m_vLimit);
  }

  // gather up all the triangles into
  // a final index buffer per section
  for (i=0; i<m_tessellationQueueCount; ++i)
  {
    m_tessellationQueue[i]->buildTriangleList();
  }
}
```

BUILDING ROAM DISPLAY GEOMETRY

As shown at the end of Listing 7.2, the final step after all sections have been queued and all triangles split is to run back through the tree and gather up the triangles for display. Just like our original terrain implementation from Chapter 6, we render each section of the terrain individually through the sorted render queue. All that remains is for us to visit each visible cRoamTerrainSection to build the vertex and index buffers needed to submit to the queue. This is performed through the buildTriangleList member function of cRoamTerrainSection.

Our implementation used the exact same vertex buffer streams found in the cTerrain base class. All that our tessellation requires is the construction of the index buffer that will define the triangles we actually render. This has some performance gain over dynamic vertex buffer creation, which would require sending much more data over the AGP bus to the video card each frame. With our implementation, vertices remain as static allocation in video card memory, and only the triangle vertex indices are updated each frame. Building this set of indices requires a simple recursion through the tree down to each leaf node. Once a leaf node is found, the triangle represented by the leaf node is added to the index buffer. When the index buffer is complete, the terrain section is ready for submission to the render queue. Listing 7.3 shows the recursive functions within `cRoamTerrainSection` that build the dynamic index buffer for display.

LISTING 7.3   Building the dynamic index buffer for ROAM section rendering.

```cpp
void cRoamTerrainSection::buildTriangleList()
{
  // lock the dynamic index buffer
  m_pIndexList = m_pIndexBuffer->lock(
    nWriteLock, 0, 0);
  m_totalIndices=0;

  // add all the triangles to the roamTerrain
  // in root triangle A
  recursiveBuildTriangleList(
    &m_rootTriangleA,
    0, 16, 16*17);

  // add all the triangles to the roamTerrain
  // in root triangle B
  recursiveBuildTriangleList(
    &m_rootTriangleB,
    (17*17)-1, 16*17, 16);

  // unlock the index buffer
  m_pIndexBuffer->unlock();
  m_pIndexList=0;
}

void cRoamTerrainSection::recursiveBuildTriangleList(
  cTriTreeNode *tri,
  uint16 iCornerA, uint16 iCornerB, uint16 iCornerC)
{
  // if there are children, we draw them instead
  if (tri->leftChild)
  {
    debug_assert(
      tri->rightChild,
      "invalid triangle node");

    uint16 iMidpoint = (iCornerB+iCornerC)>1;
    recursiveBuildTriangleList(
      tri->leftChild,
      iMidpoint, iCornerA, iCornerB);
```

```
    recursiveBuildTriangleList(
      tri->rightChild,
      iMidpoint, iCornerC, iCornerA);

  }
  else if (m_totalIndices + 3 < m_maxIndices)
  {
    // add the local triangle to the index list
    m_pIndexList[m_totalIndices++]=iCornerC;
    m_pIndexList[m_totalIndices++]=iCornerB;
    m_pIndexList[m_totalIndices++]=iCornerA;
  }
}
```

ON THE CD

To end our look at ROAM, we show one final listing. On the CD-ROM, a demonstration program can be found that uses the ROAM classes described here. This program, chapter7_demo0.exe, handles the setup and rendering of the ROAM terrain in the main.cpp file. Within this file, a small amount of extra work is performed to locate all visible terrain sections, queue them for tessellation, and then process each item in the queue. All work is performed within the member functions listed within this section, but the main.cpp file is responsible for initiating these procedures. Listing 7.4 shows the simple steps taken in the chapter7_demo0.exe program to tessellate and render the ROAM terrain.

LISTING 7.4 Managing the tessellation and rendering of a ROAM terrain. This is an excerpt from the code found in the main.cpp file of the chapter7_demo0.exe program.

```
// find all visible objects, including
// ROAM terrain sections
cSceneObject* pFirstMember =
  quadTree().buildSearchResults(
  activeCamera()->searchRect());
cSceneObject* pRenderList = pFirstMember;

// reset the ROAM terrain
m_terrainSystem.reset();

// prepare all objects for rendering
// this also adds ROAM terrain sections
// to the tessellation queue
while(pFirstMember)
{
  pFirstMember->prepareForRender();
```

```
    pFirstMember = pFirstMember->nextSearchLink();
}

// tessellate all terrain sections queued
m_terrainSystem.processTessellationQueue();

// render all objects, including the newly
// tessellated ROAM sections.
// (puts them in the render queue)
pFirstMember = pRenderList;
while(pFirstMember)
{
  pFirstMember->render();
  pFirstMember = pFirstMember->nextSearchLink();
}
```

REFERENCES

[Duchaineau] Duchaineau, M., M. Wolinski, D. Sigeti, M. Miller, C. Aldrich, and M. Mineev-Weinstein. "ROAMing Terrain: Real-Time Optimally Adapting Meshes," (available online at *www.llnl.gov/graphics/ROAM*).

[Turner] Turner, B. "Real-Time Dynamic Level of Detail Terrain Rendering with ROAM," (available online at *www.gamasutra.com/features/20000403/turner_01.htm*).

TILED GEOMETRY TECHNIQUES

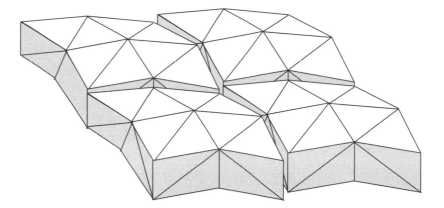

One of the perceived flaws with the ROAM method is the reliance on dynamic index buffers for display. The precision gained by making level-of-detail (LOD) decisions for each triangle yields a near-ideal set of geometry, but can generate a unique set of geometry for each camera location. Uploading the generated index buffer to the video card delivers a substantial blow to real-time performance, a matter that is only exaggerated by our rebuilding of the vertex set each frame. In addition, traditional recursion of the binary triangle tree generates individual triangles that need to be rendered. This is far less efficient than groups of triangles packaged into strips and fans for the hardware to use for cache-coherency. While generating these triangle lists from the ROAM output is not impossible, it is a daunting task for programmers new to the subject.

Instead, we turn to aggregate methods of managing terrain geometry. By this we mean techniques that perform LOD decisions on groups of triangles, rather than each individual triangle. These aggregate groups are commonly defined as squares within a regular grid covering the terrain. All LOD decisions are made at the resolution of the grid rather than on a per-triangle basis, allowing pre-made sets of geometry to be built for each grid square at various LOD levels. The benefit of these grid-based techniques is that less actual LOD computations are required at runtime, and the ready-made sets of geometry can be built to take advantage of hardware strip and fan coherency.

In this chapter, we look at two methods of working with terrain in grid increments. The first method, Chunked Terrain, was developed by Thatcher Ulrich [Ulrich] of Oddworld Inhabitants®. Ulrich's method uses a tree structure of grid cells, not unlike a quadtree, to provide increasing detail. The second method, developed by the author [Snook], uses a single grid of cells, each of which can be displayed at a precomputed LOD. Both methods rely on additional geometry placed between cells of different detail levels to hide any gaps that might appear.

CHUNKED TERRAIN

The idea of chunking terrain into squares along a regular grid is a wonderful simplification to the ROAM binary triangle tree. Where ROAM used an error metric to recursively travel down a binary tree to the desired depth, Chunked Terrain uses a similar error metric to traverse down a quadtree to the desired depth. The difference is that the result found within the quadtree node of the Chunked Terrain contains a small mesh, pre-assembled for peak rendering efficiency. While the quadtree nodes do not allow for per-triangle adjustment of the terrain geometry, the gains made in hardware efficiency far outweigh this small penalty in precision.

Figure 8.1 shows a representation of the Chunked Terrain tree described by Ulrich. At the top level of the tree, a single square is formed using two triangles. The second level of the tree contains four members, each at a higher detail level than its parent. This construction would repeat until the resolution of the underlying height map is fully represented by triangles. Just as we did with ROAM, each level of the tree is given an error metric based on the difference between the interpolated vertices and the true height data for the terrain.

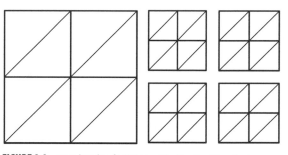

FIGURE 8.1   Two levels of LOD provided by the Chunked Terrain quadtree.

The rendering process is also identical to our implementation of the binary triangle tree within ROAM. For each node, we compare the error metric of the node with our view-dependant tolerance limit using a ratio of error over distance (see Equation 7.1). If the node is within our tolerance limit, we render the node contents and move on. If not, we step deeper into the tree and test each of the four children. This process repeats until all desired nodes in the tree have been found.

As with ROAM, we also have the issue of cracks forming within the terrain when two grid cells are rendered with different levels of tessellation. Rather than forcing neighbors to subdivide to a matching set of vertices, Ulrich provides a novel approach using a polygonal skirt around each rendered grid cell. These skirts are no more than vertically oriented triangles placed along the edge of the mesh to conceal the gap between cells. Figure 8.2 shows an example of this skirt geometry.

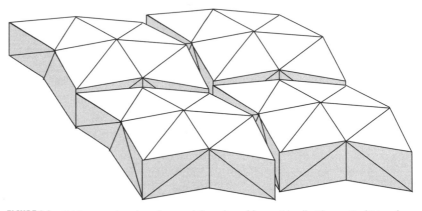

FIGURE 8.2   Skirt geometry placed around the edge of four grid cells. The vertical triangles of each skirt are shown in gray.

As Figure 8.2 shows, the vertical skirt polygons can create a discontinuity on the mesh, forming vertical peaks among the otherwise smooth mesh. At very coarse tessellations, these vertical peaks would be apparent to the user and might serve as a distraction. However, Ulrich was able to show that with a sufficiently low view-dependent tolerance, these peaks can be minimized, often to a pixel height or less, making them nearly indistinguishable from the surrounding polygons. This means that the scale and limit parameters we use to control LOD decisions will need to be adjusted to prevent these vertical polygons from becoming apparent to the user.

MANAGING CHUNKS OF GEOMETRY

The chunked terrain is stored in a set of classes derived from cTerrain and cTerrainSection. As with our ROAM implementation in the previous chapter, we derive from these classes to maintain a similar interface to manage and render the terrain. Our two new classes are cChunkTerrain and cChunkTerrainSection. As always, they represent the overall parent object of the terrain and individual grid-aligned sectors of the terrain mesh, respectively.

To facilitate the use of the chunk sections and their additional skirt geometry, we find that some additional geometry is needed by the chunked terrain system. The vertical skirt geometry requires custom index buffers to define the triangles of the skirt, and the additional vertices that define the bottom of the skirt edge. As with all of our sector-based terrain classes, we take advantage of the fact that much of this additional geometry can be shared among all the terrain sectors.

To begin, we must first create the skirt vertices. The bottom of the skirt contains vertex data that is identical to the top, except that the z-axis height value is offset by some factor. All texture coordinates and surface normals remain the same. To enable creation of the skirts, we simply duplicate our mesh vertices, copying all data and offsetting the height value of each vertex. Rather than store this new data in a separate vertex buffer, we simply double the size of the original buffer and append the new data to the end. This converts our vertex buffer into two sections, which we call *pages*. The first half of the vertex buffer (page 0) is the true surface geometry of the terrain section, while the second half (page 1) holds the same geometry offset by some vertical distance to form the bottom of the skirt geometry.

Creating a duplicated set of vertices might seem wasteful at first, but keep in mind that a skirt might be necessary both around the outside edge of our cChunkTerrainSection and within the interior of the section. We will be recursively subdividing the section into smaller squares as we traverse our internal quadtree, so skirt geometry might be needed between the interior edges of different detail levels. Storing the additional vertices as a second page of the original vertex buffer makes the new geometry transparent to the shaders. We can use the same vertex and pixel shader to draw the tiles and skirts, using index buffers to control the actual triangles rendered.

Listing 8.1 shows the additional setup required to build the vertex and index buffers. We are still using the same duel-stream approach we took advantage of in our standard and ROAM terrain, so both the shared vertices within the cChunkTerrain and the individual vertices of the cChunkTerrainSection must be duplicated. In addition, a set of skirt-defining index buffers are created by the cChunkTerrain parent class. Our continued use of section-based terrain rendering allows us to create a common set of skirt index buffers for the entire terrain, just as we did with the standard cTerrain index buffers in Chapter 6, "Basic Terrain Geometry."

LISTING 8.1   Vertex and Index buffer setup within the chunked terrain tile classes.

```
// these constant values are used in
// the code that follows. The can be
// found in the cChunkTerrain and
// cChunkTerrainSection class
// definitions
```

```cpp
enum e_index_type
{
  k_chunk = 0,
  k_skirt,
  k_totalIndexTypes
};

enum e_constants
{
  k_minTessellationShift = 2,
  k_maxDetailLevels = 4,
  k_topLod = 3,
  k_cellShift = 2,
};
#define SKIRT_HEIGHT 50.0f

bool cChunkTerrainSection::buildVertexBuffer()
{
  bool result = true;
  //
  // Build a vertex buffer and determine
  // the min\max size of the sector
  //
  cString tempName;
  tempName.format(
    "terrain_section_%i_%i",
    m_sectorX,
    m_sectorY);

  m_pSectorVerts =
    TheGameHost.displayManager().
    vertexBufferPool().createResource(tempName);

  m_worldRect.z0 = MAX_REAL32;
  m_worldRect.z1 = MIN_REAL32;

  //
  // for chunked terrain, we build a vertex buffer
  // with twice as many entries as normal. These
  // are called 'pages'. The first page is the
  // true vertex buffer, the second page is an
  // offset version of each vertex used when
  // rendering the skirts
  //
  uint32 pageSize = m_xVerts*m_yVerts;
```

```
uint32 bufferSize = pageSize<<1;

if (m_pSectorVerts)
{
  // read in the height and normal for each vertex
  cTerrain::sSectorVertex* pVerts =
    new cTerrain::sSectorVertex[bufferSize];

  for (uint16 y = 0; y<m_yVerts; ++y)
  {
    for (uint16 x = 0; x<m_xVerts; ++x)
    {
      float height =
        m_pTerrainSystem->readWorldHeight(
          m_heightMapX+x,
          m_heightMapY+y);
      cVector3 normal =
        m_pTerrainSystem->readWorldNormal(
          m_heightMapX+x,
          m_heightMapY+y);

      int vertIndex = (y*m_xVerts)+x;
      pVerts[vertIndex].height =
        height;
      pVerts[vertIndex].normal =
        normal;

      height -= SKIRT_HEIGHT;

      pVerts[vertIndex+pageSize].height =
        height;
      pVerts[vertIndex+pageSize].normal =
        normal;

      m_worldRect.z0 =
        minimum(m_worldRect.z0, height);
      m_worldRect.z1 =
        maximum(m_worldRect.z1, height);
    }
  }

  result = result &&
    m_pSectorVerts->create(
    bufferSize,
    sizeof(cTerrain::sSectorVertex),
```

```
        FLAG(cVertexBuffer::nRamBackupBit),
        pVerts);

    safe_delete_array(pVerts);
  }
  else
  {
    result = false;
  }

  return result;
}

bool cChunkTerrain::buildVertexBuffer()
{
  cString tempName;
  tempName.format("terrain_system_%i", this);

  // create the vertex buffer
  // shared by the sectors
  m_pVertexGrid =
    DisplayManager.vertexBufferPool().
    createResource(tempName);

  cVector2 cellSize(
    m_sectorSize.x/m_sectorUnits,
    m_sectorSize.y/m_sectorUnits);

  int pageSize = m_sectorVerts*m_sectorVerts;
  int bufferSize = pageSize<<1;

  cVector2 vert(0.0f,0.0f);
  sLocalVertex* pVerts =
    new sLocalVertex[bufferSize];

  // fill the vertex stream with x,y positions and
  // uv coordinates. All other data (height and
  // surface normals) are stored in the vertex
  // buffers of each terrain section
  for (int y=0; y<m_sectorVerts; ++y)
  {
    vert.set(0.0f, y*cellSize.y);

    for (int x=0; x<m_sectorVerts; ++x)
    {
```

```
        int index = (y*m_sectorVerts)+x;
        cVector2 UV(
          (float)x/(float)(m_sectorVerts-1),
          (float)y/(float)(m_sectorVerts-1));

        pVerts[index].xyPosition = vert;
        pVerts[index].localUV = UV;

        // duplicate this data into the
        // second page as well
        pVerts[index+pageSize].xyPosition = vert;
        pVerts[index+pageSize].localUV = UV;

        vert.x += cellSize.x;
      }
    }

  // now that we have built the data,
  // create one of our vertex buffer
  // resource objects with it
  bool result =
    m_pVertexGrid->create(
    bufferSize,
    sizeof(sLocalVertex),
    0, pVerts);

  safe_delete_array(pVerts);

  return result;
}

bool cChunkTerrain::buildIndexBuffer()
{
  bool result = true;
  // the default index buffer is not used
  // in chunked terrain, Instead, we build
  // an entire set of index buffers for
  // each detail level and possible
  // skirt edge

  int stride = (1<<m_sectorShift)+1;
  int stepSize = stride>k_minTessellationShift;
  int vertCount = (1<<k_minTessellationShift)+1;

  m_detailLevels = 0;
```

```
while (stepSize
  && result
  && m_detailLevels<k_maxDetailLevels)
{
  cString tempName;
  tempName.format(
    "chunk_index_buffer_%i",
    m_detailLevels);

  m_indexBufferList[k_chunk][m_detailLevels] =
    DisplayManager.indexBufferPool().
    createResource(tempName);

  result = result &&
  m_indexBufferList
    [k_chunk][m_detailLevels]->createSingleStripGrid(
    vertCount,  // width of grid
    vertCount,  // height of grid
    stepSize, // horz vertex count per cell
    stepSize, // vert vertex count per cell
    stride, // horz vertex count in vbuffer
    0);

  stepSize>=1;
  ++m_detailLevels;
}

// build an index buffer for each skirt.
// Consider each square detail level of
// the tile as a square with corners
// A,B,C & D as in the figure below

/*
   D -------- C
 ^ |          |
 | |          |
 p |          |
 o |          |
 s |          |
   A -------- B
 y
   pos x ->
*/
// the following code generates a single strip
// for each skirt following the edges
```

```
// AB, BC, CD and DA
int sideLength = (1<<m_sectorShift)+1;
int pageSize = sideLength*sideLength;

for (
  int iLevel=0;
  result && iLevel<m_detailLevels;
  ++iLevel)
{
  cString tempName;
  tempName.format(
    "chunk_skirt_index_buffer_%i",
    iLevel);

  m_indexBufferList[k_skirt][iLevel] =
    DisplayManager.indexBufferPool().
    createResource(tempName);

  int skirtSide = (1<<k_minTessellationShift)+1;
  int indexCount=skirtSide<<3;
  uint16* indexList = new uint16[indexCount];
  uint16* pIndex = indexList;

  int vStep;
  int vIndex;
  int count;
  int horzStep =
    (sideLength>iLevel)>k_minTessellationShift;
  int vertStep =
    sideLength*horzStep;

  // side AB
  vIndex=0;
  vStep = vertStep;
  for(count=0; count<skirtSide;++count)
  {
    *(pIndex++)=vIndex;
    *(pIndex++)=vIndex+pageSize;
    vIndex +=vStep;
  }

  // side BC
  vIndex -= vStep;
  vStep = horzStep;
  for(count=0; count<skirtSide;++count)
```

```
      {
        *(pIndex++)=vIndex;
        *(pIndex++)=vIndex+pageSize;
        vIndex +=vStep;
      }

      // side CD
      vIndex -= vStep;
      vStep = -vertStep;
      for(count=0; count<skirtSide;++count)
      {
        *(pIndex++)=vIndex;
        *(pIndex++)=vIndex+pageSize;
        vIndex +=vStep;
      }

      // side DA
      vIndex -= vStep;
      vStep = -horzStep;
      for(count=0; count<skirtSide;++count)
      {
        *(pIndex++)=vIndex;
        *(pIndex++)=vIndex+pageSize;
        vIndex +=vStep;
      }

      result = result &&
      m_indexBufferList[k_skirt][iLevel]->create(
        D3DPT_TRIANGLESTRIP ,
        indexCount,
        0,
        indexList);

      safe_delete_array(indexList);
    }

    return result;
}
```

TESSELLATING TERRAIN CHUNKS

With the terrain geometry in place for our chunk sections, we can now turn our attention to generating the error metrics needed to control the tessellation of the terrain and the actual rendering process. As with the

ROAM implementation of Chapter 7, "The ROAM Terrain System," we compute an error metric for each node in the tree. This error metric represents the maximum displacement error of the node and all of its children. This nested set of error metrics allows us to recursively step through the tree nodes and choose an optimal set geometry to render.

In the ROAM binary triangle tree, we had a single vertex to examine for each node. In chunked terrain, each node represents an entire grid of vertices. For each node, we must find the maximum error of the entire grid. This value becomes the displacement error value for the node, which is used by parent nodes to find the maximum error metric for a branch within the quadtree. To perform the search for the maximum grid displacement error, we add a member function to the cTerrain base class. This makes the search procedure available to methods other than the chunked terrain method we are currently building.

The procedure is a recursive examination of each triangle in the grid, and the real-world height values they approximate. The entire process is shown in Listing 8.2. Note that we use the same parameter scheme we used for building a grid-based index buffer. This allows us to determine the error metric for any grid of vertices at any level of detail.

LISTING 8.2   Finding the error metric for a grid of vertices at a specific LOD.

```
float cTerrain::computeErrorMetricOfGrid(
  uint16 xVerts,  // width of grid
  uint16 yVerts,  // height of grid
  uint16 xStep, // horz vertex count per cell
  uint16 yStep, // vert vertex count per cell
  uint16 xOffset, // starting index X
  uint16 yOffset) // starting index Y
{
  float result = 0.0f;
  int total_rows = yVerts-1;
  int total_cells = xVerts-1;

  unsigned short start_vert =
    (yOffset*m_tableWidth)+xOffset;
  unsigned short lineStep =
    yStep*m_tableWidth;

  float invXStep = 1.0f/xStep;
  float invYStep = 1.0f/yStep;

  for (int j=0;j<total_rows;++j)
```

```
{
  uint16 indexA = start_vert;
  uint16 indexB = start_vert+lineStep;
  float cornerA = readWorldHeight(indexA);
  float cornerB = readWorldHeight(indexB);

  for (int i=0; i<total_cells;++i)
  {
    // compute 2 new corner vertices
    uint16 indexC = indexA+xStep;
    uint16 indexD = indexB+xStep;

    // grab 2 new corner height values
    float cornerC = readWorldHeight(indexC);
    float cornerD = readWorldHeight(indexD);

    // setup the step values for
    // both triangles of this cell
    float stepX0 = (cornerD-cornerA)*invXStep;
    float stepY0 = (cornerB-cornerA)*invYStep;
    float stepX1 = (cornerB-cornerC)*invXStep;
    float stepY1 = (cornerD-cornerC)*invYStep;

    // find the max error for all points
    // covered by the two triangles
    int subIndex = indexA;
    for (int y=0; y<yStep;++y)
    {
      for (int x=0; x<xStep;++x)
      {
        float trueHeight =
          readWorldHeight(subIndex);
        ++subIndex;

        float intepolatedHeight;

        if (y < (xStep-x))
        {
          intepolatedHeight =
            cornerA
            + (stepX0*x)
            + (stepY0*y);
        }
        else
        {
```

```
            intepolatedHeight =
              cornerC
              + (stepX1*x)
              + (stepY1*y);
        }

        float delta = absoluteValue(
          trueHeight - intepolatedHeight);

        result = maximum(
          result,delta);

      }
      subIndex = indexA+(y*m_tableWidth);
    }

    // save the corners for the next cell
    indexA = indexC;
    indexB = indexD;
    cornerA = cornerC;
    cornerB = cornerD;
  }

  start_vert += lineStep;
}


return result;
}
```

In the `cChunkTerrainSection` objects, these error metric values computed from the vertex grid are stored in a fully expanded quadtree. This tree of error metrics is the sole representation used to form the quadtree of chunk sections. Unlike the ROAM implementation, we do not use an actual structure of pointers to represent our tree nodes. Instead, we traverse our tree by interpolating position information from the four corners of the parent node, and use the data stored in the error metric tree for testing. Listing 8.3 shows how the error metric tree is constructed.

LISTING 8.3   Building the error metric tree.

```
#define LEVEL_SIDE_LENGTH(i) (1<<i)

enum e_constants
{
```

```
      k_minTessellationShift = 2,
};

void cChunkTerrainSection::buildErrorMetricTree()
{
  // the sector shift tells us how large our
  // root node is in terms of vertices
  int shift = m_pTerrainSystem->sectorShift();
  int stride = (1<<shift)+1;

  // this information is used to setup our initial
  // step size and vertex count information
  int stepSize =
    stride>k_minTessellationShift;
  int vertCount =
    (1<<k_minTessellationShift)+1;

  // we can now step through the levels
  // of detail and determine an error
  // metric for each node of the quad
  // tree. This data is stored in the
  // error metric tree for later use
  int i;
  for (i=m_totalLevels-1; i>=0;--i)
  {
    int localStep = stepSize>i;
    int xSpan = (vertCount-1)*localStep;
    int ySpan = (vertCount-1)*localStep;

    int side_count = LEVEL_SIDE_LENGTH(i);

    for (int y=0; y<side_count;++y)
    {
      for (int x=0; x<side_count;++x)
      {
        // compute the local errorMetric.
        // m_heightMapX and m_heightMapY
        // are the pixel location in the
        // height map for this section
        float errorMetric =
          m_pTerrainSystem->computeErrorMetricOfGrid(
          vertCount,  // width of grid
          vertCount,  // height of grid
          localStep,  // horz vertex count per cell
          localStep,  // vert vertex count per cell
```

```
            m_heightMapX+
            (x*xSpan),   // starting index X
            m_heightMapY+
            (y*ySpan));// starting index Y

        // max with the errorMetric of our children
        if (i+1 < m_totalLevels)
        {
          int nextLevel = i+1;
          int nX = x<<1;
          int nY = y<<1;
          int dim = side_count<<1;

          errorMetric = maximum(
            errorMetric,
            m_errorMetricTree
              [nextLevel][(nY*dim)+nX]);
          errorMetric = maximum(
            errorMetric,
            m_errorMetricTree
              [nextLevel][(nY*dim)+nX+1]);
          errorMetric = maximum(
            errorMetric,
            m_errorMetricTree
              [nextLevel][((nY+1)*dim)+nX]);
          errorMetric = maximum(
            errorMetric,
            m_errorMetricTree
              [nextLevel][((nY+1)*dim)+nX+1]);
        }

      m_errorMetricTree[i][(y*side_count)+x] =
        errorMetric;
    }
  }
 }
}
```

Tessellating the chunked terrain is now a simple matter of examining each node in our quadtree of terrain chunks. In each node, we decide if the node itself should be drawn, or if we should instead step through and examine the four child nodes. As with the ROAM implementation, we use the ratio of error and distance to determine whether to draw a node or continue traversing the tree. The error metric values for each node in the tree are precomputed and stored in the error metric table, ready for access. To test each node, however, we still need a distance value from the node to the viewer.

The process begins by examining the root node of a cChunkTerrain Section and computing distance values to each of its four corners. Computing the distance values is a slow operation (it involves a square root calculation), but this is a one-time cost per section for each frame. As we recursively step down through the children, we interpolate these four distance values rather than perform any type of distance calculation within the children. The grid-based nature of our terrain sections makes this possible.

For each node, we determine the corner that is closest to the viewer, and use this distance value to compute the error ratio. Based on the ratio scale and limit values set by the user, we can easily determine if a given node should be drawn. As we encounter nodes to draw, we add them to a list of nodes to be drawn in the next render pass. Listing 8.4 shows highlights of the process described.

LISTING 8.4   Finding nodes to draw within a cChunkTerrainSection.

```
void cChunkTerrainSection::prepareForRender()
{
  cCamera* pCamera = TheGameHost.activeCamera();

  // compute a 2d point for each corner of the section
  cVector2 corner0(m_worldRect.x0, m_worldRect.y0);
  cVector2 corner1(m_worldRect.x0, m_worldRect.y1);
  cVector2 corner2(m_worldRect.x1, m_worldRect.y1);
  cVector2 corner3(m_worldRect.x1, m_worldRect.y0);

  cVector2 viewPoint= pCamera->worldPosition().vec2();

  // compute view distance to our 4 corners
  float distance0 = viewPoint.distance(corner0);
  float distance1 = viewPoint.distance(corner1);
  float distance2 = viewPoint.distance(corner2);
  float distance3 = viewPoint.distance(corner3);

  //clear the render list
  m_totalRenderEntries=0;

  // recursively tessellate and add
  // to the internal render list
  recursiveTessellate(
    distance0, distance1, distance2, distance3,
```

```
      0, 0, 0,
      chunkTerrain()->lodErrorScale(),
      chunkTerrain()->lodRatioLimit());
}

void cChunkTerrainSection::recursiveTessellate(
  float distA, float distB, float distC, float distD,
  int level, int levelX, int levelY,
  float vScale, float vLimit)
{
  bool split = false;

  // can we attempt to split?
  if (level+1 < m_totalLevels)
  {
    int index = (levelY*LEVEL_SIDE_LENGTH(level))+levelX;
    float errorMetric = m_errorMetricTree[level][index];

    // find the shortest distance
    float dist = minimum(distA, distB);
    dist = minimum(dist, distC);
    dist = minimum(dist, distD);

    // find the ratio of errorMetric over distance
    float vRatio = (errorMetric*vScale)/(dist+0.0001f);

    // if we exceed the ratio limit, split
    if (vRatio > vLimit)
    {
      int nextLevel = level+1;
      int startX = levelX<<1;
      int startY = levelY<<1;

      // compute midpoint distances
      float midAB = (distA + distB)*0.5f;
      float midBC = (distB + distC)*0.5f;
      float midCD = (distC + distD)*0.5f;
      float midDA = (distD + distA)*0.5f;
      float midQuad = (distA + distC)*0.5f;

      // recurse through the four children
      recursiveTessellate(
        distA, midAB, midQuad, midDA,
        nextLevel, startX, startY,
        vScale, vLimit);
```

```
                recursiveTessellate(
                  midAB, distB, midBC, midQuad,
                  nextLevel, startX, startY+1,
                  vScale, vLimit);

                recursiveTessellate(
                  midBC, distC, midCD, midQuad,
                  nextLevel, startX+1, startY+1,
                  vScale, vLimit);

                recursiveTessellate(
                  midAB, midQuad, midCD, distD,
                  nextLevel, startX+1, startY,
                  vScale, vLimit);

                // remember that we split
                split = true;

            }
        }

        // did we split?
        if (!split)
        {
          // add ourselves to the render list
          if (m_totalRenderEntries < k_maxRenderEntries)
          {
            sRenderEntry& entry =
              m_renderList[m_totalRenderEntries++];

            int lodShift = 5 - level;

            entry.level = level;
            entry.offsetX = (levelX<<lodShift);
            entry.offsetY = (levelY<<lodShift);
          }
        }
    }
```

ON THE CD

On the accompanying CD-ROM, a demo program is provided to show the chunked terrain method in action. Like all of our demonstrations provided up to this point, we do not focus on any texturing or render effects. The demo program, chapter8_demo0.exe, is a simple showcase of a small chunked terrain generated from a random height map. The height map itself is stretched over the terrain as a grayscale image to illustrate the relationship between height values stored per-pixel and the final LOD-enabled terrain.

INTERLOCKING TERRAIN TILES

The final method presented also uses a grid-based approach, this time without any tree recursion. The method, first described in *Game Programming Gems 2* [Snook], instills each grid cell with a set of prebuilt geometry at a variety of LOD levels. At the highest LOD, each grid square uses one vertex for each corresponding pixel on the height map. For each successive LOD, half the vertices are discarded, creating a lower resolution version of the mesh. This simple LOD method requires no tree information or recursion, just a simple list of possible LODs per terrain section and the error metrics that control their appearance.

To simplify storage in hardware, a single vertex buffer is used for all versions of the mesh, with individual index buffers serving to create each LOD. The index buffers define each LOD by using different vertices from the common vertex buffer. Figure 8.3 shows two detail levels built from the same vertices, using index buffers to define the triangles to be rendered.

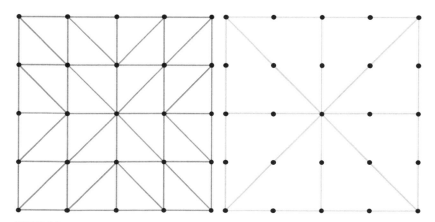

FIGURE 8.3   Using index buffers to create separate detail levels from the same set of vertices.

As with the previous methods, an error metric is calculated based on the differences between the levels of detail for each grid square. Since the grid squares are not organized in a hierarchy, we simply store a fixed number of error metrics with each cell. As we step through the cells, we check each error metric against our view-dependent tolerance value and determine the proper index buffer to use. Like Ulrich's Chunk Terrain, we perform our detail level decisions at the grid resolution rather than per triangle. However, the terrain tiles enforce a fixed stepping to this decision rather than allowing for tree recursion to further refine the mesh.

As always, we have the potential of gaps to deal with. While we could use the skirt geometry of the Chunked Terrain method to fill any gaps, the coarseness of our grid cells would make them more apparent to the end user. Instead, we need to perform some additional work to make the terrain appear to seamlessly transition between LODs. To do this, we further refine our index buffers to create gap-sealing geometry pieces that lock our tiles together.

The total set of index buffers created for a tile can be broken into two groups: body geometry and link geometry. Body pieces represent a major portion of a tile at a given detail level, with areas removed to provide space for the linking pieces to attach. Linking pieces fill the gap between adjacent body pieces to form a seamless transition. Figure 8.4 shows a pair of cells at separate LODs and the linking pieces used to connect them.

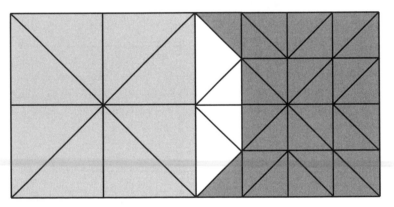

FIGURE 8.4   Two terrain tiles shown side by side with a linking piece (shown in white) used to connect them.

Using these linking pieces implies that we have a set of body pieces with notches removed from them, as shown in the right-hand tile in Figure 8.4. Given that our tiles can connect on four sides to geometry of a lower detail, we require a sct of 16 index buffers to represent each tile. Because the index buffers contain relative vertex indices only, we can create a single set of 16 to use on the entire terrain. Figure 8.5 shows the full set of 16 body pieces required for our tiles.

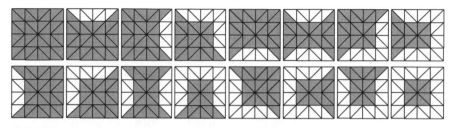

FIGURE 8.5   The 16 basic shapes needed to represent the body of each terrain tile. Open areas represent the space where linking pieces will be placed to connect to adjacent cells.

The number of linking pieces required depends on the total number of LODs available per tile. We enforce that linking pieces are placed within tiles along sides that are adjacent to lower-detail tiles. Therefore, we limit the set of linking pieces to those that can step down from one detail level to those below it. For example, Figure 8.6 shows two versions of the same linking piece, each designed to connect to an adjacent detail level that is lower than the cell containing the link.

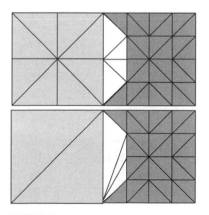

FIGURE 8.6   An example of two linking pieces designed to connect to adjacent cells of lower detail.

In the source/gaia folder on the CD-ROM, the index buffers for each of the shapes described are supplied as static data. The classes that comprise this terrain method, cTileTerrain and cTileTerrainSection, load this static data and convert it into a table of index buffers required for rendering. The vertex buffers used are the same dual-stream buffers supplied by the cTerrain and cTerrainSection base classes. No special geometry is required to facilitate our new method.

Setting up the terrain tiles is a simple matter of using the grid-based error calculation function we built earlier (see Listing 8.2) to determine a set of error metric values for the terrain section. In our sample implementation, each section can be drawn using one of four possible LODs. To pick the best LOD, we precompute a set of three error metric values for the section. These are then used during rendering to pick the proper index detail level to draw. Listing 8.5 shows the functions used to set up this data.

LISTING 8.5   Setting and using error metric values in the cTiledTerrainSection class.

```cpp
// this function builds the error metric table
void cTiledTerrainSection::computeErrorMetricTable()
{
  int vertCount =1;
  int stepCount = 8;

  for (int lod=0; lod<k_totalDetailLevels; ++lod)
  {
    // compute the local errorMetric.
    // m_heightMapX and m_heightMapY
    // are the pixel location in the
    // height map for this section.
    // m_xVerts and m_yVerts are the
    // width and height of the section
    // in vertices
    m_errorMetric[lod] =
      m_pTerrainSystem->computeErrorMetricOfGrid(
        vertCount+1,  // width of grid
        vertCount+1,  // height of grid
        stepCount-1,  // horz vertex count per cell
        stepCount-1,  // vert vertex count per cell
        m_heightMapX, // starting index X
        m_heightMapY);// starting index Y

    vertCount <<=1;
    stepCount >=1;
  }

  // make sure each error metric
```

```
    // represents all the higher lods
    m_errorMetric[1] =
        maximum(m_errorMetric[1], m_errorMetric[2]);
    m_errorMetric[0] =
        maximum(m_errorMetric[0], m_errorMetric[1]);
}


// this function chooses the best lod to draw
// using the data provided in the error metric table
void cTiledTerrainSection::prepareForRender()
{
    cCamera* pCamera = TheGameHost.activeCamera();

    // compute a 2d point for each corner of the section
    cVector2 corner0(m_worldRect.x0, m_worldRect.y0);
    cVector2 corner1(m_worldRect.x0, m_worldRect.y1);
    cVector2 corner2(m_worldRect.x1, m_worldRect.y1);
    cVector2 corner3(m_worldRect.x1, m_worldRect.y0);

    cVector2 viewPoint= pCamera->worldPosition().vec2();

    // compute view distance to our 4 corners
    float distance0 = viewPoint.distance(corner0);
    float distance1 = viewPoint.distance(corner1);
    float distance2 = viewPoint.distance(corner2);
    float distance3 = viewPoint.distance(corner3);

    // compute min distance as the test value
    float dist = minimum(distance0, distance1);
    dist = minimum(dist, distance2);
    dist = minimum(dist, distance3);

    // make sure the minimum distance is non-zero
    dist = maximum(dist, 0.0001f);

    // find the lowest lod which will suffice
    m_lod = 0;
    bool finished = false;

    float vScale = m_pTerrainSystem->lodErrorScale();
    float vLimit = m_pTerrainSystem->lodRatioLimit();

    while (!finished)
    {
        // find the ratio of variance over distance
```

```
        float variance = m_errorMetric[m_lod];
        float vRatio = (variance*vScale)/(dist);

        // if we exceed the ratio limit, move to the next lod
        if (vRatio > vLimit
          && m_lod+1 < k_totalDetailLevels)
        {
          ++m_lod;
        }
        else
        {
          finished=true;
        }
      }
    }
  }
```

The `cTiledTerrain` class contains the code that examines the neighbors of each `cTileTerrainSection` and issues the render queue entries for the body and linking pieces needed to draw each section. This source code can be found on the accompanying CD-ROM as the member function `cTiledTerrain::submitSection`. In addition to the sample source code, the CD-ROM also contains a sample application, `chapter8_demo1.exe`, which shows the interlocking terrain tiles in use.

ON THE CD

A NOTE ON LOD POPPING

Each of the methods described for handling terrain geometry suffers from popping artifacts. These are caused when an area of the terrain changes tessellation levels, causing a visible "pop" in the terrain mesh. Of the methods presented, these artifacts are least noticeable in the ROAM method, due to the rather smooth nature of the per-triangle LOD changes. Of the two grid-based approaches, the Chunked Terrain method is least likely to exhibit popping, again due to the increased resolution afforded by the tree hierarchy it uses. Popping artifacts will be most noticeable using the Interlocking Terrain Tiles method due to its much coarser grid resolution and the spontaneous appearance of linking geometry between various grid squares.

The best way to deal with the popping artifacts of all three methods is to animate, or morph, the changes between separate LOD levels over time. This reduces the jarring nature of the artifacts and gives the appearance of much smoother transitions between high and low areas of detail within the mesh. This can be used with great success in the Chunked Terrain method, virtually removing most popping artifacts. For the Interlocking Tiles method, morphing operations are less likely to yield the desirable result. The spontaneous appearance of linking pieces will cause popping to occur, even if morphing is attempted. These linking pieces use the terrain vertices in a separate manner than the regular grid, connecting different vertices into triangles to form the link piece. These new triangles change the way height values are interpolated between vertices, making it impossible to build a set of morph targets that will work in all cases. Therefore, the interlocking terrain tile method is not a realistic candidate for morphing.

When using morph targets to hide popping artifacts, the preparation for each method is the same: For each detail level, begin with vertex positions that match the surface of the previous detail level. As the viewer continues to move, slowly interpolate between these starting positions and the true position. Over time, the vertices move from their previous height values to the proper values reported by the height mesh, removing the popping effect of abrupt detail changes. To simplify the code, and make the LOD changes more apparent, the sample programs provided with this book do not attempt to morph between detail levels.

REFERENCES

[Snook] Snook, G. "Simplified Terrain Using Interlocking Tiles." *Game Programming Gems 2*, pp. 377–383, Charles River Media, Inc., 2001.
[Ulrich] Ulrich, Thatcher. "Chunked LOD," (available online at *http://tulrich.com/geekstuff/chunklod.html*).

TEXTURING TECHNIQUES

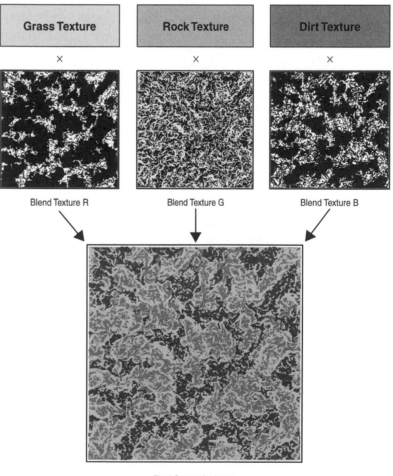

Final Composite Image

n the previous chapter, we created a simple set of terrain geometry. When rendered in wireframe, we can see the terrain level-of-detail (LOD) methods at work and begin to imagine the final landscape. The next task to overcome is texturing the terrain with realistic images to represent different ground surfaces. For this book, we will be sticking to a few basic ground surfaces: grass, dirt, rock, and snow. On older hardware, we can restrict this set even further when the number of textures available per pixel shader is severely limited—more on this later in the chapter.

The main focus of this chapter is to explore a few methods for texturing the ground, along with the pros and cons of each. In keeping with the procedural nature of noise maps used to create terrain geometry, we will also explore procedural ways to create ground textures. This allows us to continue to pursue a randomly generated terrain. Like the terrain geometry itself, we can use hand-made data or procedural solutions for greater flexibility.

A GREAT BIG BLURRY WORLD

We'll begin by quickly dismissing the simplest approach: stretch a single texture across the entire terrain. While practical from a rendering standpoint, the tradeoff in visual quality helps us quickly rule this option out. An easy way to measure visual quality is to determine the ratio of texture pixels (texels) to screen pixels for a given method. For example, imagine a section of terrain that fills the camera view. If a small texture is applied to this geometry, the bilinear filtering of this texture will result in big, blurry colors on screen. The higher the resolution of the texture, the less blurry the result; in other words, as the ratio of texture pixels to screen pixels grows, quality increases.

Our intent is to create a terrain that will span several miles. When a terrain is generated to span such a large area, the texture required to cover it and still maintain a decent texture-to-screen ratio is prohibitively large. Even a terrain that is only intended to represent a square mile would require a texture of 5280×5280 pixels just to maintain one pixel per square foot! Therefore, we might need to look at solutions that cover the terrain in multiple texture maps, rather than one large map.

This is not to say that using one large texture map to cover the terrain is unreasonable—it would be a straight-forward approach to use. Even if more robust texturing methods are used near the camera, a large texture map can still be used on distant areas of the terrain. A utility program called T2 is provided on the accompanying CD-ROM to help construct

ON THE CD

textures for use on terrain. This program allows the user to submit a height map along with various properties of the terrain desired. The program can then generate a texture of any size to use on the terrain. T2 also provides the facility to divide this large texture up into smaller pieces. When using grid-based terrain geometry such as the Chunked LOD method, having a utility program to create textures to use on individual areas of the terrain can be very useful. More information on T2 and its author, Keith Ditchburn, can be found on the Web site listed in Appendix D, "Recommended Reading."

For readers who want to use pre-made terrain textures, the T2 program is highly recommended. For this book, however, we will continue to focus on procedural methods to generate random terrain. The engine itself is oblivious to the source of the height maps used, so the output from Mr. Ditchburn's T2 program could easily be incorporated. With the pre-made route of texture generation solved, we still need to find a procedural approach.

The first idea that should have popped into your head is tiling the textures. If we created a single texture map and repeated it across the terrain several times, we could maintain a much higher texture-to-screen pixel ratio. This is true, but it would only work for homogenous surface types. If we wanted to create a terrain of 100-percent grass, we could indeed tile a high-resolution grass texture across the entire terrain. However, any repetition in the grass pattern, however subtle, would quickly become apparent when viewed repeating off into the distance. With a little artistic effort, this effect can be greatly reduced—provided that you want acre after acre of the same ground surface.

Another potential solution is a sector-based approach. Here we use multiple, unique textures arranged in a 2D grid over the terrain. Each texture represents only a small subset of the terrain, and we can maintain a high pixel ratio by increasing the resolution of these textures. In a sense, this method takes the large 5280 x 5280 pixel image we discussed earlier, and divides it into smaller images. The result is the same, using many textures to emulate a huge image. As we mentioned earlier, the T2 program is capable of generating these sector textures as well.

In practice, this approach can work quite well. However, there are a few caveats with which to contend. First, we will need to control the number of textures used in a given area. If many textures are needed to render the view from the camera, we might put quite a burden on the DirectX resource manager to continually page those textures into video memory. If all the textures required will fit into video memory, this cost is removed. However, if we use more data than video memory can hold, the DirectX resource manager will begin paging the textures into video memory as we use them, tossing older textures out to make room. This can create a situation called *thrashing*, where resources are being continually uploaded to the video card to keep up with rendering demands.

If video memory space is not a concern, there is still the potential for seams to develop between the texture images. Even if two textures are designed in a paint program to stand together side by side perfectly, there is still a potential for a seam to develop when filtering is applied. Bilinear and anisotropic filtering methods, used to magnify or minify textures as they are sampled by the pixel shader, compute a final color by sampling more than one pixel of an image and blending to produce a final result. These filters allow a texture to blur rather than become blocky as it approaches the camera. However, the filtering is applied per-texture, meaning that none of the pixels in adjacent textures will be included in the blending operation. As the edges of adjacent textures are filtered, they will create color values that do not necessarily match the filtered results of their neighbors. This can create a visual seam between two textures that would normally be seamless when placed side by side. This effect is exaggerated when texture wrapping modes (setting the texture stage state to `D3DTA_WRAP` for one or more texture coordinates) are mistakenly applied, causing the texture filter to sample pixels from the opposite edge of the texture when blending a result.

Using texture address clamping (`D3DTA_CLAMP`) rather than wrapping can reduce the appearance of seams, but the complete solution is a little trickier, and requires some tedious texture preparation. To help ensure that a texture will filter well with its neighbors, the adjacent pixels of the neighboring textures must be placed around the outside edge of each texture. By slightly insetting the UV coordinates used to map each texture onto its geometry, we can ensure that these edge pixels are never visible, but are available to the texture sampler when filtering is applied. This requires knowledge of the exact texture dimensions so that the UV coordinates can be inset one pixel in from the actual edge of the image.

Depending on the degree of filter that will be applied, a one-pixel border might not be adequate. When the textures used will be heavily filtered, a thicker border might be required. This will be the case when textures recede into the distance and the sampling pattern applied by the filter begins to reach beyond the one-pixel border. Given this potential problem, the time-consuming setup for this technique, and the fact that it still requires the same total memory footprint as the proposed 5280 x 5280 image, we will forgo this solution as well and seek something better for our landscape. However, discussing these undesirable techniques was not in vain.

BLENDING SURFACE TEXTURES

Tiling a single image across the terrain would create a monotonous, boring result, but it is a step in the right direction. Of the methods we have discussed so far, this is the clear winner in terms of potential texture-to-screen pixel quality, memory requirements, and ease of use. It stands to reason that if we can somehow incorporate multiple surface types into this technique, we can arrive at a more desirable method.

In fact, the solution we will explore involves layering this simple technique several times. Imagine if we tiled the terrain with not only a single grass texture, but other textures as well such as dirt and rock. This would create individual layers of terrain, one covered in dirt, one in rock, and one in grass. Each layer is simply a single texture repeated ad infinitum, but mixing them together would provide a very organic result.

The idea is to allow different amounts of these layers to show through in different areas of the terrain—creating a more organic result. Some parts of our terrain could allow more of the grass layer to show through, while others would appear rockier or expose the underlying dirt layer. All that is needed is a means of controlling the amount that each layer contributes to the final result.

To control the appearance of each layer, we can use a weighted average per-pixel. For each layer, we provide a weight value between 0.0 and 1.0 defining how much the layer is visible at a given location. If all the weight values are created so that the weights of all layers add up to 1.0, we can compute the final color of each pixel easily.

What we do is multiply each input texture by a visibility factor, and then sum the results. The result is a terrain that contains the high texture-to-screen pixel ratio we desire, with the ability to control the appearance of various surface types on a per-pixel basis. Figure 9.1 shows a pictorial representation of the process. In this figure, four input textures are shown. These are the three surface type textures and the blending control image. Within the blending control image, the visibility factor for each terrain surface is encoded in the red, green, and blue channels, respectively. By modulating each texture with the corresponding blend texture channel and summing the results, the final destination image can be created.

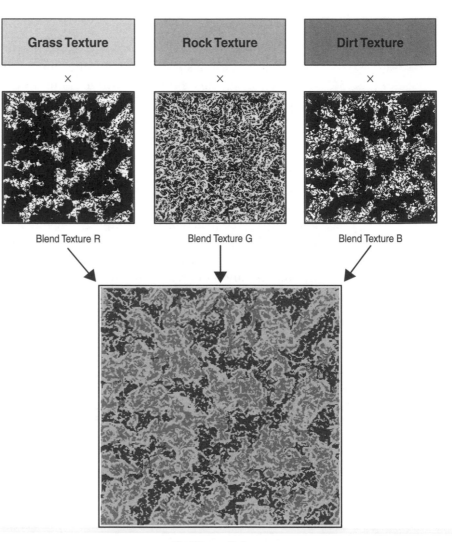

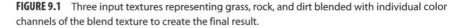

Final Composite Image

FIGURE 9.1   Three input textures representing grass, rock, and dirt blended with individual color channels of the blend texture to create the final result.

In pixel shader terms, this is a straightforward multitexture shader—which is an ideal starting point for our terrain. The pixel shader version supported by the target hardware will determine the number of textures we can blend in a single pass, so we will work with the lowest common denominator of four textures for the time being. For our initial texturing method, we will use all four to render our simple terrain in one pass.

Assume for the moment that we have three surface textures—grass, rock, and dirt—along with a fourth texture containing the blend amounts for each in the red, green, and blue color channels. Using the pixel shader shown in Listing 9.1, these textures can be blended to create the final terrain of Figure 9.2. All that remains is to create the blend texture itself, which can be done in any suitable paint program or by using a procedural technique.

LISTING 9.1   A simple pixel shader to blend three surface layers using a fourth blend texture.

```
float4 ThreeSurfaceBlend(VS_OUTPUT In)
: COLOR
{
  // sample all four textures
  float4 BlendControler =
    tex2D(LinearSamp0, In.vTex0 );
  float4 texColor0 =
    tex2D(LinearSamp1, In.vTex1 );
  float4 texColor1 =
    tex2D(LinearSamp2, In.vTex2 );
  float4 texColor2 =
    tex2D(LinearSamp3, In.vTex3 );

  // determine the amount of each surface to blend
  float4 Color0 =
    (texColor0 * BlendControler.r);
  float4 Color1 =
    (texColor1 * BlendControler.g);
  float4 Color2 =
    (texColor2 * BlendControler.b);

  // sum the resulting colors
  // and multiply by the diffuse
  // vertex color (lighting)
  return (Color0 +
          Color1 +
          Color2)
          *BlendControler.a
          *In.vDiffuse;
}
```

Creating the blend texture by hand is simple enough; simply paint the desired amount of each surface into the proper texture channel as a grayscale value. Care must be taken to ensure that the blend factors add up to 255 (white) to prevent over-saturation of the terrain when all the surface textures are blended together. To facilitate random terrain, however, we will need a runtime method to create this blend texture.

`cTerrain` stores a great deal of information about the terrain. For each pixel of the original height map, a height value and a surface normal are stored. We can use this data to generate the blend texture by defining altitudes and slope angles where we would expect to find certain types of terrain. By examining the data held in `cTerrain` and comparing it to the desired slope and altitude data, we can procedurally paint a surface blending texture. This is very similar to the functionality that the T2 utility program performs offline. The main difference is that while the T2 program produces a final texture map, we want to only create the blend texture needed to composite the final texture map in real time.

Creating the surface blend texture at the same resolution as the original height map gives us a 1:1 ratio between the data stored in the `cTerrain` class and the final blend texture. However, there is no real need to enforce such a size restriction on the blend texture. By providing a few simple functions to interpolate between the vertex data held within `cTerrain`, we can create a texture of any size equal to or larger than the original height map.

We will not be creating blend textures smaller than the height map resolution for two reasons. First, a texture of lower resolution adversely limits the way the terrain surfaces will be combined. This creates a potential for large, blocky areas of each surface type to appear. Second, interpolating across our multiple surface normals in our terrain data will yield incorrect slopes—allowing us to place terrain surfaces where they would not normally be expected.

In `cTerrain`, we add a set of functions for interpolating between the data held per-vertex for the terrain. These functions, shown in Listing 9.2, sample a set of four vertices surrounding the location in question, and interpolate them to produce a result. In the case of the surface normal interpolation, a renormalization of the result is required, since interpolating between surface normals can produce vectors that are no longer of unit length; in other words, they become denormalized as part of the calculation.

LISTING 9.2   Height and surface normal interpolation functions found within `cTerrain`.

```
float cTerrain ::calcMapHeight(
  float mapX,
  float mapY)const
{
```

```
    float fMapX = mapX * (m_tableWidth-1);
    float fMapY = mapY * (m_tableHeight-1);

    int iMapX0 = realToInt32_chop(fMapX);
    int iMapY0 = realToInt32_chop(fMapY);

    fMapX -= iMapX0;
    fMapY -= iMapY0;

    iMapX0 = clamp(iMapX0, 0, m_tableWidth-1);
    iMapY0 = clamp(iMapY0, 0, m_tableHeight-1);

    int iMapX1 = clamp(iMapX0+1, 0, m_tableWidth-1);
    int iMapY1 = clamp(iMapY0+1, 0, m_tableHeight-1);

    // read 4 map values
    float h0 = readWorldHeight(iMapX0, iMapY0);
    float h1 = readWorldHeight(iMapX1, iMapY0);
    float h2 = readWorldHeight(iMapX0, iMapY1);
    float h3 = readWorldHeight(iMapX1, iMapY1);

    float avgLo = (h1*fMapX) + (h0*(1.0f-fMapX));
    float avgHi = (h3*fMapX) + (h2*(1.0f-fMapX));

    return (avgHi*fMapY) + (avgLo*(1.0f-fMapY));;
}

void cTerrain ::calcMapNormal(
    cVector3& normal,
    float mapX,
    float mapY)const
{
    float fMapX = mapX * (m_tableWidth-1);
    float fMapY = mapY * (m_tableHeight-1);

    int iMapX0 = realToInt32_chop(fMapX);
    int iMapY0 = realToInt32_chop(fMapY);

    fMapX -= iMapX0;
    fMapY -= iMapY0;

    iMapX0 = clamp(iMapX0, 0, m_tableWidth-1);
    iMapY0 = clamp(iMapY0, 0, m_tableHeight-1);

    int iMapX1 = clamp(iMapX0+1, 0, m_tableWidth-1);
```

```
    int iMapY1 = clamp(iMapY0+1, 0, m_tableHeight-1);

    // read 4 map values from our table of
    // of data held per-vertex
    cVector3 h0 = readWorldNormal(iMapX0, iMapY0);
    cVector3 h1 = readWorldNormal(iMapX1, iMapY0);
    cVector3 h2 = readWorldNormal(iMapX0, iMapY1);
    cVector3 h3 = readWorldNormal(iMapX1, iMapY1);

    // average the results
    cVector3 avgLo = (h1*fMapX) + (h0*(1.0f-fMapX));
    cVector3 avgHi = (h3*fMapX) + (h2*(1.0f-fMapX));

    normal= (avgHi*fMapY) + (avgLo*(1.0f-fMapY));

    // re-normalize the result
    normal.normalize();
}
```

Interpolating height and surface normals across our terrain is only a small part of the task set before us. We must now define a way to control the appearance of our three potential surface types based on elevation and slope. This is actually far simpler than it sounds. First, we define our control parameters as a small structure that will be provided for each texture we want to blend. This structure can be found within the cTerrain class definition.

```
struct elevationData
    {
      float minElevation; // lowest elevation
      float maxElevation;    // highest elevation
      float minNormalZ;      // minimum z of the surface normal
      float maxNormalZ; // maximum z of the surface normal
      float strength; // overall strength (priority)
    };
```

As the elevationData structure shows, we allow each terrain surface to specify the minimum and maximum ranges for both elevation and slope. Slope is measured in terms of the z component of the surface normal. Z values close to 1.0 are vertical, depicting flat areas of the terrain, while lower surface normal z values represent steeper inclines. Setting these values to ranges between 0.0 and 1.0 allows us to map a terrain surface to cliff edges (low z values) or flat lands (high z values).

The `cTerrain` class contains a member function that can generate a blend texture using up to four `elevationData` structures as input. For each pixel of the blend texture, this function samples a height value and surface normal on the terrain and determines the blend amount of each surface type. To compute these blend factors, the routine determines individual weight values in terms of the elevation and slope ranges, and then combines the results with the overall strength of each surface type.

Weight values are calculated based on the min and max ranges supplied for elevation and slope. Terrain locations that fall within the center of the min max range are given a weight of 1.0. Locations that fall toward the min and max extents have weight values that approach zero. Weight values outside the min max range are zero. Once the weight values are calculated for both elevation and slope, the results are combined and scaled by the overall surface strength. This creates a blend factor for the surface type being tested. This procedure is repeated for all input `elevationData` structures to determine a final pixel value for the blend texture.

However, we have to enforce the limitation that all blend factors for a given pixel add up to one. This ensures that our shader will be able to combine these textures without worrying about over- or under-saturation of the final image. To enforce this rule, we maintain a sum of all the weight values calculated for each pixel of the blend texture. Before writing the actual blend factors to the pixel, we divide them by this sum. Once all the blend factors have been divided, we can be certain that they will add up to 1.0.

Again, it's a far easier process than it might seem. Listing 9.3 shows the function that performs the steps we have discussed. A quick look at the code shows this to be a straight-forward process. Note that while the blend values are computed between 0.0 and 1.0, they are converted to color values in the range (0–255) when writing them to the blending texture.

LISTING 9.3   Generating the blend image texture.

```
static float computeWeight(
  float value,
  float minExtent,
  float maxExtent)
{
  float weight = 0.0f;

  if (value >= minExtent
    && value <= maxExtent)
```

```
        {
          float span =
            maxExtent - minExtent;
          weight =
            value - minExtent;

          // convert to a 0-1 range value
          // based on its distance to the midpoint
          // of the range extents
          weight *= 1.0f/span;
          weight -= 0.5f;
          weight *= 2.0f;

          // square the result for non-linear falloff
          weight *= weight;

          // invert and bound-check the result
          weight = 1.0f-absoluteValue(weight);
          weight = clamp(weight, 0.001f, 1.0f);
        }

      return weight;
    }

    void cTerrain ::generateBlendImage(
      cImage* pBlendImage,
      elevationData* pElevationData,
      int elevationDataCount)
    {
      bool success = false;
      int x,y,i;

      // make sure there are no more than 4 structures
      elevationDataCount = minimum(elevationDataCount, 4);

      // get the blend image dimensions
      int image_width = pBlendImage->width();
      int image_height = pBlendImage->height();

      // compute the step values for uv
      // coordinates across the image
      float uStep = 1.0f/(image_width-1);
      float vStep = 1.0f/(image_height-1);
```

```
// these 4 mask values control
// which color component of the
// blend image we write to
cVector4 mask[4];
mask[0].set(1.0f,0.0f,0.0f,0.0f);
mask[1].set(0.0f,1.0f,0.0f,0.0f);
mask[2].set(0.0f,0.0f,1.0f,0.0f);
mask[3].set(0.0f,0.0f,0.0f,1.0f);

// lock all the blend image
pBlendImage->lock();

// step through and generate each pixel
for (y=0; y<image_height; ++y)
{
  for (x=0; x<image_width; ++x)
  {
    float totalBlend = 0.0f;
    cVector4 blendFactors(
      0.0f,
      0.0f,
      0.0f,
      0.0f);

    // get the elevation and surface normal
    float u = x*uStep;
    float v = y*vStep;
    float map_height = calcMapHeight(u,v);
    cVector3 normal;
    calcMapNormal(normal, u, v);

    // examine each elevationData structure
    // a compute a weight for each one
    for (i=0; i<elevationDataCount; ++i)
    {
      // compute a weight based on elevation
      float elevationScale =
        computeWeight(
          map_height,
          pElevationData[i].minElevation,
          pElevationData[i].maxElevation);

      // compute a weight based on slope
      float slopeScale =
        computeWeight(
```

```
        normal.z,
        pElevationData[i].minNormalZ,
        pElevationData[i].maxNormalZ);

  // combine the two with the relative
  // strength of this surface type
  float scale =
    pElevationData[i].strength *
    elevationScale *
    slopeScale;

  // write the result to the proper
  // channel of the blend factor vector
  blendFactors += mask[i]*scale;

  // and remember the total weight
  totalBlend += scale;
}

// balance the data (so they add up to 255)
float blendScale = 255.0f /totalBlend;

// now compute the actual color by
// multiplying each channel
// by the blend scale
blendFactors *= blendScale;

// clamp and convert to color values
uint8 r =
  (uint8) clamp(
    blendFactors.x,
    0.0f,
    255.0f);
uint8 g =
  (uint8) clamp(
    blendFactors.y,
    0.0f,
    255.0f);
uint8 b =
  (uint8) clamp(
    blendFactors.z,
    0.0f,
    255.0f);
uint8 a =
  (uint8) clamp(
```

```
            blendFactors.w,
            0.0f,
            255.0f );

        // pack and write a 32bit pixel value
        uint32 color = (a<<24)+(r<<16)+(g<<8)+b;
        pBlendImage->setColor(x,y,color);
    }
  }

  // unlock the image
  pBlendImage->unlock();
}
```

You might have noticed in Listing 9.3 that the blend texture is actually a `cImage` object, not a `cTexture`. `cTexture` is the class we would normally use to load and create image data for rendering, but because we need to write key information into specific color channels of the blend texture, we use the `cImage` class. `cImage` is a simple class for manipulating nonvideo memory DirectX surfaces of a known format, which we call "images." While `cTexture` objects can be of any format allowed by the video card (including compressed and YUV color space formats), `cImage` objects are limited to 8-, 24-, and 32-bit RGB images with a known color channel order. This makes them easier to read and manipulate than a texture that might be of some unknown color format. `cImage` textures are also restricted to system memory, preventing any potential stalls caused by locking and updating their data.

Once a `cImage` object is built, it can be used as a texture by passing it to the `uploadImage` member function of `cTexture`. This loads the image data onto the texture, performing any color space conversion or scaling necessary, thanks to the D3DX function `D3DXLoadSurfaceFromSurface`. This function provides the color conversion and scaling needed to upload our image onto the texture for use during rendering.

Using the shader from Listing 9.1 and the blend image generated by Listing 9.3, we can now render a basic terrain in a single pass on just about any video card. The entire process is shown in Listing 9.4, which contains the `InitDeviceObjects` function found within `main.cpp` from the `chapter9_demo0` program. This demo program is located on the accompanying CD-ROM.

ON THE CD

LISTING 9.4   The entire setup process for a basic, random terrain.

```
HRESULT cMyHost::InitDeviceObjects()
{
  cGameHost::InitDeviceObjects();

  // create the root node
  // for our scene and a camera
  m_rootNode.create();
  m_camera.create();
  m_camera.attachToParent(&m_rootNode);

  // setup a basic camera
  m_CameraPos.set(0.0f, 0.0f, 10.0f);
  m_camera.orientation().setRotation(
    cVector3(1.0f,0.0f,0.0f),
    cVector3(0.0f,0.0f,1.0f));
  m_camera.setProjParams(
    D3DX_PI/5.0f,
    800.0f/600.0f,
    1.0f, 1000.0f);

  // generate a random height map
  m_pHeightMap =
    displayManager()
    .texturePool()
    .createResource(cString("height map"));
  m_pHeightMap->createTexture(
    128, 128,
    1, 0,
    D3DFMT_A8R8G8B8,
    D3DPOOL_MANAGED);
  m_pHeightMap->generatePerlinNoise(
    0.01f, 5, 0.6f);

  // create a terrain from this map
  m_terrainSystem.create(
    &m_rootNode,
    m_pHeightMap,
    cRect3d(-500.0f,
        500.0f,
        -500.0f,
        500.0f,
        -250.0f,
        250.0f),
    3);
```

```
// load our render method
m_pRenderMethod =
  TheGameHost
  .displayManager()
  .renderMethodPool()
  .createResource("terrain method");
m_pRenderMethod->loadResource(
  "media\\shaders\\simple_terrain.fx");

// generate three elevation structures
cTerrain ::elevationData elevation[3];

// grass (all elevations and slopes)
elevation[0].minElevation = -250;
elevation[0].maxElevation = 250;
elevation[0].minNormalZ = -1.0f;
elevation[0].maxNormalZ = 1.0f;
elevation[0].strength = 1.0f;

// rock (all elevations, steep slopes)
elevation[1].minElevation = -250;
elevation[1].maxElevation = 250;
elevation[1].minNormalZ = 0.0f;
elevation[1].maxNormalZ = 0.85f;
elevation[1].strength = 10.0f;

// dirt (high elevation, flat slope)
elevation[2].minElevation = 50;
elevation[2].maxElevation = 250;
elevation[2].minNormalZ = 0.75f;
elevation[2].maxNormalZ = 1.0f;
elevation[2].strength = 20.0f;

// generate the blend image
cImage* pBlendImage;
pBlendImage =
  displayManager()
  .imagePool()
  .createResource(cString("image map 3"));
pBlendImage->create(
  256,
  256,
  cImage::k_32bit);

m_terrainSystem.generateBlendImage(
```

```
    pBlendImage,
    elevation, 3);

pBlendImage->randomChannelNoise(
  3, 200, 255);

// upload the blend image to a texture
m_pBlendMap =
  displayManager()
  .texturePool()
  .createResource(cString("image map"));

m_pBlendMap->createTexture(
  256, 256,
  1, 0,
  D3DFMT_A8R8G8B8,
  D3DPOOL_MANAGED);

m_pBlendMap->uploadImage(pBlendImage);
safe_release(pBlendImage);

// load the ground surface textures
m_pGrass =
  displayManager()
  .texturePool()
  .createResource(cString("grass"));
m_pRock =
  displayManager()
  .texturePool()
  .createResource(cString("rock"));
m_pDirt =
  displayManager()
  .texturePool()
  .createResource(cString("dirt"));

m_pGrass->loadResource(
  "media\\textures\\grass.dds");
m_pRock->loadResource(
  "media\\textures\\rock.dds");
m_pDirt->loadResource(
  "media\\textures\\dirt.dds");

// create a surface material
// and load our textures into it
m_pSurfaceMaterial =
```

```
    displayManager()
    .surfaceMaterialPool()
    .createResource(cString("ground material"));
m_pSurfaceMaterial->setTexture(0, m_pBlendMap);
m_pSurfaceMaterial->setTexture(1, m_pGrass);
m_pSurfaceMaterial->setTexture(2, m_pRock);
m_pSurfaceMaterial->setTexture(3, m_pDirt);

// give the render method and material to the terrain
m_terrainSystem.setRenderMethod(m_pRenderMethod);
m_terrainSystem.setSurfaceMaterial(m_pSurfaceMaterial);
return S_OK;
}
```

NATURE IS NOISY

One limitation of our single-pass terrain system is that it can only handle a maximum of three surface types. We impose a limit of four textures per pass for this simple method in order to remain compatible with lower-end video cards. However, astute readers will notice that we use all four channels of the blend texture. Why do we use four channels to blend three textures? Because we can.

Repetitive textures will destroy the visual appeal of any terrain engine. Nature itself is a very organic, nonrepeating thing—and our terrain engine is not. The easiest way to battle the repetitive nature of our surface textures is to introduce some random noise. Whenever we have the opportunity to add a little randomness to our terrain, we seize it whole-heartedly. This is the case with the fourth channel of our blend texture. Our simple terrain shader only needs three channels to blend the surface images, so we fill the remaining fourth channel with some random noise. Looking back at Listing 9.4, you will notice a call to the cImage function randomChannelNoise. This function adds some random values to channel 3 of the blend image (alpha). Looking back at Figure 9.1, we can see that this alpha value is used to modulate the final color generated by the shader. By setting some random values into this channel of the blend image, we can bring some nonrepeating randomness to the terrain. To exaggerate the effect, try extending the range of random values.

FRAME BUFFER COMPOSITING

Given more texture channels per pass, we could obviously make a more interesting terrain. For cards that support more than four textures per pass, we can blend more surface types and introduce more randomness to the overall presentation. As always, more is better, so we will end this chapter by introducing the concept of frame-buffer blending—something we will use extensively later in the book.

Even with the limitation of four textures per pass, we can still blend a full set of four surface types if we render in more than one pass. The additional passes will reduce overall rendering speed, but the effect is well worth the cost. For our second demo program in this chapter, we will generate a full set of four blending values and add a bit of snow to the terrain.

We will use all four channels of the blend image to control the surface texture mixing, so we will have to find another way to introduce randomness to the terrain. Luckily, if we divide into two passes, we also free an additional texture slot per pass. The first pass will blend textures one and two (grass and rock, in our case), and the second pass will add on the final two surfaces (dirt and snow). This takes three textures per pass (blend texture plus two surfaces), so we have a complete slot open for our use.

This new texture can be used for a variety of things. We could consider creating an overlay for the entire terrain. Imagine a yellow brick road winding around the hills. To do this, we would need a fairly high resolution texture that contains an alpha mask to control where it is visible on the terrain. We could also use it to render cloud shadows over the terrain. If the texture were filled with large areas of softened noise, modulating the terrain colors with this image would give the impression of cloud shadows. Animating the UV coordinates would give this effect a sense of motion.

For the time being, a yellow brick road is not of interest to us, and we will be addressing clouds later in the book. In this second demo, we will fill this texture with four individual noise patterns—one geared specifically to each surface type. This allows us to add noise to the grass, rock, dirt, and snow that fits better with each terrain type. In a paint program, we can add individual detail elements to the channels of our noise texture. For grass, we use a stippled pattern that fits with the blades of grass. For the rock surface, we use larger, pitted-looking noise patterns. Dirt and snow are given noise channels to suit them as well.

In the revised shader, we perform two passes for pixel shader 1.1 hardware. The first pass renders the grass and dirt, and the second pass handles the rock and snow. In each pass, the proper channel of blend texture and noise texture are also used to augment the final color produced. Listing 9.5 shows the revised pixel shader code. This code can also be

ON THE CD   found in the `chapter9_demo1` program on the accompanying CD-ROM, which also shows the revised `InitDeviceObjects` function used to incorporate snow into our terrain.

The shaders appear a little cryptic, which is an unfortunate side effect when using HLSL code for pixel shader 1.1 targets. Pixel shader version 1.1 only allows for eight total arithmetic instructions in each shader. Even the most straightforward HLSL code will often exceed this limit and fail to compile. However, packing instructions together into what appears to be more cryptic commands allows the HLSL compiler a little more freedom to generate better code. As odd as it sounds, it is a handy little trick that works.

For example, our intent is to multiply the blend and noise textures together, and then apply individual channels of this result to each of our surface textures. The straightforward code would read something like this:

```
//after reading 4 textures…
//combine blend and noise textures
Float4 r0 = t0*t3;
// use a dot with vRedMask to isolate the
// red channel of r0 and multiply with t2
t2= t2* dot(r0, vRedMask);
// do the same with the blue channel
// and the texture held in t1
t1= t1* dot(r0, vBlueMask);
// combine the two results with the
// diffuse color of the vertex
return (t1+ t2)* In.vDiffuse;
```

Unfortunately, the HLSL compiler will generate more than eight instructions from this code (as of DirectX 9.0), making the shader fail on older hardware. Expanding r0 where it appears in the code seems to alleviate the problem for the compiler, and allows it to generate the proper number of instructions. Hence, the more cryptic lines actually compile to less code. Expanding r0 into what it represents (t0*t3) does the trick.

```
t2= t2* dot((t0*t3), vRedMask); // dot with red mask
  t1= t1* dot((t0*t3), vBlueMask); // dot with blue mask

  return (t1+ t2)* In.vDiffuse;
```

LISTING 9.5   Adding an additional terrain surface by expanding to multiple render passes.

```
float4 TwoSurfacePass0(VS_OUTPUT11 In) : COLOR
{
  const  float4 vC0 //red mask
    =float4(1.0f,0.0f,0.0f,0.0f);
  const  float4 vC1 //blue mask
    =float4(0.0f,0.0f,1.0f,0.0f);

  float4 t0 = tex2D(LinearSamp0, In.vTex0 );
  float4 t1 = tex2D(LinearSamp1, In.vTex1 );
  float4 t2 = tex2D(LinearSamp3, In.vTex2 );
  float4 t3 = tex2D(LinearSamp5, In.vTex3 );

  t2= t2* dot((t0* t3), vC1);
  t1= t1* dot((t0* t3), vC0);

  return (t1+ t2)* In.vDiffuse;
}

float4 TwoSurfacePass1(VS_OUTPUT11 In) : COLOR
{
  const  float4 vC0 //green mask
    =float4(0.0f,1.0f,0.0f,0.0f);
  const  float4 vC1 //alpha mask
    =float4(0.0f,0.0f,0.0f,1.0f);

  float4 t0 = tex2D(LinearSamp0, In.vTex0 );
  float4 t1 = tex2D(LinearSamp2, In.vTex1 );
  float4 t2 = tex2D(LinearSamp4, In.vTex2 );
  float4 t3 = tex2D(LinearSamp5, In.vTex3 );

  t1= t1* dot((t0* t3), vC0);
  t2= t2* dot((t0* t3), vC1);

  return (t1+ t2)* In.vDiffuse;
}

technique MultiPassTerrain
{
    pass P0
    {
      CULLMODE = CW;
      ZENABLE = TRUE;
      ZWRITEENABLE = TRUE;
      ZFUNC = LESSEQUAL;
```

```
    AlphaBlendEnable = false;

    // shaders
    VertexShader
      = compile vs_1_1 VS11();
    PixelShader
      = compile ps_1_1 TwoSurfacePass0();
}

pass P1
{
  CULLMODE = CW;
  ZENABLE = TRUE;
  ZWRITEENABLE = TRUE;
  ZFUNC = LESSEQUAL;

    // add this pass with the
    // previous one
    AlphaBlendEnable = true;
    SrcBlend = one;
    DestBlend = one;
    BlendOp = add;

    // shaders
    VertexShader
      = compile vs_1_1 VS11();
    PixelShader
      = compile ps_1_1 TwoSurfacePass1();
}
}
```

III

EXTENDING THE ENGINE

At this point, we can begin an exploration of more advanced terrain rendering topics. We have a basic terrain up and running with geometry control and a procedural texturing method. Behind the scenes, we have created a robust render queue that can handle multipass rendering efficiently. The stage is set for more complex ideas to emerge.

In this final section, we integrate some new features into the engine to handle robust lighting, vegetation, and the sky. To facilitate some of these effects, we will need to revisit and extend our core render pipeline. In addition, we adhere to backward compatibility with vertex and pixel shader 1.1. In some cases, this will limit our options, but this is a necessary cost for widespread compatibility.

In Chapter 4, "Gaia Engine Overview" we eluded to the fact that our models housed a collection of cEffectFile objects, called cRenderMethod. Until this point, we have only used a single render method to display each object: the shader loaded into the default stage of each cRenderMethod. In this section, we will begin rendering the scene in multiple stages. In each stage, the proper shader within the cRenderMethod will be used to draw the objects' contribution to the render stage.

The cGameHost is the governor of the render stages. As the objects are instructed to add themselves to the render queue, they query the cGameHost to find out which stage of rendering is taking place. The objects then submit the proper cEffectFile to the render queue, or skip rendering if the cRenderMethod does not contain an entry for the current stage. As we will see later, this allows us to render a frame in multiple stages, giving each object the opportunity to employ a unique shader for each stage.

We begin in Chapter 10, "Big Sky Country," by turning our attention skyward. Although not as interesting as the terrain geometry methods, the sky and far background play a pivotal role in the appearance of our final scene. To make things more interesting, we will also explore some procedural cloud methods and the gratuitous lens flare effect that so many outdoor games choose to use.

We revisit the sky in Chapter 11, "Rendering Outdoor Scenes," as we look into a robust lighting system for our engine. We use an atmospheric lighting system to provide a more realistic lighting model for our scene. Where applicable, we add simple bump mapping and shadow buffer use to aid in lighting the scene. This is where we will begin using the multi-stage pipeline and customized shaders for each individual stage.

With the sun shining bright, it makes sense to begin populating the scene with foliage. In Chapter 12, "The 3D Gardener," we will look at some easy ways to add grass, plants, and trees to the environment. We will explore simple billboards and volumetric impostors to handle most of the work. In keeping with the procedural nature of this book, we will show how models of groundcover can be procedurally warped to nestle into the landscape.

We conclude the book by adding a simple water shader to surround our island. This involves converting our height map into an island, and then forming the mesh pieces that will form the water. This final step in our exploration of terrain rendering concludes the book, but not the usefulness of the subjects we have covered.

CHAPTER

10

BIG SKY COUNTRY

B y far, the most important thing about a terrain engine is the ground. As we saw in the previous two chapters, various methods for representing the ground geometry and visual appearance are paramount to creating a realistic display. In this chapter, we turn our attention skyward to bring a little atmosphere to our terrain engine (pun intended).

We will begin by looking at basic environment mapping techniques that allow us to surround our landscape with imagery. From there, we will look into procedurally generating some of the textures used to represent the sky and cloud volumes, and show how they can be used together to represent a convincing scene.

SKY BOX METHODS

The *sky box* is the venerable workhorse of atmospheric rendering. Used in just about every landscape engine and outdoor game, the sky box can represent a complete 360-degree view around the camera with great success. To begin our exploration into sky rendering, we will begin by implementing a simple sky box.

The sky box is simply a box placed around the camera so that the camera is at the exact center of the box. Figure 10.1 shows this relationship. By mapping textures to the inside of each face of the box, a complete scene around the camera's viewpoint can be generated. Constructing such a sky box would require a simple set of eight vertices (one for each box corner) and six textures. These six textures would represent the view from the camera to each face of the sky box. The image place on the top face of the box represents the view above the camera; the image on the bottom of the box shows the view below the camera, and so on.

To render the simple sky box, we could simply render each face of the box using the appropriate texture. When all faces have been rendered, the screen will be filled with a panoramic view of the distant scenery surrounding the camera. Of course, great care needs to be taken to ensure that the six individual texture maps are seamless in nature, and were carefully created to represent the proper view.

Cube environment mapping makes the entire process a simple, one-step rendering pass. Cube environment maps can be thought of as a pregenerated sky box in texture form. The cube map actually contains six textures, one for each side of the cube. DirectX provides support for cube maps in the form of an `IDirect3DCubeTexture9` object. This class is a variety of textures that effectively allows us to group six textures into a single object. Figure 10.1 shows how these six textures are arranged to form the sides of the cube.

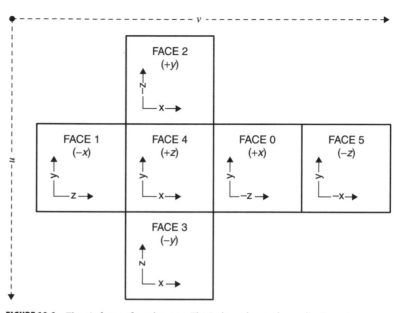

FIGURE 10.1   The six faces of a cube map. The index value and coordinate system are shown for each face.

To render with a cube environment map, we use 3D texture coordinates. Unlike regular texture mapping, the cube map coordinates represent a view vector from the center of the cube. This view vector is used by the hardware to determine which side of the cube to sample from to produce a final color value. In Figure 10.2, a sample cube is shown with a viewpoint in the center. The vector shown, being a normalized view direction, would map directly to a set of 3D texture coordinates to sample the cube map.

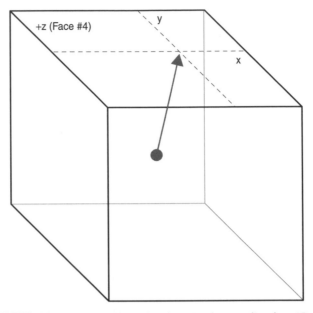

FIGURE 10.2   Viewing angles within the unit cube map directly to 3D cube map texture coordinates. Here, a vector maps to the (*x, y*) location shown on Face #4. This is the positive *z* face of the cube map.

Most commercial 3D rendering packages contain methods to generate the textures needed to construct a cube environment map. These individual textures can then be assembled into a single `dds` cube map texture file using the DirectX Texture Tool program provided with the DirectX SDK. On the CD-ROM several cube map files are provided in `source\bin\media\textures` to help you get started.

In the engine, our `cTexture` class is prepared to represent both regular and cube texture maps, making their use transparent to the remainder of the engine. A quick look at the `cTexture` interface shows a few additional methods for dealing with cube maps. The two main functions are `createCubeTexture` and `uploadCubeFace`. The first function allows us to create a cube map from scratch, and the second function provides a means to upload individual cImage objects to the six cube map faces. When loading a `dds` file, the `cTexture` class will determine if the `dds` file contains a regular or cube texture map, and perform the proper construction routine for each.

In addition to supporting cube textures, we require a class to handle the sky box itself. Gaia contains such a class, aptly named `cSkyModel`. This class handles the simple task of loading the sky box geometry (a simple unit cube) and rendering it on demand. Note that the geometry for the sky box need not be to scale. In fact, our sky box geometry is only two world units across each side. Since our rendering of the sky box is a special-case scenario, we create a separate camera matrix for "unit space." This is essentially a view matrix from the camera that is centered at the origin and comprises the view distance range of 0.01 to 2.0 world units.

The cCamera object is already equipped to generate this view matrix for unit space. This matrix is the combination of a view from the world matrix facing in the direction of the camera and a refined projection matrix. The projection matrix inherits the cameras viewing angle and aspect ratio, but restricts the near and far plane to that of our unit space. These two matrices are combined into what is called the sky box matrix within the class. This is the matrix we will use to render our sky box. Listing 10.1 shows the creation of the sky box view matrix within the cCamera class.

LISTING 10.1   Building a sky box viewing matrix within the cCamera class.

```
void cCamera::setProjParams(
    float fFOV,
    float fAspect,
    float fNearPlane,
    float fFarPlane )
{
    // remember attributes for
    // the projection matrix
    m_fFOV       = fFOV;
    m_fAspect    = fAspect;
    m_fNearPlane = fNearPlane;
    m_fFarPlane  = fFarPlane;

    // create the regular projection matrix
    D3DXMatrixPerspectiveFovLH(
        &m_matProj,
        fFOV,
        fAspect,
        fNearPlane,
        fFarPlane );

    // create a unit-space matrix
    // for sky box geometry.
    // this ensures that the
    // near and far plane enclose
    // the unit space around the camera
    D3DXMatrixPerspectiveFovLH(
        &m_matUnitProj,
```

```
                fFOV,
                fAspect,
                0.01f,
                2.0f );
    }

    void cCamera::recalcMatrices()
    {
        // sky boxes use the inverse
        // world matrix of the camera (the
        // camera view matrix) without
        // any translation information.
        m_matSkyBox = inverseWorldMatrix();
        m_matSkyBox._41 = 0.0f;
        m_matSkyBox._42 = 0.0f;
        m_matSkyBox._43 = 0.0f;

        // this is combined with the unit
        // space projection matrix to form
        // the sky box viewing matrix
        D3DXMatrixMultiply(
            &m_matSkyBox,
            &m_matSkyBox,
            &m_matUnitProj);

        // remaining camera setup code...
    }
```

The sky box itself is embodied by the simple `cSkyModel` class. This class contains the sky box geometry (a simple cube loaded from disk) and pointers to the `cEffectFile` and `cSurfaceMaterial` objects used to draw the sky box. Unlike regular scene geometry, we do not place our sky box in the render queue. Sky boxes are usually rendered at key moments in the scene drawing process, so we equip the `cSkyModel` class with on-demand rendering. In most cases, the sky box is rendered prior to any other geometry. Since the sky box always fills the display, it is often used to overwrite any depth or color information currently in the render target. By rendering the sky box first, the program can effectively skip any screen-clearing operations.

However, as the sky box grows more complex, it might actually be beneficial to render it last. Such is the case when a complex pixel shader is used to render the sky box. In these cases, doing a standard screen-clearing operation and rendering the scene geometry prior to the sky box will ensure that portions of the sky box obscured by the landscape are not

rendered. The decision of when to render the sky box requires some testing to determine the best timing.

Once the sky box is built, rendering is a very simple matter—especially since we have already built the classes that perform most of the
work (cEffectFile and cSurfaceMaterial). Refer to the main.cpp file of
the chapter10_demo0 project on the CD-ROM to see the full setup and
rendering process for the sky box. Listing 10.2 shows the simple effect file
used to render the sky box. In this shader, the sky box coordinates are
simply converted to 3D texture coordinates that are used to reference the
cube map texture. Since our cube geometry is a simple two-unit wide box
centered at the origin, we know that its vertices will map directly to 3D
texture coordinates in the –1.0 to 1.0 range.

ON THE CD

LISTING 10.2   The simple_skybox.fx effect file.

```
//
// Simple Sky Box Shader
//

// transformations
float4x4 mWorldViewProj: WORLDVIEWPROJECTION;

// the cube map
texture tex0 : TEXTURE;

struct VS_INPUT
{
  float4  Pos : POSITION;
};

struct VS_OUTPUT
{
    float4 Pos  : POSITION;
    float4 vTex0: TEXCOORD0;
};

VS_OUTPUT VS(const VS_INPUT v)
{
  VS_OUTPUT Out = (VS_OUTPUT)0;

  // transform the vert
  float4 pos = mul(v.Pos, mWorldViewProj);

  // output with z equal to w
```

```
    // to force to farthest possible
    // z value into the depth buffer
    Out.Pos = pos.xyww;

    // a slight swizzle is nessesary
    // to convert the verts to
    // 3D texture coords
    Out.vTex0 = v.Pos.yzxw;

      return Out;
}

// cube map coordinates should not wrap
sampler LinearSamp0 =
sampler_state
{
    texture = <tex0>;
    AddressU  = clamp;
    AddressV  = clamp;
    AddressW  = clamp;
    MIPFILTER = LINEAR;
    MINFILTER = LINEAR;
    MAGFILTER = LINEAR;
};

float4 CubeMap(VS_OUTPUT In) : COLOR
{
  // return the cube map texture
  return tex3D(LinearSamp0, In.vTex0 );
}

technique BasicCubeMap
{
    pass P0
    {
      // no culling
      CULLMODE = NONE;

      // do not test z,
      // just overwrite it
      ZENABLE = TRUE;
      ZWRITEENABLE = TRUE;
      ZFUNC = always;

      // also clear any stencil
```

```
        StencilEnable = true;
        StencilFunc = always;
        StencilPass = replace;
        StencilRef = 0;

        AlphaBlendEnable = false;

        // shaders
        VertexShader = compile vs_1_1 VS();
        PixelShader  = compile ps_1_1 CubeMap();
    }
}
```

THE SKY DOME

The main drawback to the sky box technique is that it is difficult to animate textures on. Being a box with images mapped on each face, it becomes problematic to try to animate something like cloud movement across the sky. This is due to the nature of the cube map we are using, and the fact that our geometry only offers eight basic vertices to texture map between. In truth, we could use any type of geometry we desire for the sky and still make use of cube map textures. What we give up is the ability to map directly between vertex and texture coordinates for cube map sampling.

As an alternative to the sky box, we will move next to the sky dome. As the name suggests, this is a dome that is placed over the camera. Our dome is not a true hemisphere, however. To better enable 2D texture animation across the sky for scrolling clouds, we will use a flattened hemisphere. Figure 10.3 shows this type of geometry. Flattening the dome means less distortion when 2D texture maps are applied. As shown in Figure 10.3, this also prevents the edges of the dome from becoming vertical. If we used a true hemisphere for our dome, scrolling clouds would appear to sink straight down at the edges of the dome rather than recede into the distance.

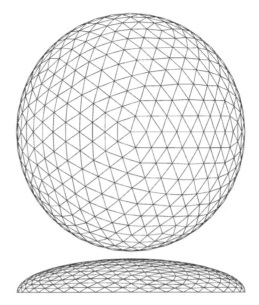

FIGURE 10.3   A top and side view of the sky dome geometry.

The only changes the dome adds to our rendering process is that we need to return to clearing the display each frame, and we must now perform an extra normalization step in the vertex shader. Clearing is needed again because there is no bottom side to our dome, and since the dome is no longer one unit away from the camera at each vertex, we must normalize the vector from the camera to each vertex to create cube map coordinates.

In the code, `cSkyModel` is equipped to load a dome model when requested. Apart from this change in geometry, there is no difference between using a box or a dome to represent the sky. As mentioned before, the vertex shader that uses the sky dome must be augmented to perform vector normalization when creating the cube map coordinates, as shown in Listing 10.3.

LISTING 10.3   The `simple_skydome.fx` vertex shader. The rest of the effect file is identical to Listing 10.2.

```
VS_OUTPUT VS(const VS_INPUT v)
{
  VS_OUTPUT Out = (VS_OUTPUT)0;

  // transform the vert
```

```
    float4 pos = mul(v.Pos, mWorldViewProj);

    // output with z equal to w
    // to force to farthest possible
    // z value into the depth buffer
    Out.Pos = pos.xyww;

    // a slight swizzle is nessesary
    // along with normaliztion
    // to convert the verts to
    // 3D texture coords
    Out.vTexO.xyz = normalize(v.Pos.yzx);
    Out.vTexO.w=1.0f;

    return Out;
}
```

ANIMATED CLOUDS

Before introducing another demo to show the sky dome in action, we will add a little more interest to the sky by creating an animated cloud layer. To animate a sky full of clouds, we will combine multiple noise maps scrolling at different rates across the sky dome. The mixture of these noise maps will continually change the shape of the clouds as they march across the sky.

In the pixel shader, we add an additional texture. This is a simple noise texture that contains grayscale noise in each color channel. We will sample this texture twice in the pixel shader, reading two separate noise values. The noise channels within the texture are divided into two frequencies. The red, green, and blue channels contain the cloud images themselves—a simple noise pattern of wispy cloud shapes. In the alpha channel, we place a different noise frequency that will be used to perturb the cloud shapes as they move. Figure 10.4 shows an example of these two texture channels.

The animation provided by the two noise layers is a simple modulation of the two. Provided that the texture mapping coordinates animate at lightly different rates, the overlapping noise textures will produce clouds that change shape as they are modulated together. Essentially, these textures can be seen as two masks being combined in the sky. Clouds appear where the white areas of the two masks overlap. As the two noise textures slide across the sky at different rates, the shapes created by the overlapping mask areas will continually evolve.

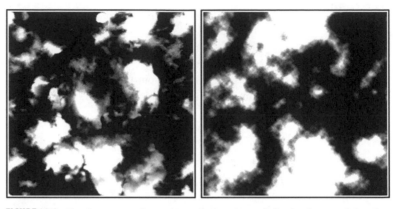

FIGURE 10.4 Two images used together to form animated clouds when modulated together.

When rendering the cloud map, we take care to mask out the clouds around our horizon map. As the clouds approach the edge of our dome, they will appear to move downward toward the horizon. Because the cloud textures are projected downward onto our dome, they would appear on the top and bottom halves of the dome if unmasked. To account for this, we add an alpha channel to our cube map of the horizon. In the sample cube map used in the demo, this alpha channel fades the clouds away as they approach the mountain imagery depicted in the horizon map. This fades the clouds out as they reach the horizon, and prevents the clouds from being drawn over the distant scenery images.

The work is done in the pixel shader, as shown in Listing 10.4. The background map (a simple mountain range cube map) and cloud layers are sampled, and then combined to form the final sky dome. To create the clouds, the two cloud layers are modulated together and masked with the background alpha channel. This result is then added to the background image to produce the final result. Figure 10.5 shows a sample image of our sky, as shown in the `chapter10_demo1.exe` program located on the accompanying CD-ROM.

ON THE CD

LISTING 10.4   The `simple_skydome.fx` pixel shader used to combine the cloud maps with the background image.

```
float4 CloudShader(VS_OUTPUT In) : COLOR
{
  // sample the cube map and clouds
  float4 background= tex3D(LinearSamp0, In.vTex0 );
  float4 cloud0= tex2D(LinearSamp1, In.vTex1 );
```

```
float4 cloud1= tex2D(LinearSamp1, In.vTex2 );

// modulate the clouds together and
// mask with the background alpha
float4 cloud_layer =
  cloud0 * cloud1.a * background.a;

// sum and return the results
return background + cloud_layer;
}
```

FIGURE 10.5   A sample image of the cloud rendering method.

LENS FLARE

When a conventional camera is pointed toward a light source, secondary reflections of light rays within the optics of a camera can create lens flare. Lens flare appears as translucent shapes and bright spots in the camera image. In real-world photography, this is often considered a nuisance. In video games, it is a feature we often exploit to emulate the appearance of outdoor photography. Even though the lens flare effect is often overused, its usefulness in bringing realism to a rendered display cannot be discounted.

In photography, lens flare is created when a bright light source shines directly into a camera lens assembly. In these cases, the light overpowers any anti-reflective coatings on the lenses and begins to bounce around the assembly. The secondary reflections caused by the light source become evident in the form of bloom and geometric shapes. However, something so chaotic can be easily modeled in 2D.

Not all lens flare behaves the same way, but we find that we can make a sweeping generalization to create a believable effect. In most cases, the position of the lenses within a camera creates lens flare as a collection of shapes oriented in a straight line. This line connects the projected position of the light source to its inverted position across the center of the lens. For our engine, this equates to drawing a line from the screen position of the light source through the center of the screen. The length of the line is equal on either side of screen center, as shown in Figure 10.6.

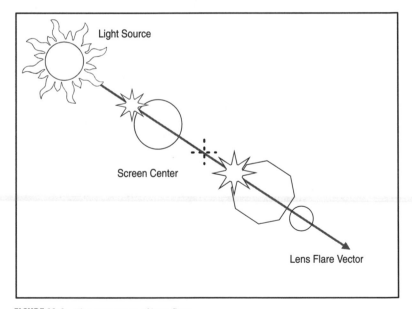

FIGURE 10.6   The 2D vector of lens flare.

What remains is to determine the size and position of the shapes that will form our lens flare effect. The first shape is the easiest. At the exact center of the light source (in screen space), the over-saturation of light rays traveling through the camera creates a bloom, or sunburst, of bright white. In photography terms, this is akin to the overexposure of film at the projected position of the light. Regardless of the light color, this bloom will often be over-saturated to the point of being white, but the bloom will taper off to the true color of the light along each of the spokes it creates.

The remaining shapes are dictated by the distances present between camera lenses, the number of aperture blades present in the camera, and any prism effects created by the edge of each lens. Film type can also play a role, controlling the color shift of the lens flare. Video cameras also have their own signature flare effects, often bleeding red and blue color bands horizontally. In short, there is a myriad of potential flare causes in each camera, and attempting to model them realistically would be a needless burden on our engine.

As it turns out, the true causes of lends flare are irrelevant to us. Rather than attempt to model the true inter-reflections of light rays through a lens assembly, we find that we can build a believable lens flare model from sheer observation. Therefore, we won't focus on the true optics of the effect, just the final outcome. We will use a preset collection of shapes to produce our lens flare effect, allowing only the position and color of the light source as parameters for the effect.

We begin by creating a series of textures containing the shapes of common lens flare items. These are translucent images that will use their alpha channels to control their opacity on screen. Because lends flare is a screen-based effect, we can simply blend these images over our scene to create the final display. The lens flare textures include sunburst stars, circles, and octagons. You can find these textures on the CD-ROM in

ON THE CD

source\bin\media\textures\lens_flare.dds (see Figure 10.7).

To arrange these shapes in various sizes, we will use a hard-coded table of relative size and position information. These table entries record the size of each shape relative to the brightness of the light source, and their position along the lens flare vector. As the vector is stretched, maintaining the relative positions of each shape will spread them apart along the vector creating realistic motion of the lens flare. Rendering is just a simple matter of placing these textures on billboard cards using the position and size information. When rendered as additive, alpha blended overlays on the screen, they will create a dramatic effect.

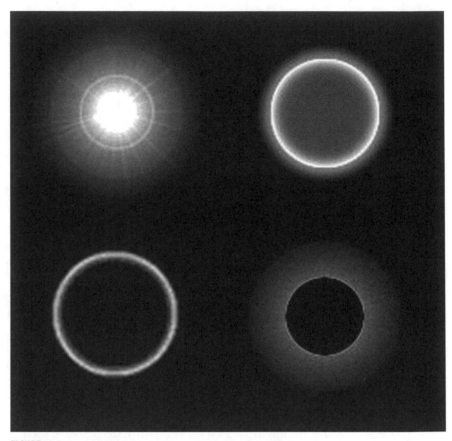

FIGURE 10.7   Sample images used to create the lens flare effect.

In the engine, we add a simple class to our lighting system to handle lens flare events based on the position of the sun. This class, `cLensFlare`, determines the screen position for the light source in screen coordinates each frame. When the center of the light source is within the screen boundaries, this class will construct and render the lens flare shapes. Like our sky box, we need to control when this will occur. Our lens flare sprites must be the last items rendered on screen, and they must be rendered in the same order to blend consistently. Therefore, the `cLensFlare` rendering calls should only be used after the scene itself has been rendered.

One glaring omission from the `cLensFlare` implementation is occlusion. When the sun goes behind a cloud or tree limb, no light rays reach the camera lens and the flare effects subside. In our engine, we do not provide a means of detecting all of the possible sun occluders. We can, however, make some basic assumptions from the angle of the sun to turn off lens flares after sunset. True occlusion would involve casting rays from the camera to the light source and testing for collisions that obscure the light. Even if these tests are performed, the procedural method we use for the cloud layer will make cloud obstruction difficult to test for.

One potential solution would be to render the scene into an off-screen buffer using a narrow camera frustum focused on the sun. For this session, the sun would be rendered as a bright white sphere, and all other objects as black silhouettes. This will result in a final image that contains a center pixel of white when the sun is visible and black when it is not. If we used this as a texture during our lens flare rendering, we could sample this center texel and modulate the visibility of the lens flare shapes by its value. When the sun is visible, this white texel will allow the flare cards to be drawn. As the texel fades to an obscured black, the lens flare cards will fade as well.

Implementation details for lends flare rendering and the `cLensFlare` class can be found on the accompanying CD-ROM. The demo application `chapter10_demo2` shows the basic lens flare technique in action.

ON THE CD

RENDERING OUTDOOR SCENES

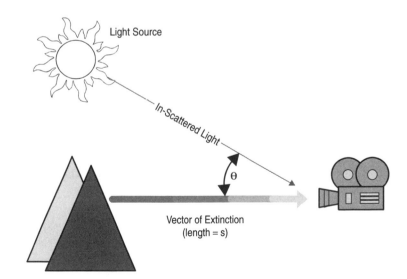

At this point in the development of our engine, we begin to use some features we have ignored until now. Back in Chapter 4, "Gaia Engine Overview," we eluded to the fact that our models contained collections of `cEffectFile` objects (our stand-in for the D3D Effect File). Even though we had the capacity to store multiple sets of HLSL shaders for each model, we have limited ourselves to just one. This has allowed us to get a basic engine up and running without concerning ourselves too much with bump mapping, lighting, and other extensions to the engine.

In this chapter, we begin to use those additional HLSL shaders to great effect. By the time we finish, we will have a better lighting model in place along with bump maps to enhance our objects and complete the scene. Each of these additions will take place in its own stage of the render process, isolated from the other stages. This allows us to focus on the application of each stage one at a time, using customized shaders within each object's `cRenderMethod` as needed.

A Multistage Approach

The multi-stage approach to rendering is simply a way to reduce the overall workload by dividing it into discreet steps. For example, in this chapter we will add lighting, shadows, and bump mapping to the engine. Each of these will exist as a unique render stage so we can render each individually. In the first stage, we render all the object bump maps; in the second stage, we add shadows; and in the third stage, we layer on the final lighting model. The reasons why we render in this order will become more apparent as we progress through the chapter.

Using multiple stages helps us add features we normally could not provide on all video cards. Older video cards that have limited multitexturing capability are simply ill equipped to try to composite textures, apply bump maps, and display the effects of atmospheric light in a single session. To enable these features, a multi-stage approach is necessary. The results of each stage are then combined to create the final image.

We have two basic options to perform this final composition of the render stages. We could render the results of each stage to an individual render target, and then use a final stage to source each image as a texture. This stage would be responsible for combining the images to produce the final on-screen image. The downside of this method is that each stage requires a unique render target, which must also be in a format compatible for use as a texture in the final stage. To maintain a decent pixel-to-screen ratio, we would also have to enforce that these render targets be of similar size (or larger) than the final display. For high-resolution full-screen display modes, this can consume a large amount of video memory.

The second option is to layer each stage directly into the frame buffer. In this manner, we use alpha blending operations to continually composite the output of each stage into the final image. Alpha blending the layers as they are rendered restricts the type of effects that can be performed using this technique, but it is a much simpler technique to employ and requires no additional video memory for render targets. This is the approach we will use within this section of the book. While not as flexible as compositing individually rendered images, it can still be used to provide a high-quality image using the effects we have planned.

As we discuss each of the stages we will be creating in this chapter, we will show how they can be layered into the frame buffer using alpha blending. For readers who want to try the multi-target approach, this information will still be useful in building your final compositing render stage. For the book, we tend to lean toward the solution that will fit more video cards. If you know that your particular video card is capable of more, we certainly encourage you to experiment with the multi-target approach.

As usual, we use the cGameHost object as our central information provider. To govern the render stages, the cGameHost object maintains the index of the current stage being rendered. To begin a new stage, we need only to inform the cGameHost of the new stage and render the objects within view of the camera. As these objects submit themselves to the render queue, they will query the current render stage from the cGameHost and submit the proper shaders in their render queue entry. In fact, the objects have been performing this task all along; the cGameHost has simply been reporting that they should use their default shaders.

To understand the multi-stage approach, we will examine each stage in the order in which they are applied. We will begin with a simple ambient color stage, and then add bump mapping. In the final stage, we will discuss a robust outdoor lighting model that uses an approximation of light passing through the earth's atmosphere for greater realism. This brings us to a total of the stages for our demonstration: ambient, bump map, and lighting. The results of each stage are layered into the frame buffer to produce the final result.

AMBIENT LIGHT

The first stage is by far the simplest. In this stage, we modulate the texture maps covering an object with a simple ambient color value. This color value represents the amount of ambient light in our scene. It fills the frame buffer with a set of base values for each pixel in the scene. Later, when we render the illumination of each model, we will add the lighting results to these base colors.

We also take advantage of the simplicity of this stage to set up the depth buffer. The ambient pass will execute quickly, making it a perfect candidate for writing depth values into the *z* buffer. Future stages, which are more complex in nature, can be set up to use the z>$> buffer values written in this initial stage. No further writing to the *z* buffer will be necessary. This helps increase the efficiency of the later stages.

Listing 11.1 shows a sample effect file used to render the ambient light contribution for our terrain. In this shader, the texture maps are combined using the blend method we defined earlier. The final color is multiplied against a constant ambient hue to produce the final base color.

LISTING 11.1   A sample HLSL shader used to write values to the *z* buffer and set up the base color for each pixel using simple ambient lighting.

```
//
// Simple Terrain Shader
// Using Ambient Light
//

// transformations
float4x4 mViewProj: VIEWPROJECTION;

// terrain section offsets
float4 posOffset : posScaleOffset =
 {1.0, 1.0, 0.0f, 0.0f};
float4 texOffset : uvScaleOffset =
 {1.0, 1.0, 0.0f, 0.0f};

// texture maps used
texture tex0 : TEXTURE; // blend
texture tex1 : TEXTURE; // surface 0
texture tex2 : TEXTURE; // surface 1
texture tex3 : TEXTURE; // surface 2

// the ambient light color
float4 ambient_light =
 {0.3f,0.3f,0.6f,0.0f};

struct VS_INPUT
{
```

```
    float2  Pos    : POSITION0;
    float2  UV     : TEXCOORD0;
    float  ZPos    : POSITION1;
};

struct VS_OUTPUT
{
    float4 Pos   : POSITION;
    float2 vTex0  : TEXCOORD0;
    float2 vTex1  : TEXCOORD1;
    float2 vTex2  : TEXCOORD2;
    float2 vTex3  : TEXCOORD3;
};

VS_OUTPUT VS(const VS_INPUT v)
{
  VS_OUTPUT Out = (VS_OUTPUT)0;

  float4 combinedPos = float4(
    v.Pos.x,
    v.Pos.y,
    v.ZPos,
    1);

  combinedPos.xy += posOffset.zw;

  Out.Pos = mul(combinedPos, mViewProj);

  Out.vTex0 =
    (v.UV+texOffset.zw)*texOffset.xy;
  Out.vTex1 = v.UV;
  Out.vTex2 = v.UV;
  Out.vTex3 = v.UV;

    return Out;
}

sampler LinearSamp0 = sampler_state
{
    texture = <tex0>;
    AddressU  = clamp;
    AddressV  = clamp;
    AddressW  = clamp;
    MIPFILTER = LINEAR;
    MINFILTER = LINEAR;
```

```
            MAGFILTER = LINEAR;
    };

    sampler LinearSamp1 = sampler_state
    {
        texture = <tex1>;
        AddressU  = wrap;
        AddressV  = wrap;
        AddressW  = wrap;
        MIPFILTER = LINEAR;
        MINFILTER = LINEAR;
        MAGFILTER = LINEAR;
    };

    sampler LinearSamp2 = sampler_state
    {
        texture = <tex2>;
        AddressU  = wrap;
        AddressV  = wrap;
        AddressW  = wrap;
        MIPFILTER = LINEAR;
        MINFILTER = LINEAR;
        MAGFILTER = LINEAR;
    };

    sampler LinearSamp3 = sampler_state
    {
        texture = <tex3>;
        AddressU  = wrap;
        AddressV  = wrap;
        AddressW  = wrap;
        MIPFILTER = LINEAR;
        MINFILTER = LINEAR;
        MAGFILTER = LINEAR;
    };

    float4 PS(VS_OUTPUT In) : COLOR
    {
      // sample all four textures
      float4 BlendControler = tex2D(LinearSamp0, In.vTex0 );
      float4 texColor0 = tex2D(LinearSamp1, In.vTex1 );
      float4 texColor1 = tex2D(LinearSamp2, In.vTex2 );
      float4 texColor2 = tex2D(LinearSamp3, In.vTex3 );

      // determine the amount of each surface to blend
```

```
    float4 Color0 = (texColor0 * BlendControler.r);
    float4 Color1 = (texColor1 * BlendControler.g);
    float4 Color2 = (texColor2 * BlendControler.b);

    // sum the resulting colors
    // and multiply by the ambient
    // light color
    return (Color0 + Color1 + Color2)
      *BlendControler.a * ambient_light;
}


//
// This technique outputs ambient color
// while filling the z buffer with
// depth values
//
technique AmbientTerrainShader
{
    pass P0
    {
      CULLMODE = CW;
      ZENABLE = TRUE;
      ZWRITEENABLE = TRUE;
      ZFUNC = LESSEQUAL;

      AlphaBlendEnable = false;
      AlphaTestEnable = false;

      // shaders
      VertexShader = compile vs_1_1 VS();
      PixelShader  = compile ps_1_1 PS();
    }
}
```

BUMP MAPPING

Up until this point, we have not used bump maps. Provided that the video card supports the additional texture slots, per-pixel bump mapping could be applied to the scene in the standard fashion during our regular rendering pass. When we find ourselves limited by an older video card, we must find a way to incorporate bump maps as a separate render stage. To do so, we will forgo true per-pixel bump mapping and use an alpha blending technique to apply the bump maps to the scene as our second render stage.

True bump mapping involves the use of a texture map that contains surface normals. These normals are written into the texture so that their x, y, and z component values are quantified as red, blue, and green color values. Bump mapping is performed in the pixel shader by first converting the light vector to texture space in a vertex shader, and then performing a dot product of this vector with the surface normal stored in the bump map texture. The result is a per-pixel scalar value used to modulate the amount of light arriving at each pixel.

Given that the output of a bump map pass is a scalar value used to control the amount of light on a given pixel, we can simply render these bumps out as grayscale lighting modifiers. In this sense, the dark side of a bump created by the normal map texture creates a mini-shadow in our destination alpha channel. When the final lighting stage is applied, the scalar values in the alpha channel will control how much light is blended into the final scene

To visualize this, imagine that we rendered our model using traditional per-pixel bump mapping and a chalky-white diffuse texture. This would produce a rendered image of a gray scale model that is bright white in the areas that receive light and darker gray in the areas that do not. The bump maps would all be apparent in the image, creating highlights and recesses as shades of gray. This is the exact data that we add to the destination alpha channel.

In the final stage, lighting values are calculated for the model without regard to the surface normals. In a sense, we prepare the lighting as if the model was illuminated on all sides. As the illuminated colors are written to the frame buffer, they are modulated with the alpha values we have already placed there from our rendering of the bump maps. This cancels out the contribution of the light on darker areas of the model, producing the final bump-mapped result. The result is not true per-pixel dot product bump mapping, but it does provide a decent approximation.

Setting up the bump map stage requires some intervention in the source code. The bump map stage only outputs values to the destination alpha channel. This imposes two restrictions. First, the destination buffer must contain an alpha channel. Second, we must ensure that the bump mapping stage only outputs values into this alpha channel, leaving the red, green, and blue color channels of the destination buffer intact.

The first restriction is easy to satisfy. As display modes are enumerated at program startup, each is passed through a virtual function for verification by the application. In programs that rely on destination alpha, we simply reject all display modes that do not contain at least 8 bits of alpha channel. Performing the test is handled by overloading the virtual function `ConfirmDevice` provided by the DirectX Application Framework class `CD3DApplication`. Our own `cGameHost` class is derived from this framework base class, so we can simply overload the `ConfirmDevice` function of our `cGameHost` object. Listing 11.2 shows an example function that will approve only those display modes that are compatible with the bump map method.

LISTING 11.2   Rejecting display modes that are not compatible with the alpha-channel bump map method.

```
HRESULT cGameHost::ConfirmDevice(
    D3DCAPS9* pCaps,
    DWORD behavior,
    D3DFORMAT display,
    D3DFORMAT backbuffer)
{
    // we require an alpha channel in the backbuffer
  if (backbuffer != D3DFMT_A8R8G8B8)
  {
   return E_FAIL;
  }

  // allow the base class to continue
  // verification of the device
  return cGameHost::ConfirmDevice(
    pCaps,
    behavior,
    display,
    backbuffer );
}
```

The second restriction is also handled by the `cGameHost` class. Recall that the `cGameHost` is notified of the beginning and ending of each render stage. This gives us an opportunity to set any render states or execute any custom code on which the stages rely. In the case of bump mapping, we need to notify DirectX not to render any output to the red, green, or blue color channels of the destination. Our sole output will be the alpha channel value that we will later use to attenuate our lighting contribution to the scene.

In the `cGameHost` class, a simple render state change is added to the render stage notification functions to limit the pixel shader color output to the alpha channel. Listing 11.3 shows the two functions within the `cGameHost` class that perform these state changes.

LISTING 11.3   Limiting output to the alpha channel during bump map rendering.

```
void cGameHost::beginRenderStage(uint8 stage)
{
  debug_assert(
    stage < cEffectFile::k_max_render_stages,
    "invalid render stage");

  m_activeRenderStage = stage;

  if (m_activeRenderStage ==
    cEffectFile::k_bumpMapStage)
  {
    // during the bump map stage,
    // we write only to the alpha
    // channel of the destination
    d3dDevice()->SetRenderState(
      D3DRS_COLORWRITEENABLE,
      D3DCOLORWRITEENABLE_ALPHA);
  }
}

void cGameHost::endRenderStage()
{
  if (m_activeRenderStage ==
    cEffectFile::k_bumpMapStage)
  {
    // re-enable rendering to all
    // color channels
    d3dDevice()->SetRenderState(
      D3DRS_COLORWRITEENABLE,
        D3DCOLORWRITEENABLE_ALPHA|
        D3DCOLORWRITEENABLE_BLUE |
        D3DCOLORWRITEENABLE_GREEN|
        D3DCOLORWRITEENABLE_RED);
  }

  m_activeRenderStage = 0;
}
```

One last subject to address is bump mapping our procedural terrain. Recall from Chapter 9, "Texturing Techniques," that we blend multiple texture maps to create our final terrain. Each of these texture maps represents a different ground surface such as grass, rock, dirt, and so forth. It would stand to reason that we would prefer to have a separate bump map for each of these surface types as well, using the same blending scheme to combine the bump maps across the terrain.

This creates a bit of a problem on older video cards. Remember that bump mapping requires the use of normal maps. Normal maps, by definition, contain surface normals encoded as color information. If we combine these color channels using texture-blending operations, the result is not guaranteed to remain a surface normal. This will produce visible artifacts in the resulting bump map. What is required is the renormalization of these combined surface normals, something older video cards (those using pixel shader version 1.x) are incapable of.

The only recourse for these older video cards is to convert the blend texture to a mask image. Rather than smoothly blending between normal maps, we will create a mask that only allows one of the blended maps to contribute to each pixel. This allows us to mix the bump maps of various surface types without the need to renormalize the result. To convert the blend texture, we simply examine the blend factors stored in each color channel. The largest value found is set to 1, and all other channels are cleared to 0. This effectively converts the blending texture into a hard-edged mask suitable for combining surface normals.

The conversion function `convertToBumpMask` is added to the `cImage` class. This is the same class we used to construct the original blend texture for our terrain. Listing 11.4 outlines the process of examining each color channel of the blend texture and finding the highest value. This becomes the mask channel that will allow only one surface normal to appear on screen for each pixel rendered.

LISTING 11.4   Converting terrain texture blending data to hard-edges mask information.

```
void cImage::convertToBumpMask()
{
  int pitch;
  uint8* pBits = lock(0, &pitch);

  if (pBits)
  {
    uint8* pOut = pBits;
    for (uint16 y=0;y<m_height;++y)
    {
      for (uint16 x=0;x<m_width;++x)
      {
        uint32 color;
        getColor(x, y, color);
```

```
        uint8 r = color&0xff;
        uint8 g = (color>8)&0xff;
        uint8 b = (color>16)&0xff;
        uint8 a = (color>24)&0xff;

        // there can be only one!
        if (r>=g && r>=b && r>=a)
        {
          r=0xff; g=0; b=0; a=0;
        }
        else if (g>=r && g>=b && g>=a)
        {
          g=0xff; r=0; b=0; a=0;
        }
        else if (b>=r && b>=g && b>=a)
        {
          b=0xff; r=0; g=0; a=0;
        }
        else
        {
          a=0xff; r=0; g=0; b=0;
        }
        color = (a<<24)+(b<<16)+(g<<8)+r;
        setColor(x, y, color);
      }

      pBits += pitch;
    }
  }
  unlock();
}
```

Listing 11.5 shows the effect file used to combine the normal maps using the newly made mask texture. Note that to convert the incoming light vector into texture space for bump mapping, a binormal and tangent vector must be computed. Our terrain vertex data does not contain this information, so we perform a set of cross-product operations using the surface normal to approximate the binormal and tangent vectors. These vectors are used to transform the light vector to texture space for the per-pixel dot product operation.

LISTING 11.5   Two sample HLSL pixel shader functions used to composite terrain bump maps. One renormalizes blended surface normals, and the other relies on the blend mask to prevent surface normals from being combined.

```
// Pixel Shader 1_x is incapable of
// normalizing a vector. We are
// relying on the fact that the mask
// texture has been setup to allow only
// one of the bump map textures to appear
// on screen - preventing the need to
// renormalize the surface normals
float4 PS_1x(VS_OUTPUT In) : COLOR
{
  // sample all four textures
  float4 mask = tex2D(LinearSamp0, In.vTex0 );
  float4 texColor0 = tex2D(LinearSamp1, In.vTex1 );
  float4 texColor1 = tex2D(LinearSamp2, In.vTex2 );
  float4 texColor2 = tex2D(LinearSamp3, In.vTex3 );

  // determine the amount of each surface to blend
  float4 Color0 = (texColor0 * mask.r);
  float4 Color1 = (texColor1 * mask.g);
  float4 Color2 = (texColor2 * mask.b);

  float4 normal = Color0+Color1+Color2;

  // compute the per-pixel dot product
  // and output the result
  return saturate(dot(
    (In.vLightVec-0.5f)*2.0f,
    (normal-0.5f)*2.0f));
}

// Pixel Shader 2_x is icapable of
// normalizing a vector. We can use
// a regular blend texture here and
// normalize the result prior to
// performing the dot product
float4 PS_2x(VS_OUTPUT In) : COLOR
{
  // sample all four textures
  float4 mask = tex2D(LinearSamp0, In.vTex0 );
  float4 texColor0 = tex2D(LinearSamp1, In.vTex1 );
  float4 texColor1 = tex2D(LinearSamp2, In.vTex2 );
  float4 texColor2 = tex2D(LinearSamp3, In.vTex3 );
```

```
// determine the amount of each surface to blend
float4 Color0 = (texColor0 * mask.r);
float4 Color1 = (texColor1 * mask.g);
float4 Color2 = (texColor2 * mask.b);

float4 normal = normalize(Color0+Color1+Color2);

// compute the per-pixel dot product
// and output the result
return saturate(dot(
  (In.vLightVec-0.5f)*2.0f,
  (normal-0.5f)*2.0f));
}
```

APPROXIMATING OUTDOOR LIGHT

The effect of atmosphere on light, sometimes called *aerial perspective*, can be summed up into two phenomena. First, light traveling through our atmosphere loses much of its color saturation as distances increase. It also shifts color slightly, as the atmosphere absorbs or scatters a proportional amount of the color spectrum as light passes through it. The absorption and scattering mainly removes colors in the blue spectrum—nearly 10 times more than red or green. Another way to think of this is that as light passes through our atmosphere, it sheds much of its blue color and scatters it in all directions.

The second phenomenon is that this scattered light becomes a type of light source of its own. Light rays scattered by the atmosphere provide additional color in the angles in which they are scattered. This is known as the *in-scattering* of light. Again, since mainly the blue component of the light was scattered, the in-scattered light source tends to maintain a blue tint. This is not always true, but it is a generality that we can use in crafting our lighting system.

We can witness these occurrences with a quick trip outside. The sky, which is a mixture of semitransparent gasses beneath a black void, appears blue to us as the sun shines through it. As light rays from the sun pass through the atmosphere, they shed their blue color and scatter it. Some of this scattered light reaches our eye, making the atmosphere above our heads appear blue. The light rays that reach the ground have shed their blue color in proportion to the distance traveled through the atmosphere. This is more apparent as the sun approaches the horizon, and must cast light tangentially through more of the atmosphere. This shedding of blue light makes the color of the light rays shift to red as it nears the horizon—giving us a deep red glow at sunrise and sunset.

Ample academic research has been done on the correct modeling of light through our atmosphere and through airborne particles in general. Most notable among this work is the research provided by A. J. Preetham and Nathaniel Hoffman [Preetham and Hoffman]. In their research, Preetham and Hoffman provide an accurate model for depicting the effects of daylight on outdoor scenery. Their respective papers (see References or Appendix D, "Recommended Reading") provide detailed analysis of the effects of aerial perspective and how it can be applied to outdoor scenery. Rather than rehash their work here, we suggest their reading material for more information.

What we will cover is the application of the method they provide. In doing so, we will use some constant values for our color shifting and light scattering formulas that are derived from the work presented by Preetham and Hoffman. We do not provide the details in how these constants are derived, since this would require a more detailed explanation of light passing through particulate matter and aerosols. Instead, we will take the constants calculated by Preetham and Hoffman at face value and look at how they can be used within our scene.

First, we will take a shortcut and emulate the effects of atmosphere on the color of sunlight itself. While the color of sun at various times of day can be calculated with great accuracy [Preetham] for any date or time of day, we find that for most applications, this is not truly necessary. In our engine, the sun will travel the same arc each day, and we do not take seasonal changes into account. Therefore, the color change in sunlight can be easily precomputed and interpolated over the course of the day. We make an additional simplification by declaring that the sun will travel directly overhead, reaching the highest position (zenith) at noon. At this point, the sun will be as bright as possible with a slight yellow tint. This is to emulate the vertical sunlight rays passing through the least amount of atmosphere during the noon hour. At the horizon line, we will ramp the color of sunlight toward red for both sunrise and sunset. This emulates the rays of the sun passing through a greater amount of the atmosphere as they reach a horizontal angle.

To manage our outdoor lighting data, we provide a new class called `cLightManager`. This class is responsible for managing all scene lighting conditions, and is globally available as a member of the `cGameHost` singleton. A preprocessor definition is also provided to allow objects to access the light manager using a simple macro named `LightManager` that accesses the singleton. For the time being, out light manager will be responsible for our sole light, the sun. Should we ever need to add additional lights to the environment, the `cLightManager` class would prove to be a convenient host for that data as well.

Within the `cLightManager`, we track the passage of time in radian units. For every 2pi unit of time, the sun will make a full pass around our world. We standardize on the sun revolving around the world *x*-axis (the positive *z*-axis is the vertical axis in our sample scene), so computing a directional vector for the sun is a matter of computing the sine and cosine of the time value, and using those numbers as the *x* and *z* values of the directional vector to the sun. The `cLightManager` class handles this as part of its update function.

Once a vector to the sun is calculated, the *z* component (vertical height of the sun) can be used to shift between our noon and horizon sunlight colors. These colors are held as constant values within the `cLightManager` class. At the creation of the class, we compute the noon and horizon sunlight colors using the formula provided by Preetham [Preetham], and then store these two values for interpolation. For greater accuracy, we could compute these values each frame as the sun moves, but our interpolation provides a much faster approximation. The `cLightManager` class contains the member function `computeSunlightColor` that is used to generate the two interpolated sunlight hues during construction of the class. This function could also be used on a per-frame basis if a more precise sunlight color is desired.

With the color of sunlight determined by the CPU, the remaining task is to build a structure of information that the vertex shader can use to render with this light under a set of atmospheric conditions. As stated earlier, light passing through the atmosphere undergoes two processes. As light from a rendered vertex passes through the atmosphere, it undergoes a change in hue. This represents the loss of color over distance, known as *extinction*. In addition to extinction, a certain amount of the sunlight being scattered within the atmosphere reaches our eye. This adds color to the point being rendered and is known as *in-scattering*. Figure 11.1 shows a visual representation of each. Note that extinction is a function of distance, and in-scattering is mainly controlled by the angle between the view direction and the sun.

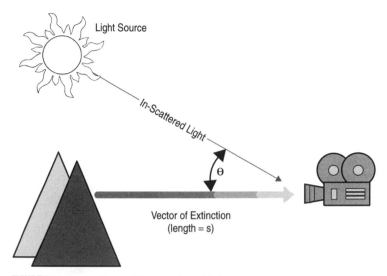

FIGURE 11.1   Extinction and In-scattering of light.

Extinction is a way of representing the light that is lost by particulate matter in the air absorbing or scattering light on its way to the viewer. We represent the overall extinction using Equation 11.1. In this formula, s is the distance between the viewer and the point in question. β_r and β_m are two coefficient values that describe the amount of light scattering present in the atmosphere. These coefficients represent two models of representing the scattering of light known as Rayleigh scattering and Mie scattering. A thorough explanation of both can be found in [Preetham and Hoffman]. For our use of these terms, we need only understand that Rayleigh scattering represents the scattering effect of miniscule particles, while Mie models the effects of larger, spherical particles. The combination of both systems culminates in our final scattering formula.

$$F_{ex}(s) = e^{-\left(\beta r + \beta m\right)s}$$

(11.1)

Stated more succinctly, Formula 11.1 shows that extinction (F_{ex}) is a function of distance (s). Note that distance is a real-world value, typically 0–5000 meters or so, not a view-space or projected distance value. Extinction is calculated by adding the coefficients for Rayleigh and Mie scattering ($\beta_r+\beta_m$), multiplying by distance, and then computing the negative exponential of that product. In the code, we use preset constant values for Rayleigh and Mie coefficients, but allow them to be scaled to produce different atmospheric effects. Some experimentation is necessary to see the effects of Rayleigh and Mie scattering on sunlight, but these are easier to understand in the context of in-scattering.

In-scattering is the measurement of sunlight that is reflected by particles in the air toward the viewer. In a sense, this is a measurement of the
color provided by the particles themselves. The formula to determine the
amount of in-scattering present at a given location is a function of both
the distance to the viewer and the angle between the sunlight arriving at
the point and the view direction. This is a fairly involved computation, as
shown in Equation 11.2.

$$L_{in}(s,\theta) = E\left(1 - F_{ex}(s)\right)\frac{\beta_r(\theta) + \beta_m(\theta)}{\beta_r + \beta_m} \tag{11.2}$$

This nasty-looking formula shows in-scattered light (L_{in}) to be a function of both distance and angle to the sun. E represents the color of the
sun, which is multiplied against 1 minus the extinction value defined by
Equation 11.1. The Rayleigh and Mie coefficients are to create a ratio that
further attenuates the light of the sun—modeling the actual light color
reflected by particles at the given location. The denominator of this ratio
is a sum of the two coefficients, but the numerator requires some additional processing, as shown in Equations 11.3 and 11.4.

$$\beta_r(\theta) = \frac{3}{16\pi}\beta_r(1 + \cos^2\theta) \tag{11.3}$$

$$\beta_m(\theta) = \frac{1}{4\pi}\beta_m\left(\frac{(1-g)^2}{(1+g^2-2g\cos(\theta))^{3/2}}\right) \tag{11.4}$$

Lighting formulas don't get much scarier than this. Equations 11.3
and 11.4 compute the angular coefficients for Rayleigh and Mie given an
angle between the viewing direction and the path of sunlight. These formulas approximate the light that particles bounce in various directions,
and attempt to deduce the amount of this light collected at a specific
viewing angle. For the Mie coefficient, a scalar value (g) is used to control
the effect of theta over the final coefficient. Higher values for g (between
0 and 1) have the effect of reducing the angular range of light emitted
from the particles. In the case of the sun, this can have the visual effect of
reducing the amount of particulate glow around the sun. Again, the papers by Preetham and Hoffman are a good source for understanding how
these formulas are derived. For our purposes, we will continue to look
mainly at their implementation.

As suggested by [Hoffman], a pixel shader can do the job of calculating the effects of both extinction and in-scattering by modulating the
scene color with the extinction value and adding any in-scattered light.
The formula for this is shown in Equation 11.5. Simply stated, the final
output color is based on distance and angle to the sun. The original color

(L_o) is multiplied by the result of the extinction function. The in-scattered light is then added to this product to produce the final color.

$$L(s,\theta) = L_o F_{ex}(s) + L_{in}(s,\theta) \qquad (11.5)$$

The difficulty comes in generating extinction and in-scattering values to provide to the pixel shader. A fairly sizable vertex shader is required to calculate the extinction and in-scattering values per vertex for the pixel shader to use. A listing for this vertex shader, derived from the shader originally presented by Hoffman and Preetham, is shown in Listing 11.6. We place this function within a header file so it can be used by multiple HLSL shaders.

LISTING 11.6   A light scattering vertex shader that calculates extinction and in-scattering as diffuse and specular colors.

```
//
// This shader assumes a world-space vertex is
// provided, and distance values represent
// real-world distances. A set of pre-
// calculated atmospheric data is provided
// in the atm structure. See the source code
// on the CD-ROM to view the calculations
// used to setup these constants
//

// calculate eye vector and world
// distance using a world vertex
// and camera position.
float3 eyeVector = vCameraPos - worldPos;
float s = dot(eyeVector, eyeVector);
s = 1.0f/sqrt(s);
eyeVector.rgb *= s;
s = 1.0f/s;

// compute cosine of theta angle
float cosTheta = dot(eyeVector.rgb, sun_vec.rgb);

// compute extinction term E
// -(beta_1+beta_2) * s * log_2 e
float4 E = -atm.vSumBeta1Beta2 *
  s * atm.vConstants.y;
E.x = exp(E.x);
E.y = exp(E.y);
E.z = exp(E.z);
```

```
E.w = 0.0f;

// Compute theta terms used by in-scattering.
// compute phase2 theta as
// (1-g^2)/(1+g-2g*cos(theta))^(3/2)
// notes:
// theta is 180 - actual theta
//(this corrects for sign)
// atm.vHG = [1-g^2, 1+g, 2g]
float p1Theta = (cosTheta*cosTheta)
  +atm.vConstants.x;
float p2Theta = (atm.vHG.z*cosTheta)
  +atm.vHG.y;
p2Theta = 1.0f/(sqrt(p2Theta));
p2Theta = (p2Theta*p2Theta*p2Theta)
    *atm.vHG.x;

// compute in-scattering (I) as
// (vBetaD1*p1Theta + vBetaD1*p2Theta) *
// (1-E) * atm.vRcpSumBeta1Beta2
//
// atm.vRcpSumBeta1Beta2 =
// 1.0f/ (Rayleigh+Mie)
float4 I = ((atm.vBetaD1*p1Theta)+
          (atm.vBetaD2*p2Theta))
          *(atm.vConstants.x-E)
          *atm.vRcpSumBeta1Beta2;

// scale in-scatter and extinction
// for effect (optional)
I = I*atm.vTermMultipliers.x;
E = E*atm.vTermMultipliers.y;

// reduce in-scattering on unlit surfaces
// by modulating with a monochrome
// Lambertian scalar. This is slightly
// offset to allow some in-scattering to
// bleed into unlit areas
float NdL = dot(v.Norm, sun_vec);
I = I*saturate(NdL + 0.33f);

// apply sunlight color
// and strength to each term
// and output
Out.vI.xyz = I*sun_color*sun_color.w;
```

```
Out.vI.w = NdL*NdL;

Out.vE.xyz = E*sun_color*sun_color.w;
Out.vE.w = NdL;
```

As noted in the shader, a structure of precalculated values exists containing all the atmospheric data. On the application side, we define a class to construct this data using runtime values. This allows the ratio of Rayleigh to Mie particle coefficients to be adjusted, as well as scaling the final values for light extinction and in-scattering. The `cLightScattering Data` object serves this need within the code, and is a member of our `cLightManager` object. This class assembles all the atmospheric coefficients, and performs as much precalculation on this data as possible. The entire set of atmospheric data is then uploaded en mass as a structure to the effect file being used.

We allow for runtime tuning of the atmospheric conditions to allow for experimentation. Increasing the coefficients is akin to adding more of the particles they represent to the atmosphere, which can have considerable visual impact. For example, the Raleigh coefficient represents miniscule particles and transparent gasses. We can think of these as water droplets. Adding more tends to scatter more blue light into the sky and increase the overall glow of the sun. The Mie coefficient represents much larger particles. One example of this is pollution. As the Mie coefficient is increased, in-scattered light created from these large particles tends to create a gray, murky haze in the air—much like smog or an overcast sky. The demo program `chapter11_demo0`, located on the accompanying CD-ROM, allows for experimentation with these values.

ON THE CD

The downside of light scattering is that our implementation relies on fine tessellation of the sky model to create a smoothly interpolated result. If we knew the exact values we wanted to use for light scattering, we could remove our vertex shader dependence and precalculate extinction and in-scatter tables as textures. For extinction, we could define a one-dimensional texture that contains the extinction values for a given distance range. In-scattering could be represented by a standard 2D texture, with one axis representing the distance range and the other the angle to the sun.

BRINGING IT ALL TOGETHER

To see the effects provided by all three of the stages added in this chapter, view the demonstration program `chapter11_demo0` on the accompanying

CD-ROM. This demonstration incorporates all three of our new render stages to produce a final result. In the source code, the scene is rendered three times. Each time, a new render stage value is given to the `cGameHost` object. This causes all objects rendered to submit the proper shaders into the render queue. Each shader is equipped with the proper alpha blending information needed to combine its output into the frame buffer.

REFERENCES

[Preetham] Preetham, A. J., P. Shirley, and B. Smits. "A Practical Analytic Model For Daylight." Siggraph proceedings 1999, (available online at *www.cs.utah.edu/vissim/papers/sunsky*).

[Hoffman] Hoffman, N., and A. J. Preetham. "Rendering Outdoor Light Scattering in Real Time," (available online at *www.ati.com/developer/dx9/ATI-LightScattering.pdf*).

THE 3D GARDENER

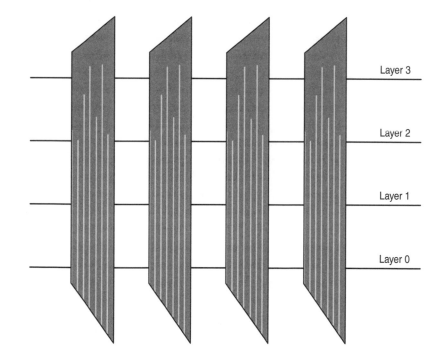

Layer 3

Layer 2

Layer 1

Layer 0

B ringing our multi-stage render pipeline into the engine sets the stage for us to begin populating the world with objects. In this chapter, we look at some easy ways to bring groundcover, plants, and trees into the environment. We do this to bring additional realism to our scene. We do not delve too deeply into managing the geometry of objects, such as dynamic level-of-detail (LOD) generation. Instead, we will instill our geometry class, cModelResource, with the ability to hold discrete versions of the model at different levels of detail.

We do this because our models will be shared throughout the map. Even though we might load one model of an oak tree, we will use it in various places on the map. Our cSceneModel objects contain the per-instance data for each tree, and refer to a common cModelResource where the actual geometry is stored. Because multiple cSceneNodes will be referencing the same model, using a dynamic LOD representation for the model geometry becomes difficult.

Although fast, dynamic LOD methods such as the one used by the D3DX progressive mesh object (ID3DXPMesh) are not normally considered applicable to this situation. Each time the detail level of these dynamic meshes is changed, the internal geometry is recomputed. This is a one-time cost per change in LOD that is fast enough for occasional use. In our scenario, we will have many cSceneModel objects trying to use a common mesh object at different levels of detail. Using progressive meshes such as ID3DXPMesh to store this geometry would cause us to update the detail level of the source mesh for each tree rendered. This could amount to hundreds of progressive mesh updates per frame, becoming very inefficient.

Luckily, we have already alleviated this concern with our use of the render queue. As models are added to the queue for rendering, they also place their desired LOD as a 4-bit number. This allows us to specify 16 levels of detail for each object. As the render queue sorts the entries by render method and model indices, it will also sort similar LOD values together for each model. Since these LOD values are simply a part of the overall sorting value being used, this functionality comes for free as part of the sort we are already performing. As the sorted queue entries are rendered, we can rest assured that instances of each model that use the same LOD version will be grouped together, allowing us to reduce the number of times we must process the progressive mesh.

For our purposes, we will allow for the use of standard ID3DXMesh objects and ID3DXPMesh objects interchangeably. Our class object, cModelResource, can contain either type of object within the frame tree of mesh containers it holds. cModelResource provides a simple member function, setLOD, which can be given a value between 0 and 16; 16 being the highest LOD. Using ID3DXPMesh objects will reconfigure the geometry held within the progressive mesh using the interface methods provided by the D3DX library. When standard ID3DXMesh objects are used, as they have been in every demo presented so far, the setLOD member function does nothing.

In each of the methods presented next, dynamic LOD using ID3DXPMesh objects is assumed to be used wherever applicable. The fact that progressive meshes are used does not impact the methods themselves, since they would work with either type of mesh. What follows are rendering tricks that you can use to enhance the look of low polygon models in general, especially those used to represent small plants and groundcover. For large objects, such as trees, we rely solely on the ID3DXPMesh to provide LOD management.

VEGETATION IMPOSTORS

In this book, we consider an impostor to be a low-detail object that is rendered to give the appearance of one having much more detail. The simplest and most common representation of an impostor is the billboard. A billboard is merely a flat plane, usually comprised of just a few triangles, onto which a pre-rendered view of a highly detailed object is placed. If the image contains an alpha channel, a simple alpha test can be used to hide portions of the billboard that are not meant to be seen. For example, the DirectX SDK contains a sample program that shows the images of trees placed on billboards in a sample 3D environment. Even though each tree is really just a flat card, the alpha-tested image placed on the card gives the look of a more detailed tree.

When a single billboard is used, it must be continually rotated to face the camera. When a billboard is visible on-edge, the effect is lost and the paper-thin construction of the billboard is exposed. Our cCamera object contains a matrix that can be used to rotate billboards to face the camera for just this purpose. The next problem to contend with is that we have just one image to place on the billboard. Even though we can rotate the geometry to prevent the camera from seeing the edge of the billboard, we will continually show the same image to the camera regardless of the billboard's orientation. This will make our objects appear to spin as the camera passes them by because the camera is always shown the same viewing angle of the object.

One potential way to fix this problem is to use multiple billboards to represent each object. To do this, we arrange several billboards around an axis, so that each card is facing in a unique direction. Figure 12.1 shows this billboard assembly from above, looking down on a set of billboard cards arranged in a radial pattern. On each card, we place a pre-rendered view of the object from the direction perpendicular to the billboard. Since we cover multiple viewing angles with individual cards, there is no need to rotate the cards to face the camera. Instead, while rendering the billboard set, we compute the dot product of each billboard with the viewing angle. Only the card that is most perpendicular to the view vector (i.e., the highest dot product result) is drawn (see Figure 12.1).

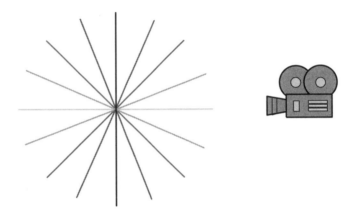

FIGURE 12.1 Multiple billboard cards used to impersonate a more detailed model. As seen from above, eight billboards are used to display the object. The card most perpendicular to the camera (shown in black) is the only one visible.

Using the multi-billboard technique also requires generating the textures needed to place on each card. In a 3D Software package, an object must be rendered from multiple angles—one for each billboard card desired. To better facilitate rendering of the billboard set, we will group all the cards together into a single model. This will allow us to render the entire set at once, using a vertex shader to decide which cards are visible to the viewer. An additional setup step is required to map our textures to this object.

Rather than using the pre-rendered object textures individually, we can combine them into a single texture map. Each of the billboard cards is then given a set of texture coordinates to read the proper area of this texture map. If we can ensure that there is an ample gap between each image containing alpha-tested transparency, we can render our new impostor as one model and one texture map.

One of the nice properties of this method is that it is completely transparent to the game engine. All the setup is performed offline—creating the composite texture and billboard assembly. The effect file handles the determination of which faces to draw, leaving no responsibilities for the engine. To our game engine, these impostors are just models with surface materials and render methods like any other. No special code is needed to create or manage these objects.

One oversight with this method is lighting. The billboard cards themselves are flat planes, and will be lit as flat planes by the lighting model. Using bump maps to give the appearance of a more volumetric object can help hide these problems, but we will never be able to approximate what true lighting of a highly detailed object could provide.

GRASS IS MOTHER NATURE'S FUR

Short blades of grass can be drawn using a technique not unlike fur rendering. A common way to render fur-covered objects is to use concentric shells of geometry, each a little larger than the one before it. Into each shell, a texture map is applied. This texture map contains a stippled color pattern for the fur, and a per-pixel height value for each hair. These height values are stored in the alpha channel of the texture. The texture represents the cross section of the fur, and the height at which each hair stands.

When rendered, each shell uses an alpha test to determine which pixels to draw. The reference alpha values used to test each shell layer is the minimum height of a hair stand that could reach the shell layer. Using this test, only those pixels that represent hair that intersects the plane of the shell are drawn. When these shells are stacked, the effect is a convincing appearance of hair on an object.

This technique is directly applicable to short blades of grass. If we rendered an area of the landscape multiple times, raising the ground slightly with each pass, we could apply the same technique. Figure 12.2 shows a cross section of our terrain using four shell layers. These represent us drawing the terrain four times, raising the ground slightly with each pass. Onto each of these layers a texture map is placed. This texture map contains a per-pixel height value for blades of grass. Each of these blades is depicted as a bar chart in Figure 12.2. On each layer, we only want to draw the blades of grass that are at least as tall as the layer itself. An alpha test value is associated with each layer representing its height. Only those pixels that contain an alpha value greater than the layer's reference value are drawn. In Figure 12.2, these are shown as the highlighted lines on each layer.

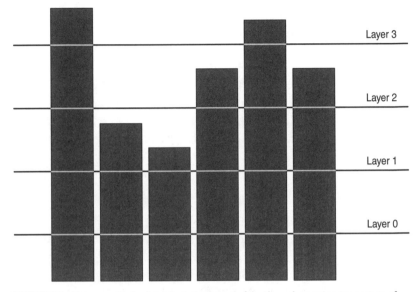

FIGURE 12.2   Using multiple alpha-tested planes to fake the volumetric appearance of grass.

The result is the appearance of blades of grass created by the parallax provided by the individual layers. Each layer only rendered the cross section of a blade of grass, but together they form the illusion of a complete blade. Another way to picture this is as a stack of coins. Each pass over our terrain draws a single coin, but layered on top of each other, they give the appearance of an entire stack.

The technique breaks down when viewed in profile. As Figure 12.2 shows, there is a perceivable gap between each layer. When we try to use this effect to crest a hill, the appearance of grass at the apex of the hill might appear stippled and disjointed. This is because the viewing angle allows us to see between the layers, where no grass is drawn. To hide this artifact, we must add vertically oriented polygons to the system that contain a profile view of the grass. Then, as the viewing vector approaches a parallel angle to the stacked grass layers, these profile polygons will prevent the camera from seeing the gaps. Figure 12.3 shows a representation of these profile polygons.

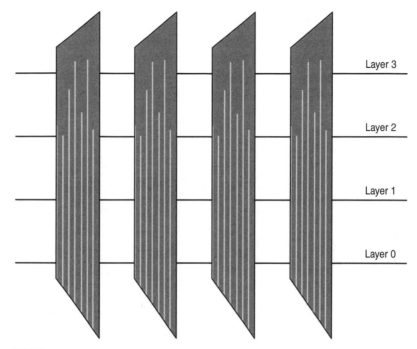

FIGURE 12.3   Profile cards used to prevent viewers from seeing between the layered grass planes.

This technique is easy to demonstrate using flat planes, but our terrain is far from flat. Assuming that we create a model that contains a set of grass layers and vertical profile planes, how could we use this within the rolling hills of our terrain? The answer lies in the next technique, which we can use for grass as well as other objects.

AMBER WAVES OF GRAIN

To draw low-lying objects on our terrain, such as grass or other types of vegetation, we must accurately map them to the contours of the terrain itself. If we rendered small, individual models, this would be a simple matter of looking up the height and surface normal for the terrain point below each object and using this information to reorient the objects on the ground. This would allow us to render small, individual models along the surface of the terrain. While this method would work, it is far from efficient.

To work more efficiently, we need a way to render larger models and deform them along the surface of the terrain. These larger models could contain multiple representations of smaller objects. For example, our layered grass model is a good candidate for this method. Rather than try to render each layer and profile card individually, we can group them together into larger models and deform them along the surface of the ground.

We do this using patch deformation, which involves using a grid of values to deform a model. Each of our groundcover models, examples of which might be the grass layer system or a small group of plants, is created to fit within a square patch of ground. The size can vary, but the technique works best if the models remain small. Below the model, we sample a 4x4 grid of height and surface normals from the terrain. If the models are designed to be 4x4 terrain units large, then sampling these values is a simple lookup into the tables of height and surface normals stored with the `cTerrain` object.

These 16 values are then given to the vertex shader for deformation. As the model vertices are rendered, we determine which grid cell they lie in within our 4x4 set of data. Once the grid cell is determined, we interpolate the four corner values of the cell to find the final vertical height and surface normal of the vertex in question. When this technique is applied to all of the model vertices, the result is a model warped to fit the contours of the terrain.

ON THE CD

In the demonstration program `chapter12_demo0`, we use this technique for small plants and grass patches. Listing 12.1 shows a sample HLSL function that you can use to perform the deformation. In the source code, additional patch-deforming routines can be found that also interpolate the surface normals to ensure that deformed groundcover geometry is properly lit.

LISTING 12.1   The patch-deforming vertex shader used to map objects to the contours of the terrain.

```
// declare a 4x4 grid of
// world heights and
// surface normals
struct PatchPoints
{
  float4 normh[16] ;
};
PatchPoints pc : patchCorners;

// a function to deform vertices
// using the patch height values
void PatchDeform(
    in out float3 Pos,
```

```
    uniform float4x4 mWorld)
{
  // note:
  // we assume the source model is
  // scaled to fit within a 3x3 unit
  // box.

  // Find the x,y integer position
  // and cell-based scalars
  int x;
  int y;
  float sx = modf(Pos.x, x);
  float sy = modf(Pos.y, y);

  // compute the index into our 4x4
  // array of values and read the
  // four corner values of the cell
  // we are in
  int index = (y*4)+x;
  float4 z0 = pc.normh[index];
  float4 z1 = pc.normh[index+1];
  float4 z2 = pc.normh[index+4];
  float4 z3 = pc.normh[index+5];

  // interpolate between the
  // four corners using sx and sy
  float4 zl = lerp(z0,z1,sx);
  float4 zh = lerp(z2,z3,sx);
  float4 zi = lerp(zl,zh,sy);

  // convert our point to world
  // space and offset by the
  // interpolated height in zi
  Pos = mul(float4(Pos, 1), mWorld);
  Pos.z = Pos.z+zi.w;
}
```

13

OCEAN WATER

 ×  =

n this final chapter, we move away from the landmass and add a completely different surface type to our engine: water. More specifically, we will be creating a body of ocean water that can be used throughout our environment. Doing so will require some mathematically intense animation on the CPU to create the dynamic motion of deep ocean waves. This animation will be applied to a dynamic mesh of vertices that will comprise our ocean surface.

We will be presenting the mathematics involved without diving too deeply into the calculations that must be performed. While we will provide an overview of the work being performed, a detailed explanation of the mathematic principles being employed is beyond the scope of this book. Appendix D, "Recommended Reading," contains references to further reading on the topics we will discuss here.

The first step is to prepare our landmass for water. We will flood our landscape with water at a certain elevation, allowing it to exist across the entire environment. Water will therefore be visible wherever the land mass dips below our sea level elevation. This allows us to border our island with water and allow lakes to appear within the valleys of our terrain. Once we have prepared the terrain for the appearance of water, we will examine the water system itself and an overview of the math involved with animating deep ocean waves.

Knowing the underlying math principles is one thing, but implementing them in an efficient manner is another. In bringing the ocean into our environment, we will discuss some key methods to animate the ocean mesh over time without bringing the frame rate to a crawl. Once the geometry is complete, we will continue on to craft the shader used to render the water. This will complete the effect and define our final demonstration program for this book. The chapter concludes by presenting this demo along with a few thoughts on further extensions the reader might want to consider.

AN ISLAND AT SEA

Our terrain has always had a ragged edge to it. The edge of the height map data used to construct the terrain marked the edge of our world. One last addition to the engine is to surround our map with water. This involves first adjusting our terrain, and then adding the water element to the scene.

To begin, our map must become an island. This means that we must ensure that all vertices around the edge of our height map are submerged. Otherwise, the ragged edge of our world would remain. Forming the island is easiest to do before the terrain is actually constructed. At the bitmap level, we can make adjustments to the height map itself used to form the island. To create the island, we simply iterate over the height map and modulate each entry with a value to control height. If done correctly, we can pull the edge values of the map below sea level to ensure that our terrain slips beneath the water before abruptly ending.

To do this we apply a height-scaling value across the height map that will force pixels closer to the edge of the bitmap toward zero. We use a nonlinear falloff to compute this value, so pixels in the center of the height map will be largely untouched. To do this, we construct a vector from the pixel in question to the center of the map. We then compute the length of this vector to derive our distance from the map center. We scale this distance by half the bitmap resolution to create a value in the 0 to 1 range. We then square the value for nonlinear falloff. Our final height map scale is then one minus this value.

Figure 13.1 shows a bitmap representation of these values. Computed per pixel, the scalars generated would resemble the grayscale image shown here. By multiplying each pixel of this bitmap against our height map, we effectively pull the edge of our map below sea level.

FIGURE 13.1 Using control values per pixel to form an island out of a height map.

As Figure 13.1 shows, our application of the procedural island adjustment can result in very circular island shapes. A second look at the process shows an easy remedy for this. Our use of a 2D vector from the map center point to each height map location has essentially created a second height map against which we multiply the original. This is the exact process shown in Figure 13.1. Rather than generate this modulation map on a per-pixel basis using 2D vectors, we could simply pregenerate some appealing island shapes and store them as height map files on the hard drive. Once we generate the procedural height map for our random terrain, we simply multiply it against one of these island templates to adopt the contoured shape of the island.

We take this approach in `chapter13_demo0.exe` provided on the accompanying CD-ROM. The result is a terrain that is still randomly generated in terms of its elevations and texture mapping, but adopts its overall island shape from a pregenerated texture. The ease of use far outweighs the loss of a truly random terrain. If more randomness is desired, the reader is encouraged to experiment with adding noise or layering multiple island templates.

THE WATER TILE

Before we examine how the water will be animated, we need to decide the best way to account for the large amount of surface area we want to cover with water. In our implementation, we want to surround our island terrain with water, and allow the water to appear wherever the landmass descends below sea level. This effectively means that the water could potentially be anywhere on the map—and can extend into the horizon as far as the eye can see. This creates an interesting problem.

How can we ensure that the water surface exists throughout the entire environment? Obviously, we would not want to create the geometry required to cover our entire terrain with water that extends into infinity in all directions. However, the ocean water must appear as if it does extend this far. To solve this problem, we use the same solution we used for the other element of our terrain that exists across the entire environment: the sky.

Recall from Chapter 10, "Big Sky Country," that our sky model is really a tiny façade placed around the camera position. When rendered, this gives the appearance of distant scenery and clouds encircling the viewer. Our ocean water is no different, and we can use a similar technique to display an endless sea of ocean water around the viewer. The difference is that while the sky model was rendered in camera space, effectively disconnecting from the environment, the water must appear as if it is an integral part of the landscape.

To create an endless body of water, we us a piece of geometry that can be tiled across the environment. This geometry will represent an area of water of some fixed dimension. To create the appearance of more water, we simply draw the tile repeatedly, offsetting it to new world positions each time. By rendering the tile in every visible position, we can give the appearance of an endless sea. This allows us to draw as many water tiles as the camera can see without actually maintaining any persistent data for each water-covered location. The world-aligned bounding box containing the cameras view frustum is applied to a world grid of water tile locations. For each world grid location that intersects the camera frustum, a water tile is drawn.

ANIMATING WATER

Many techniques have been published over the years regarding the animation of ocean waves and general fluid surfaces. Interestingly, these techniques have been researched in both computer graphics academia and oceanographic literature. In both cases, researchers provide methods to model and approximate the fluid dynamics responsible for water surface behavior. For our purposes, we will focus on just one of these techniques. See Appendix D for further reading.

To be clear, our intent is to approximate the motion of deep ocean waves, not actually simulate one based on physical parameters. Our ocean tile geometry is repeated over the entire camera view space, so our method of animation must also tile seamlessly. This means that our solution must be very artificial in nature. The method involves using a Fast Fourier Transform (FFT) to combine many octaves of sinusoidal waves to deform a patch of geometry into something with a very wave-like appearance. This type of effect has been used with great success in many commercial 3D packages as well as in the motion picture industry.

We will provide an overview of the technique here, focusing on how it can be applied for real-time performance. The mathematics principles used to generate the actual waves are beyond the scope of this book, so we provide only a brief overview of the concepts here. Further explanation can be found in papers provided by Jerry Tessendorf [Tessendorf], Lasse Staff Jensen and Robert Golias [JensenGolias]. In addition, some background reading on Gaussian random numbers and Fourier Transformations is beneficial in understanding the mathematics principles involved.

In short, the technique is not based on any attempt to model ocean water through physical simulation. Instead, a series of sinusoidal waves are combined to displace a set of vertices in a grid. The model specifies the manner in which the amplitudes and phases of these sinus waves are generated, which is based on observation and statistical analysis of the real sea. An FFT is performed in two dimensions (vertically and horizontally across the vertex grid) to sum the sinus waves into displacement values for the vertex grid. When animated over time, the result is a patch of undulating waves that closely resembles real ocean waves.

The most beneficial property is that using an FFT provides a result that tiles in all directions. This allows us to apply the FFT-based animation method to our wave tile and ensure that we can still draw the tile repeatedly across a large environment. It should be noted that methods related to the combination of sine waves have been applied directly to vertex shaders [ShaderX], but we do not consider this ideal for our situation. We will render the same water tile geometry multiple times, so it makes sense to perform the computations once on the CPU to set up a dynamic vertex buffer, and then use a minimal vertex shader to translate the tile to a set of desired world positions. Performing any wave-deformation work in the vertex shader would cause the sine wave computations to be executed redundantly each time the water tile is drawn.

We should also note that our implementation of the FFT-animation method is based on an example provided by Carsten Wenzel [Wenzel]. Wenzel's example wave application, which can be found both on his own Web site and the NVIDIA developers relations Web page (both are listed in Appendix D), demonstrates the use of the FFT-based animation method to animate a patch of water on a frame-by-frame basis. Our implementation is a variation of Wenzel's work, adding distributed processing of the FFT to achieve better runtime performance.

We also further simplify the technique by producing only height values to deform the mesh. Animation of a vertex grid in relation to ocean waves is typically performed to produce two effects. First, the height of each vertex on the grid is adjusted to produce the wave form. Second, the vertices are typically offset along the water surface to better approximate the choppy nature of some ocean waves. In our implementation, we speed up the process by producing height values only. This removes a great deal of the computation required.

Before we can apply the FFT, we must create the initial set of data and animate it. We follow the suggestion made by Tessendorf and use a Phillips spectrum to create a set of amplitudes and phases for the sinus waves based on wind and wave height parameters. The use of the Phillips spectrum creates a set of initial data that has been shown to closely approximate the appearance of real ocean waves when combined with two draws from a Gaussian random number generator. Using a Gaussian random number generator (provided in the core library file `random_numbers.cpp`), this method defines the state of our ocean waves at time 0. The first step is to compute the Phillips spectrum based on input wave and wind parameters. The equation used is shown in Equation 13.1

$$P_h(\mathbf{K}) = a \frac{\exp\left(-1/(kl)^2\right)}{k^4} \left|\hat{K} \cdot \hat{W}\right|^2 \qquad (13.1)$$

where
K = vector of wave motion
k = magnitude of vector **K**
$\hat{K}$ = normalized vector **K**
$\hat{W}$ = wind direction
l = maximum wave height
a = constant value controlling wave height

As shown in Equation 13.1, the initial set of data for each wave is defined by the direction of travel for the wave, its magnitude, and the global wind vector. In addition, some limitations are imposed by the equation. The constant scalar (a) controls the overall outcome of the equation, allowing us to exaggerate the waves or diminish them with larger and smaller values of (a). The final portion of the equation, where the absolute value of the dot product of the normalized vectors for **K** and **W** is computed, controls wave height in relation to the wind direction. It effectively removes any components of the wave that travel perpendicular to the wind direction, but allows portions of the wave traveling with the wind and against the wind to remain. The maximum wave height value (l) is also a limiting factor. This value can be computed using Equation 13.2.

$$l = \frac{v^2}{g} \tag{13.2}$$

where
v = wind speed
g = gravitational constant (9.81)

To create the final set of data for our initial state, the Phillips spectrum is combined with two draws from a random number generator to create some random wave variations. A Gaussian generator is used for aesthetic purposes, since it has been shown that Gaussian-generated values tend to follow the observed data for ocean waves. Although other forms of distributed random numbers would also work, we again follow Tessendorf's suggestion and use a Gaussian generator. Our example Gaussian generator is shown in Listing 13.1.

LISTING 13.1   Gaussian random number generation for setting up ocean wave amplitude and phase.

```
//: GaussRandom
//------------------------------------------------
//
// Generatres a gaussian random number using
```

```
//   the polar form of the Box-Muller transformation
//
//----------------------------------------------://

// The polar form of the Box-Muller transformation
// is capable of generating two random gauss values
// in one pass. We provide a method to captolize on that
// since we need our Gaussian values in pairs
// to build complex numbers
void gaia::GaussRandomPair(
  float& result_a, float& result_b,
  float dMean, float dStdDeviation)
{
  float x1, x2, w, y1, y2;

  do {
     x1 = 2.0f * random_unit_float() - 1.0f;
     x2 = 2.0f * random_unit_float() - 1.0f;
     w = x1 * x1 + x2 * x2;
  } while ( w >= 1.0f );

  w = sqrtf( (-2.0f * logf( w ) ) / w );
  y1 = x1 * w;
  y2 = x2 * w;

     result_a = ( dMean + y1 * dStdDeviation );
     result_b = ( dMean + y2 * dStdDeviation );
}
```

Not shown in Listing 13.1 is the function `random_unit_float()`. This simple function generates a random floating-point value in the range (0,1). Any means of generating this value can be used. Our specific implementation is shown in the sample source code within the file `random_numbers.h` on the accompanying CD-ROM.

Using the Gaussian generator, we can assemble our initial set of data. To perform this task, we employ yet another horrific-looking equation. As shown in Equation 13.3, this equation combines two random numbers from our Gaussian generator with the previous results of the Phillips spectrum to define our initial set of waves at time 0. To facilitate the application of the FFT later, we create this set of amplitude data in the Fourier domain.

$$\tilde{h}_O\left(\mathbf{K}\right) = c(\xi_r + \xi_i)\sqrt{P_h(\mathbf{K})} \qquad (13.3)$$

where

$$\xi_r, \xi_i = \text{Gauss random values generated with mean 0 and} \qquad (13.3)$$
$$\text{standard deviation 1}$$

$P_h(\mathbf{K})$ = Phillips spectrum for vector $\mathbf{K}$

c = constant value $\dfrac{1}{\sqrt{2}}$

The result when Equation 13.3 is performed over a set of $\mathbf{K}$ vectors is a list of complex numbers representing phase and amplitude for the sinusoidal waves we will be combining. In the example source code, we use the x and y locations of the vertex grid to compute 2D vectors for $\mathbf{K}$. Therefore, we have the same number of distributed $\mathbf{K}$ vectors as we do vertices.

To animate the data, we use angular frequencies of each vector K to compute sine and cosine values over time. These values are then applied to the complex numbers originally computed by Equation 13.3 to animate our waves in motion. Given a set of angular frequencies stored in an array, and a set of Equation 13.3 results, we can perform the animation using the code in Listing 13.2. In this listing, a set of complex numbers m_colH0 has already been generated using Equation 13.3 along with a set of angular frequencies for each wave vector $\mathbf{K}$. Because we derived $\mathbf{K}$ from our vertex positions, we can also use the positions as a lookup value into the table of frequencies and complex numbers. These lookups are performed with simple inline functions that convert the vector components i and j into array index values. The sComplex data type is a simple structure containing the real and imaginary components of a complex number.

LISTING 13.2   Animating the Fourier-domain table for water waves.

```
void cOceanManager::animateHeightTable()
{
  for(int j = -k_half_grid_size;
    j< k_half_grid_size;
    ++j )
    {
      for(int i = -k_half_grid_size;
      i< k_half_grid_size;
      ++i )
      {
        float fAngularFreq=
        m_colAngularFreq[ getIndex(i,j)]
```

```
               * m_fTime;
               float fCos=Cosine(fAngularFreq);
               float fSin=Sine(fAngularFreq);

               int indexFFT = getIndexFFT(i,j);
               int indexHO = getIndexHO(i,j);
               int indexHOn = getIndexHO(-i,-j);

               // update the tale of complex numbers
               // affecting water surface height.
               m_colH[indexFFT].real=
               ( m_colHO[indexHO].real
                 + m_colHO[indexHOn].real ) * fCos -
                     ( m_colHO[indexHO].imag
                 + m_colHO[indexHOn].imag ) * fSin;

               m_colH[indexFFT].imag=
               ( m_colHO[indexHO].real
                 - m_colHO[indexHOn].real ) * fSin +
                     ( m_colHO[indexHO].imag
                 - m_colHO[indexHOn].imag ) * fCos;
           }
       }
   }
```

The last step is to convert the Fourier-space data back into the spatial domain while combining the effects of each sinus waveform. The FFT does all of this for us, but as fast as an FFT is, we find we need greater efficiency to animate our water in real time. First, let's examine what the FFT is comprised of, and then we will show how to perform the work more efficiently using some linear interpolation. Fully explaining the theory behind the FFT is beyond the scope of this book. Instead, we will deal directly with the computation of the FFT as shown in Listing 13.3.

In Listing 13.3, the number of real and imaginary numbers provided is known to be k_grid_size (the dimension of our vertex grid). A second value, k_log_grid_size, is also precomputed as an iteration controller for the FFT. These constants make more sense when the source code is looked at as a whole, rather than out of context within Listing 13.3. On the accompanying CD-ROM the entire process of generating, animating, and performing the FFT can be found in the cOceanManager class.

ON THE CD

LISTING 13.3   Performing the FFT on a set of real and imaginary numbers.

```
void cOceanManager::FFT(float* real, float* imag )
{
    long nn,i,i1,j,k,i2,l,l1,l2;
    float c1,c2,treal,timag,t1,t2,u1,u2,z;

    nn = k_grid_size;

    // bit reversal
    i2 = nn > 1;
    j= 0;
    for(i= 0;i< nn - 1; ++i )
    {
        if(i<j)
        {
            treal = real[i];
            timag = imag[i];
            real[i] = real[j];
            imag[i] = imag[j];
            real[j] = treal;
            imag[j] = timag;
        }

        k = i2;
        while( k <=j)
        {
            j-= k;
            k >= 1;
        }

        j+= k;
    }

    // Compute the FFT
    c1 = -1.0f;
    c2 = 0.0f;
    l2 = 1;
    for( l = 0; l < k_log_grid_size; ++l )
    {
        l1 = l2;
        l2 <<= 1;
        u1 = 1.0;
        u2 = 0.0;
        for(j= 0;j< l1; ++j )
        {
```

```
for(i= j;i< nn;i+= 12 )
{
    i1 =i+ l1;
    t1 = u1 * real[ i1 ] - u2 * imag[ i1 ];
    t2 = u1 * imag[ i1 ] + u2 * real[ i1 ];
    real[ i1 ] = real[i] - t1;
    imag[ i1 ] = imag[i] - t2;
    real[i] += t1;
    imag[i] += t2;
}

z =  u1 * c1 - u2 * c2;
u2 = u1 * c2 + u2 * c1;
u1 = z;
}

c2 = sqrt( ( 1.0f - c1 ) / 2.0f );
c1 = sqrt( ( 1.0f + c1 ) / 2.0f );
}
}
```

As shown in Listing 13.3, while the FFT lives up to its reputation as a fast transform, it still requires an ample amount of computation. For our water tile, we also need to perform the FFT in two dimensions: once across the horizontal rows of source data, and once down each column of source data. This yields a final set of data that is the conglomeration of all wave information in a two-dimensional grid.

Rather than try to perform all the calculations and update our dynamic vertex buffer with the result each frame, we can cheat a little with linear interpolation. In this method, we animate the table once every n ticks. During the period before the next animation update, we compute all the necessary FFT operations and update the vertex buffer. This distributes the entire calculation over a fixed number of game ticks. For a smooth display, we interpolate between the updated set of vertices and the previous set. Therefore, while we work behind the scenes to generate the next set of vertices, the water continues to animate by interpolating between two sets of vertices previously generated.

With the extra time gained, we can also add a second FFT to generate surface normals for our water geometry—a problem we have ignored until this point. Just as we used the FFT to generate a set of height offsets for our vertices, the same method can be used to generate surface normals for each point on the grid. Details can be found in the example source code on the accompanying CD-ROM. Given these new additions to the

ON THE CD

overall process, we define our update scheme using the code shown in Listing 13.4. Again, this code is taken out of context. Each function called by the switch statement can be found within the cOceanManager class in the example code.

In Listing 13.4, a tick counter is used to iterate over the stages of water animation. This value is updated once per game tick. Each time the update function is called, the proper stage of the animation process is performed and this counter is incremented. When the final stage is reached, the results are written to a one of two vertex buffers. For each frame, an interpolation value is updated with a scalar value that will be used to blend between the two vertex buffers in the vertex shader. This produces a constantly animating result on screen from our periodic animation of the water mesh.

LISTING 13.4   Distributing the update process for ocean water over time.

```
enum eProcessingStages
{
  k_animateHeight = 0,
  k_animateNormal,
  k_heightFFTv,
  k_heightFFTh,
  k_normalFFTv,
  k_normalFFTh,
  k_uploadBuffer,
  k_rotateBuffers,
  k_total_process_stages,
};

void cOceanManager::update()
{
  debug_assert(
    m_tickCounter >= k_animateHeight,
    "invalid tick counter");
  debug_assert(
    m_tickCounter < k_total_process_stages,
    "invalid tick counter");

  switch(m_tickCounter)
  {
    case k_animateHeight:
      m_fTime =
        applicationTimer.elapsedTime()*0.15f;
      animateHeightTable();
```

```
      break;
  case k_animateNormal:
    animateNormalTable();
    break;
  case k_heightFFTv:
    verticalFFT(m_colH );
    break;
  case k_heightFFTh:
    horizontalFFT(m_colH );
    break;
  case k_normalFFTv:
    verticalFFT(m_colN );
    break;
  case k_normalFFTh:
    horizontalFFT(m_colN );
    break;
  case k_uploadBuffer:
    fillVertexBuffer(
      m_pAnimBuffer[m_activeBuffer]);
    break;
  default:
    ++m_activeBuffer;
    if (m_activeBuffer
      >= k_total_water_meshes)
    {
      m_activeBuffer = 0;
    }
    break;
};

// compute the interpolation factor for
// the vertices currently in use
m_fInterpolation = //0.0f;
  (float)(m_tickCounter+1)
  /(float)(k_total_process_stages);

++m_tickCounter;
if (m_tickCounter == k_total_process_stages)
{
  m_tickCounter = k_animateHeight;
  m_fInterpolation = 0.0f;
}
}
```

RENDERING WATER

Now that the ocean water mesh is being efficiently animated over a series of frames, we can examine how we will texture and illuminate the water surface. The first step is to determine the base water color. Here we perform another approximation based on observation. As a gross generalization, ocean water can be said to interpolate between two colors based on the viewing angle. When looking across water (over the crest of a wave), the ocean water takes a greenish hue. When looking directly into the body of water, the color is a deep blue. The first step in our vertex shader is to compute the viewing angle and use this to interpolate between two constant color values.

Next, we need to deal with the surface of the water. In addition to our animated surface normals, we will be applying a normal map to the water surface to simulate tiny surface waves. Both of these properties need to be considered when computing the final addition of reflected light on the water surface. Just as with out terrain bump-mapping pass, we compute binormal and tangent vectors for each vertex and use these to transform the light vector into texture space. In addition, we compute a half-angle vector for specular lighting and convert this to texture space as well.

In the pixel shader, dot products are computed with both vectors against the surface normal read from the bump map. In the diffuse case, the light vector result is used to modulate our interpolated water color. In the specular case, the result is raised to a specular power and then modulated with the current color of the sun. This creates a water surface with diffuse, view-dependent coloration and a glistening highlight from reflected sunshine.

To further enhance the technique, we animate the normal map texture coordinates. The base texture address is calculated by applying a simple scale value to the world vertex position. This is offset by the horizontal components of the surface normals to create an undulating motion that expands and contracts with the crest of each wave. Two reads of the normal map are performed at different scales to add further motion to the miniscule waves. One read is used to create the diffuse result, and the second is used for the specular result.

The result is a reasonable approximation of an opaque water surface. Listing 13.5 shows the complete effect file used to generate our ocean water. On the accompanying CD-ROM, the demonstration program chapter13_demo0 displays our new ocean system. Further implementation details can be found within the source code for this application.

ON THE CD

LISTING 13.5   The ocean water effect file.

```
//
// Ocean Water shader
//
#include "light_scattering_constants.h"

// transformations
float4x4 mWorldViewProj: WORLDVIEWPROJECTION;
float4 posOffset : posScaleOffset
  = {1.0f, 0.0f, 0.0f, 0.0f};
float4 vCameraPos: worldcamerapos;
float4 sun_color: suncolor
  = {0.578f,0.578f,0.578f,0.0f};

float4 sun_vec: sunvector =
  {0.578f,0.578f,0.578f,0.0f};
float4 xAxis =
  {1.0f, 0.0f, 0.0f, 0.0f};
float4 vOne =
  {1.0f, 1.0f, 1.0f, 0.0f};
float4 vHalf =
  {0.5f, 0.5f, 0.5f, 0.0f};

float3 waterColor0 =
  {0.15f, 0.4f, 0.5f};

float3 waterColor1 =
  {0.1f, 0.15f, 0.3f};

texture tex0 : TEXTURE;

struct VS_INPUT
{
  float2  Pos   : POSITION;
  float   ZPos0 : POSITION1;
  float2  Norm0 : NORMAL0;
  float   ZPos1 : POSITION2;
  float2  Norm1 : NORMAL1;
};

struct VS_OUTPUT
{
  float4 Pos  : POSITION;
  float3 Col  : COLOR0;
  float3 T0   : TEXCOORD0;
```

```
    float3 T1    : TEXCOORD1;
    float3 T2    : TEXCOORD2;
    float3 T3    : TEXCOORD3;
};

VS_OUTPUT VS(VS_INPUT v)
{
  VS_OUTPUT Out = (VS_OUTPUT)0;

  // offset xy and interpolate
  // z to get world position
  float3 worldPos =
  float3(
    v.Pos.x+posOffset.z,
    v.Pos.y+posOffset.w,
    lerp(v.ZPos0, v.ZPos1, posOffset.x));

  // transform and output
  Out.Pos =
    mul(float4(worldPos, 1), mWorldViewProj);

  // interpolate normal
  float2 nXY = lerp(v.Norm0, v.Norm1, posOffset.x);
  float3 normal = normalize(float3(nXY, 24.0f));

  // compute tex coords using world pos
  // and normal for animation
  float3 uvBase =
    float3(
      worldPos.x*0.01f,
      worldPos.y*0.01f,
      0.0f);

  float3 uvAnim = normal * 0.1f;
  Out.T0 = uvBase + uvAnim;
  Out.T1 = (uvBase * 0.5f) - uvAnim;

  // compute binormal and
  // tangent using cross products
  float3 tangent = xAxis.yzx *  normal.zxy;
  tangent =
    (-normal.yzx * xAxis.zxy) + tangent;

  float3 binormal = normal.yzx *  tangent.zxy;
  binormal =
```

```
      (-tangent.yzx * normal.zxy) + binormal;

   // transform the sun vector to texture space
   float3 lightVec;
   lightVec.x = dot(sun_vec, binormal);
   lightVec.y = dot(sun_vec, tangent);
   lightVec.z = dot(sun_vec, normal);

   // normalize the light vector
   // and output
   Out.T2 = normalize(lightVec);

   //compute the view vector
   float3 camera_vec = vCameraPos - worldPos;
   float s = length(camera_vec);
   camera_vec = normalize(camera_vec);

   // transform the view vector to texture space
   float3 viewVec;
   viewVec.x = dot(camera_vec, binormal);
   viewVec.y = dot(camera_vec, tangent);
   viewVec.z = dot(camera_vec, normal);

   // normalize the view vector
   viewVec = normalize(viewVec);

   // compute the half-angle vector
   float3 half_angle_vec =
     (viewVec + lightVec)*0.5f;

   // normalize the half vector
   // and output
   Out.T3  = normalize(half_angle_vec);

   // color interpolator is the dot product
   // of the view vector with the normal
   float cosTheta =
     saturate(dot(-camera_vec, normal));
   Out.Col =
     lerp(waterColor0, waterColor1, cosTheta);

   return Out;
}

sampler LinearSamp0 = sampler_state
```

```
{
    texture = <tex0>;
    AddressU  = wrap;
    AddressV  = wrap;
    AddressW  = wrap;
    MIPFILTER = LINEAR;
    MINFILTER = LINEAR;
    MAGFILTER = LINEAR;
};

float4 PS(VS_OUTPUT In) : COLOR
{
  // composite bump maps
  float3 bump0 =
    (tex2D(LinearSamp0, In.T0 )-0.5f)*2.0f;
  float3 bump1 =
    (tex2D(LinearSamp0, In.T1 )-0.5f)*2.0f;
  float3 bump =
    (bump0+bump1)*0.5f;

  // compute base diffuse color
  float3 baseColor =
    dot(bump, In.T2) * In.Col;

  // compute specular component
  float specFactor =
    dot(bump, In.T3);
  float3 specColor =
    specFactor * specFactor *
    specFactor * specFactor * sun_color;

  // combine and output
  return float4((baseColor+specColor), 1.0f);
}

technique OceanWater_1_1
{
  pass P0
  {
    CULLMODE = CW;
    ZENABLE = TRUE;
    ZWRITEENABLE = TRUE;
    ZFUNC = LESSEQUAL;

    AlphaBlendEnable = false;
```

```
        AlphaTestEnable = false;

        // shaders
        VertexShader = compile vs_1_1 VS();
        PixelShader  = compile ps_1_1 PS();
    }
}
```

THE END OF THE ROAD

With the ocean surrounding our little island, our sample environment is complete. We examined many different techniques to generate, manage, and render our 3D landscape using DirectX 9. We looked at various geometry management schemes for the terrain, implemented procedural landscape creations, and used atmospheric lighting to further enhance the overall display.

There is still ample subject matter out there to incorporate into this engine. With this final chapter complete, we invite the reader to continue delving into these topics, using the engine provided with this book as a springboard for new rendering and geometry management ideas. We suggest perusing Appendix D "Recommended Reading" to uncover further reading on terrain rendering topics.

REFERENCES

[Tessendorf] Tessendorf, J. "Simulating Ocean Water." Siggraph 2001 Course notes, (available online at *http://home1.gte.net/tssndrf/index. html*).

[JensenGolias] Jensen, L. S., and R. Golias. "Deep-Water Animation and Rendering," Gamasutra Article, (available online at *www.gamasutra. com/gdce/2001/jensen/jensen_01.htm*).

[ShaderX] Isidoro, J., A. Vlachos, and C. Brennan. "Rendering Ocean Water." *ShaderX*, Wordware Publishing, Inc. 2002, pp. 347–356.

[Wenzel] Wenzel, C. "Ocean Scene," (available online at *http:// meshuggah.4fo.de/OceanScene.htm*).

APPENDIX

A

GAIA UTILITY CLASSES

ON THE CD

Below the terrain rendering methods we explored in earlier chapters lies a core set of support libraries that provide a foundation for the application. Rather than load the front of the book with introductory chapters explaining each system, we provide an overview of each component here. As you read through the source code on the CD-ROM, you can turn to this section for an explanation of the classes you will encounter.

MONITORING BIT FLAGS

Often, we will find ourselves in need of storing a bunch of Boolean values within an object. Although we think of Booleans as being polar true\false values, they still consume a full 32 bits of data for storage. Why? Since the most efficient storage type on the PC is an integer, Booleans end up being inflated to integer size.

This is not a big deal when you use an occasional Boolean in your code, but once you store more than one Boolean value as a class member, the wasted space begins to pile up. The last numeric tool is more of a container class. However, since it is a container of bits, we treat it as a simple numeric data type. A container class used to assemble Boolean values as bit flags can make more efficient use of space and allow the setting, clearing, and testing of multiple Boolean values simultaneously.

At its core, the bit field is nothing more than a simple numeric variable whose bits are being used as separate flags. The positive side of this is that we can do bulk operations on the flags by using bitwise operations (AND, OR, NOT, etc.) on the host variable. The negative side is that we are limited by the size of the host variable we choose.

For simplicity's sake, we are going to stick to the common data types. This means we are limited to a 32-bit value as our largest possible host value. Our bit field class can therefore store a maximum of 32-bit flags and still allow effortless testing and manipulation of the flags. Now, you could adventure into 64-bit integer values as host types, or extend the class to contain multiple host variables, but to keep the class simple, we will stick with the 32-bit flag limitation.

To make the code more readable, we need to define the difference between a bit and a flag. Some programmers use the two terms interchangeably, so we'll spell out the terms used by the engine. If you think of a 32-bit value as an array of single-bit values, then a "bit" is identified by its index into the array, and a "flag" is the numeric value of the array. For example, take an empty bit field and set bit number 3; the bit field now has a flag value of 8 (1000 in binary is decimal 8). Bits can only represent a single Boolean value, while flags can represent an entire set at once. Given the previous flag of 8, set bit number 2. The bit field now has a combined flag value of 12 (binary 1100), which shows both bits 2 and 3 as being set to true.

This is incredibly useful because we can now test multiple bit flags using bitwise operators on flag values. To test whether the first three bit flags are set in a bit field, simply compute the value [`bit_field&7`]. If the result is equal to 7, then all three bits are set. If the result is nonzero, then at least one of the three flags is set. The `cBitField` class makes this easier by providing a set of member functions for setting and testing individual bits and combined flag values. The class itself is a template, so it can use any host variable type specified by T. `Typedefs` for common flag container sizes are listed after the class definition. Highlights of the class are shown in Listing A.1.

LISTING A.1   Highlights of the `cBitFlags` template class found in core\bit_flags.h.

```
template <class T>
class cBitFlags
{
public:

    T value;

    // Creators...
    cBitFlags();
    cBitFlags(T data);
    cBitFlags(const cBitFlags& Src);
    ~cBitFlags();
```

```
    // Operators...
    cBitFlags& operator=( const cBitFlags& Src);
    cBitFlags& operator=( T Src);
    operator T() {return(value);};
    bool operator&(T test);
    bool operator==(const cBitFlags& Src)const;
    bool operator!=(const cBitFlags& Src)const;

    // Mutators...
    void set(T settings);
    void clear();
    void setFlags(T settings);
    void clearFlags(T settings);
    void setBit(int bit, bool setting=true);
    void clearBit(int bit);

    // Accessors...
    bool isEmpty()const;
    bool testBit(int bit)const;
    bool testFlags(T test)const;
    bool testAny(T test)const;

    int totalBits()const;
    int totalSet()const;
};

// common flag typedefs
typedef cBitFlags<uint8> u8Flags;   // 8 bits of flags
typedef cBitFlags<uint16> u16Flags; // 16 bits of flags
typedef cBitFlags<uint32> u32Flags; // 32 bits of flags

// to set a bit flag to be true, we OR in it's flag value
template <class T>
inline void cBitFlags<T>::setBit(int bit)
{
    value |= (1<<bit);
}

// to set a bit flag to be false, we AND with a mask to
// clear the bit
template <class T>
inline void cBitFlags<T>::setBit(int bit)
{
    value &= ~(1<<bit);
}
```

```
// setting multiple bits is a simple OR with the provided
// flag value
template <class T>
inline void cBitFlags<T>::setFlags(T settings)
{
    value |= settings;
}

// clearing multiple flags is a simple AND with the inverted
// flag value
template <class T>
inline void cBitFlags<T>::clearFlags(T settings)
{
    value &= ~settings;
}

// to test a single bit, we shift it up to create a flag to
// compare
template <class T>
inline bool cBitFlags<T>::testBit(int bit)const
{
    return(value & (1<<bit) ? true : false);
}

// return true if all the provided flags are set
template <class T>
inline bool cBitFlags<T>::testFlags(T test)const
{
    return((value & test) == test);
}

// return true if any of the provided flags are set
template <class T>
inline bool cBitFlags<T>::testAny(T test)const
{
    return(value & test ? true : false);
}
```

THE SINGLETON CLASS

A singleton, as far as class objects are concerned, is a type of class of which only one instance can exist. This is commonly used for management classes used to control systemwide resources. For example, class objects designed to manage system memory, texture space, or audio playback would be good candidates for the singleton method. Having more than one object managing such resources would add a level of complexity to the application, and can easily be avoided using singletons.

If the desire is to have only one instance of a class, why not simply add a class definition and create a single, global instance of that class? In truth, this is a perfectly reasonable way to handle the situation. Creating a class containing static member functions would also work, providing global access to all methods and members and thereby enforcing a single interface to some system resource. There are many ways to emulate what singletons can do, but each adds its own set of caveats that we can avoid.

Using a single, globally defined instance of a class object would indeed create a single interface for managing a given resource, but the order of construction is undefined. In many cases, there is an order of construction for system managers that must be honored; for example, memory and file managers might have to be constructed prior to a texture manager. Using class objects declared as global instances makes controlling this construction order a little problematic. Additional initialization methods would need to be created to handle construction order at some point during the applications startup procedures.

Singletons provide all the benefits of the alternative methods, with a higher degree of control over construction and destruction. In essence, all the singleton method provides is a way to enforce that only one instance of an object can exist at any time, and that the active instance is globally available to anyone who needs to communicate with it. This is achieved with a simple template interface that any class can derive from in order to become a singleton. Listing A.2 shows the simple singleton template class used within the core library as defined in `core\singleton.h` on the accompanying CD-ROM.

ON THE CD

LISTING A.2   The singleton template class.

```
template <class T>
class Singleton
{
public:

    // the singleton must be constructed
    // with a reference to the controlled object
    Singleton(T& rObject)
    {
        debug_assert(!s_pInstance,
            "only one instance allowed");
```

```
            s_pInstance = &instance;
    }

    // the singleton accessor
    ~Singleton()
    {
        debug_assert(s_pInstance,
            "no instance available");

        s_pInstance = 0;
    }

    // the singleton accessor
    static T& instance()
    {
        debug_assert(s_pInstance,
            "no instance available");
        return (*s_pInstance);
    }

private:

    // Data...
    static T* s_pInstance;

    // Nonexistant Functions...
    Singleton( const Singleton& Src);
    Singleton& operator=( const Singleton& Src);

};
template <class T> T* Singleton<T>::s_pInstance = 0;
```

As shown in Listing A.2, the singleton is really nothing more than a method of managing a pointer to a class object. Because only one class pointer is allowed to exist, the singleton enforces that a single, unique instance of the managed class is available to all callers. The managed class object is provided as the template parameter T at the time of construction. A pointer to the managed class is then stored within the static member s_pInstance, and returned via the member function instance() to anyone who needs it. Enforcement is handled using the debug_assert macro, which mimics the standard assert() function. If a second instance of the singleton object is ever created, or if someone tries to access the managed class pointer before it is initialized, an assertion message box will halt the application.

To create a class managed by the singleton method, simply derive the class from the singleton template and provide the managed class as the template parameter. During the construction of the managed class, pass a reference of it into the constructor of the singleton template base class. From this point on, a pointer to the managed class will be stored within the singleton base class, globally accessible via the `instance()` member function. The managed class is now guaranteed to have only one instance active at a time, and its interface is globally available to the application.

Here is an example of the singleton template in use:

```
// an example class managed via the singleton template
class MyClass : public Singleton<MyClass>
{
    public:

        // when MyClass is constructed, it must construct
        // the singleton base class as well
        MyClass() : Singleton(*this) {};
        ~MyClass() {};

        void SomeFunction();
};

// global access to the managed class is available
// from the static member function, instance().
MyClass::instance().SomeFunction();

// or we can use a pre-processor definition
// to make access to MyClass more convenient
#define MYCLASS MyClass::instance()

// the definition can then be used just as if
// it were a class itself.
MYCLASS.SomeFunction();
```

At some point within the application, a single instance of the managed class must be created, and this must occur prior to any call to the managed class interface. Whether the instance is created in the global space, as a local variable, or via explicit calls to new and delete does not matter. The important concern is the timing of its construction and destruction to ensure that the interface is available at the time it is called.

STRINGS

Text strings are an often-overlooked subject in computer games. While they might seem unimportant for most 3D games, text can still play a vital role in any adventure or role-playing game. A good string class is also useful when adding a user-input console or text-based scripting system. For the purpose of this book, the `basic_string` class provided by the Standard Template Library (STL) is employed to do most of the work. To reinforce our desire for portability, all text manipulation within the engine is done with international markets in mind.

We use the `tchar` data type to provide transparent support for both 8-bit character sets and Unicode-compatible 16-bit character sets. This is an easy way to provide international text display support using the generic text functions provided in the Win32 SDK. The Microsoft runtime library provides a great deal of flexibility by using generic text functions that automatically reroute to the ANSI single-byte character set (SBCS), localizing multibyte character sets (MBCS), or Unicode character set methods as needed.

By providing the desired character support as a preprocessor definition, the programmer can choose which character set the application will use. By default, the engine will be configured to use the standard 8-bit ANSI character set. To change this, simply add the preprocessor definitions `_UNICODE` or `_MBCS` to the project settings. This will define the `tchar` data type to the proper bit size and remap all generic text functions to their proper specialized counterparts. More information on the generic text functions can be found in the Win32 SDK documentation, or by examining the `tchar.h` header file provided with the Win32 development library.

For the generic text paradigm to work, some careful planning is required for static text. All static text that is intended for display or use with string-manipulating functions must be created with the macro `_text` to enforce the proper character set. For example, to declare a static string of text:

```
tchar my_string[] = _text("Some Text");
```

When `_UNICODE` is defined, this macro will provide the static string in wide-character format (16 bits per character instead of the usual 8), allowing it to remain compatible with Unicode-based text functions. When `_UNICODE` is not defined, the macro has no effect and the string is left in the default state.

Strings that appear in the resource file associated with the application need no conversion. By default, resource strings are encoded in Unicode format for portability. When the Win32 LoadString function is used to load the resource string into a tchar buffer, the proper character set conversion is applied automatically. Therefore, if all static game text resides in the resource file, or is declared within the code using the _text macro, compliance with international character sets becomes as easy as recompiling with the _UNICODE or _MBCS definitions.

The wrapper class created to hold string data in our core library is cString. This class is built upon the STL string class basic_string and also mimics some of the functionality found in the MFC class CString by providing additional operators for appending strings and equality operators for comparisons. The wrapper class also adds member functions for loading resource strings, formatting text, and performing case-independent string compares. Just like the generic text functions, cString can be compiled for ANSI or Unicode support using the same preprocessor definitions. The code can be found on the accompanying CD-ROM in the core\string.h header file, and the basic cString interface is shown in Listing A.3.

ON THE CD

LISTING A.3   The cString wrapper class derived from the STL basic_string implementation.

```
class cString: public TEXT_BASE_CLASS
{
public:

    // Creators...
    inline cString(){};
    cString(const cString& rhs);
    explicit cString(const TEXT_BASE_CLASS& rhs);
    explicit cString(tchar c);
    cString(const tchar *s, ...);
    ~cString(){};

    // cast the string directly to a tchar pointer
    inline operator const tchar*()const;

    // copy data from various source types
    cString& operator=(const cString& rhs);
    cString& operator=(const TEXT_BASE_CLASS& rhs);
    cString& operator=(const tchar *s);
    cString& operator=(tchar c);
```

```
    // append data from various sources
    cString& operator+=(const cString& rhs);
    cString& operator+=(const TEXT_BASE_CLASS& rhs);
    cString& operator+=(const tchar *s);
    cString& operator+=(tchar c);

    // test equality and inequality (case sensitive)
    bool operator==(const cString& rhs);
    bool operator!=(const cString& rhs);

    // test without case sensitivity
    bool compareNoCase(const cString& rhs);

    // operator that allows cString to be used
    // as an STL map key value
    bool operator<(const cString& rhs);

    // format the string from optional parameters
    void __cdecl format(const tchar* text, ...);
    void __cdecl format(const tchar* text, va_list arglist);
};
```

As you can see in Listing A.3, the interface for cString is sparse. The entire wrapper interface does little more than add a few extra functions to make string use a little easier. Because the class is derived from the STL basic_string class, it inherits the STL interface for most of the basic string functions. Operations such as erasing the string, searching for substrings, and determining the length of the string are provided in the base class interface.

One important idea to keep in mind with the STL base class is that, like the MFC CString class, basic_string will perform its own internal memory allocations as needed. The use of string manipulation functions can lead to a large amount of memory allocations and memory copy operations behind the scenes—especially as strings grow in size. To alleviate this problem, we will get into the habit of using the basic_string function reserve.

The reserve function allows us to pre-allocate memory space, providing a workspace in which all further appending operations can place new additions to the string. Wherever we can estimate the final string size, pre-reserving the memory space will allow us to perform multiple operations on the string without causing unnecessary memory operations.

SYSTEM DATA

Certain builds of the game engine contain processor-specific optimizations; such as the Intel Streaming SIMD Extensions (SSE). These types of instructions are only valid on the processors that support them. Asking the end user which type of processor he has is not a dependable way to address this problem, so we are forced to query the host CPU ourselves to determine what instruction sets are supported. While we are at it, we will inquire about the host operating system and available system memory, both of which can determine the application we run or the data sets we want to load.

For example, we could build a specific version of the game executable for use on Microsoft Windows XP using the SIMD instruction set, and another version that is more OS and CPU agnostic. We would then use a separate application to query the host operating system and processor, and then launch the optimal version of the actual game executable. Although the end user is provided with multiple game executables, the launcher application ensures that the best program is used for the host system.

Furthermore, the game executables themselves can determine the amount of system memory available on the host system and load the proper set of game data. On machines with limited memory, smaller textures and geometry models can be loaded. When more room is available, larger, more detailed data sets are loaded. This helps to ensure the best possible experience for the end user.

This method can also be extended, albeit with a bit of a gamble, to enable the game to run in an enhanced mode on future processors. Perhaps there is a software effect that we can't afford to do on current hardware very often. When more powerful processors are detected, we can allow the game to perform these actions more frequently, thereby helping the game scale to future hardware. For example, imagine that our title uses animated textures read from some type of video file. On current hardware, we limit playback to 10 or 12 frames per second. This gives us ample time to decode the next frame on the CPU before it is needed, but the final animation is a little choppy because of the low playback rate. However, the game is released with a version of the animated texture video at 30 fps and 60 fps in addition to the 10 fps version we are using by default. When a super-fast processor is detected in the future, the game can opt to use one of the more costly video files, thereby increasing the quality of our game with the new processor.

To query information about the system hosting the application, we define a class, cSystemData, designed to gather the information and store it in a way we can reference easily. Information such as processor type, resident operating system, and available system memory is contained within this class, along with an estimate of the system's processor speed. This data allows us to determine the proper version of our game executable to launch, and the proper data set to load. `cSystemData` contains a function called `querySystemInformation` that will gather the information we are looking for. The source code is shown in Listing A.4.

The first step is to determine the amount of system memory resident on the host machine, and the amount of memory currently available to our application. While one could argue that virtual memory systems provide a near infinite amount of system memory, performance will still suffer dramatically if portions of your application's data are swapped out to a file on the hard drive. Therefore, it's always best to know how much system RAM is available for use.

The Win32 SDK provides a function to report everything we would ever need to know about system memory: `GlobalMemoryStatus`. This function fills a structure with information about system and virtual memory resident on the host machine. The structure, `MEMORYSTATUS`, contains the data shown next. Within the `querySystemInformation` function, we poll the system for this information and store the information we need within the `cSystemData` class.

```
typedef struct _MEMORYSTATUS { // mst
        DWORD dwLength;         // sizeof(MEMORYSTATUS)
        DWORD dwMemoryLoad;     // percent of memory in use
        DWORD dwTotalPhys;      // bytes of physical memory
        DWORD dwAvailPhys;      // free physical memory bytes
        DWORD dwTotalPageFile;  // bytes of paging file
        DWORD dwAvailPageFile;  // free bytes of paging file
        DWORD dwTotalVirtual;   // user bytes of address space
        DWORD dwAvailVirtual;   // free user bytes
    } MEMORYSTATUS, *LPMEMORYSTATUS;
```

The members we are most interested in are `dwTotalPhys` and `dwAvailPhys`, which hold information about the total amount of system memory resident on the host computer, and how much of that memory is available for us to use. If the total physical memory on the host system is less than what our game requires, we will need to inform the user and exit the application. If the total amount of memory satisfies our constraints, but our required amount of memory is not currently available, we need to warn the user that the performance of our game will suffer if external applications are not closed to free up more memory.

The next step is to determine the host operating system. While it is somewhat rare to create code that will run on some versions of Windows but not others, there are a few cases where this will happen. Windows NT introduced some functions that are not available within Windows 95. These are mainly extended versions of existing functions such as `Find-FirstFileEx` and `GetDiskFreeSpaceEx`, but there is also enhanced support for multithreaded application under NT that does not exist under earlier versions of Windows. If your application wants to use such functions, you must ensure that the proper operating system is present.

Again, a simple function call tells us what we want to know. The function, `GetVersionEx`, fills a structure containing data about the host operating system. Our responsibility is to convert the major and minor build numbers reported in this structure to data we can use. For our purposes, we create an enumeration of known Windows versions containing the following members:

```
enum WINDOWS_VERSIONS
    {
        UNKNOWN =0,
        WINDOWS_95,
        WINDOWS_95_SR2,
        WINDOWS_98,
        WINDOWS_98_SR2,
        WINDOWS_ME,
        WINDOWS_NT,
        WINDOWS_2K,
        WINDOWS_XP,
        // the final value is for
        // versions of windows
        // yet unreleased
        WINDOWS_FUTURE
    };
```

The enumeration is laid out in a numerical order that we can use to our advantage. The assumption is that each version is backward compatible to all lower versions listed in the enumeration. `WINDOWS_98` is backward compatible with `WINDOWS_95`; `WINDOWS_NT` is backward compatible with `WINDOWS_98`, and so on. If we know which of these enumerated values represents our minimum requirement, we can quickly determine whether the current OS is compatible with our needs. When these conditions are not met, we will need to inform the user and exit the application. Within the `querySystemInformation` function, shown in Listing A.4, the major and minor build numbers reported by `GetVersionEx` are converted into our enumerated version numbers.

There is ample information available on identifying the system processor contained in the host machine. Performing such a test requires using assembly-language instructions to poll the CPU for information. Most of this information is published by the processor manufacturers, and in articles such as Rob Wyatt's Gamasutra.com article on processor detection from July 1999 [Wyatt]. These references provide more detailed information on how to poll the host processor for identification.

Rather than identify the CPU itself, we only need to determine what it supports. If we have processor-specific code in our executable, it would be best to test directly for support of the code rather than the CPU's brand and model name. In the case of the Intel SSE instruction set, chips from multiple vendors will support these instructions. Working to determine whether the CPU is a genuine Intel Pentium III (or above) will no longer suffice. Newer processors such as AMD Athlon XP also support the SSE instruction set, and will support the code we want to run. Future processors might support these instructions as well, so vendor information becomes largely irrelevant.

The key to CPU feature identification is the assembly-language instruction CPUID. This instruction is the gateway to interrogating the CPU, and can be used to retrieve the processors name, features, and, in some cases, its serial number. For our purposes, the feature set is all we require, but we must first determine if the CPUID instruction itself is supported.

To determine if the CPUID instruction is supported, we test bit number 21 of the EFLAGS register. If this flag can be modified by software, the CPUID instruction is supported. This should also be true for any hardware vendor that supports CPUID on their products.

As shown in the cpu_supports_cpuid function within Listing A.5, a little assembly-language gets the job done by retrieving the contents of the EFLAGS register using the PUSHFD instruction. The routine then toggles the bit in position 21, and then uses the POPFD instruction to write the modified value back into the EFLAGS register. It then retrieves the contents of EFLAGS using a second PUSHFD instruction, and checks whether the value of the ID bit is indeed the value we set. If so, then we have proven that bit 21 of the EFLAGS register is writable, and the CPUID instruction is available.

Once CPUID support is found, we can continue checking for the features we need. The CPUID function can perform multiple tasks and retrieve different sets of information. For our purposes, we need CPUID to tell us which features the CPU supports. This is done by loading the value 1 into the EAX register prior to calling CPUID. Setting this value in EAX requests a set of feature bit flags from CPUID, which are placed into the register EDX. By copying the contents of EDX into our own 32-bit flag variable, we can determine the features supported. This operation is shown in the `get_cpu_feature_flags` function in Listing A.5. The 32 flags reported by CPUID are listed in Appendix C, "Programming Reference Sheets."

The flags we need to test are those that signal the features we want to use. These include bits number 25 and 26, signaling CPU support for the Intel SSE and SSE2 instruction sets. However, for these two features the CPU query is not enough. Even if these bits are set by the CPU, we still need to determine if the operating system allows the operations. We do this the lazy way by attempting to call the functions and trapping any exceptions that signal their failure. If the calls create exceptions, the host operating system does not support these extensions. Listing A.5 contains two functions used to determine SSE and SSE2 support: `os_supports_sse_instructions` and `os_supports_sse2_instructions`.

The last piece of information we want to track is a speed estimate for the host CPU. This is useful if we want to tune some of the CPU-dependant functions in our game, such as artificial intelligence operations or any non-hardware rendering effects. Unfortunately, gathering information about the actual CPU speed is not an exact science. Using the CPU's own resident counter, we can determine the exact number of CPU clock cycles that occur over a set period of time, but even that degree of information is not truly correct.

To read the elapsed clock cycles back from the CPU, we use the `rdtsc` instruction in assembly-language. This instruction stands for Read Time Stamp Counter, and it fills two 32-bit registers with a grand total of 64 bits of counter information. The counter is incremented at the rate of the processor's speed. For example, a 1GHz processor would increment the counter roughly 1,000,000 times per second. Given this information, we can sample the counter twice, and look at how much the counter increased over time. This gives us a rough estimate of the processor speed.

The reason why this is a rough estimate is that we are performing a sample of the CPU counter over time, and any method we use to determine the passage of real time will be somewhat inexact. Another reason is that the CPU speed itself might fluctuate. Such is the case with many modern mobile processors that allow the CPU speed to decrease when demand is low. This is one way in which mobile processors conserve power. Therefore, our speed rating for the CPU is useful as a guideline only, not an exact benchmark.

Listing A.6 shows the basic CPU speed test operation. This function also uses the `cTimer` class to determine how much actual time has passed while the function retrieves two values from the `rdtsc` instruction. Determining the speed of the host processor is then a simple matter of dividing the number of CPU cycles elapsed by the time spent gathering the data.

This calculates an estimation of clock cycles per second, which should be nearly identical to the speed rating of the CPU.

LISTING A.4   Gathering system information.

```
void cSystemInfo::querySystemInformation()
{
    MEMORYSTATUS    MemStatus;
    OSVERSIONINFO   OSVersion;

    // read the memory status
    MemStatus.dwLength = sizeof (MemStatus);
    GlobalMemoryStatus(&MemStatus);

    // read the OS Version data
    OSVersion.dwOSVersionInfoSize =
        sizeof(OSVersion);
    GetVersionEx(&OSVersion);

    // fill in our data members
    m_physicalMemory=
        MemStatus.dwTotalPhys;
    m_totalMemory=
        MemStatus.dwAvailPhys
        + MemStatus.dwAvailPageFile;

    //
    // Figure out which OS this is
    //
    if (OSVersion.dwPlatformId==
                VER_PLATFORM_WIN32_WINDOWS)
    {
        m_osVersion.Build=
            LOWORD(OSVersion.dwBuildNumber);

        m_platform=WINDOWS_95;

        if (m_osVersion.MinorVersion==0
            && m_osVersion.Build>950)
        {
            m_platform=WINDOWS_95_SR2;
        }
        else if (m_osVersion.MinorVersion==10)
        {
```

```
                m_platform=WINDOWS_98;
        }
        else if (m_osVersion.MinorVersion>10)
        {
                m_platform=WINDOWS_ME;
        }
    }
    else if (OSVersion.dwPlatformId==
                VER_PLATFORM_WIN32_NT)
    {
        m_osVersion.Build
            =OSVersion.dwBuildNumber;

        if (m_osVersion.MajorVersion<4)
        {
                m_platform=WINDOWS_NT;
        }
        else if (m_osVersion.MajorVersion == 4)
        {
                m_platform=WINDOWS_2K;
        }
        else if (m_osVersion.MajorVersion == 5)
        {
                m_platform=WINDOWS_XP;
        }
        else
        {
                m_platform=WINDOWS_FUTURE;
        }
    }
    else
    {
        m_platform          =UNKNOWN;
        m_osVersion.Build =OSVersion.dwBuildNumber;
    }

    //
    // Check for extended CPU facilities
    //
    m_cpuFlags = get_processor_flags();

}
```

LISTING A.5 Assembly-language functions for determining CPU features.

```
bool cpu_supports_cpuid()
{
    uint32 result=0;
    _asm{
        pushfd                      // Get original EFLAGS
        pop        eax
        mov        ecx, eax
        xor        eax, 200000h // Flip ID bit in EFLAGS
        push       eax          // Save new EFLAGS value
        popfd                   // Replace current EFLAGS
        pushfd                  // Get new EFLAGS
        pop        eax          // Store new EFLAGS in EAX
        xor        eax, ecx
        jz         THE_END      // Failure - NO CPUID

        // The processor supports the CPUID instruction.
        mov            result,1
    THE_END:
    }

    return (result ? true:false);
}

u32Flags get_cpu_feature_flags()
{
    u32Flags result=0;
    if(cpu_supports_cpuid())
    {
        _asm
        {
            pushad
            mov     eax,1              ; select feature flags
            cpuid
            mov     result,edx
            popad
        }
    }
    return (result);
}

// report if OS allows Intel SSE extensions
bool os_supports_sse_instructions()
{
```

```
        __try
        {
            __asm
            {
                pushad;
                // attempt an SSE call
                orps xmm1,xmm1;
                popad;
            }
        }
        __except(1)
        {
            return(false);
        }

        return(true);
}

// report if OS allows Intel SSE2 extensions
bool os_supports_sse2_instructions()
{
        __try
        {
            __asm
            {
                pushad;
                // attempt an SSE2 call
                paddq xmm1, xmm2
                popad;
            }
        }
        __except(1)
        {
            return(false);
        }

        return(true);
}

u32Flags get_processor_flags()
{
    u32Flags result=get_cpu_feature_flags();

    // if the SSE flags are set,
    // double-check with the OS
```

```
        if (result.testBit(25))
        {
            if (!os_supports_sse_instructions())
            {
                result.clearBit(25);
            }
            else
            {
                if (result.testBit(26))
                {
                    if (!os_supports_sse2_instructions())
                    {
                        result.clearBit(26);
                    }
                }
            }
        }
        return result;
}
```

LISTING A.6   Assembly-language functions for determining CPU speed.

```
void cSystemInfo::readCPUCounter(uint64 *pCounter)
{
    _asm
    {
        RDTSC
        mov edi, pCounter
        mov DWORD PTR [edi], eax
        mov DWORD PTR [edi+4], edx
    };
}

void cSystemInfo::computeProcessorSpeed()
{
    uint64 startTime, endTime;
    cTimer localTimer;

    // start the timer
    localTimer.start();
    // sample the cpu counter
    readCPUCounter(&startTime);
    // waste some time
    Sleep(100);
    // resample the cpu counter
```

```
    readCPUCounter(&endTime);
    // stop the clock
    localTimer.stop();

    // compute the CPU speed
    // as ticks per millisecond
    uint64 sampleDelta =
        endTime - startTime;
    uint32 elapsedMilliseconds =
        localTimer.elapsedMilliseconds();
    m_processorSpeed =
        (uint32)sampleDelta/elapsedMilliseconds;
}
```

ASSERT, WARNINGS, AND COMMENTS

The top priority for any suite of debugging tools is the humble assert macro. Assertions are a useful tool in checking assumptions within the code and trapping for error cases before they evolve into hard-to-find bugs. Essentially, the macros take some condition and panic if the condition turns out to be false. The panic is displayed in the form of a message box displayed on screen to show the failed assertion. Given the code assert($x==5$), a message box will appear if x does not equal 5 at the time the assert macro is processed. The Standard C library provides an assert macro that does an amiable job of trapping error cases, but it falls short in two key areas.

First, when the common assert macro traps an error, it puts up a message box with very little information. The only data presented to the user is the condition that caused the assert macro to fail. In practice, this could mean that the code assert ($x==17$) would trigger the panic case when $x!=17$ and display something cryptic like "Assertion Failed! Expression: $x==17$" in a message box. The information, while factual, is not very useful.

In fact, the only time the assert macro is useful is when the application is running within a debugging environment, or Just-In-Time debugging is enabled on the host machine. If either is true, the message box provides a button that will break into the code and grant the opportunity to inspect the problem. This is where the second shortcoming becomes apparent, because the break point actually resides inside the file assert.c, where the assert functionality lives. Since the application project usually does not contain the standard library's assert.c file, the first thing Visual C++ presents is a file dialog box asking for the location of assert.c. After canceling the file search dialog box and navigating up the call stack, the actual line of code that triggered the assertion can be found. Granted, these extra steps to get to the root of the problem are a minor annoyance, but they are a nuisance we can easily remove.

Given the goals of providing more useful information and granting the ability to break on the exact line of code containing the condition we are testing, the next step is to forge a replacement for the standard assert macro. Luckily, other programmers have been annoyed by the shortcomings of the standard C assert, and an ample list of good replacement ideas is available to us already. As with many areas of game programming, there are always others out there seeking answers to the same problems.

John Robbins, author of the "Bug Slayer" column for *Microsoft Systems Journal*, wrote about the idea of a Super Assert in his February 1999 article [Robbins]. Among other innovations, he added a complete stack trace to the output message box. Armed with call stack information, a programmer could deduce what had caused the error while running the application outside a debugging environment. This is common in beta testing, where the testers might not have full debugging environments at their disposal.

Steve Rabin contributed an article to the book *Game Programming Gems* [Rabin] that builds upon Robbins' work. His additions included adding clipboard-pasting functionality to the debug output, so the error text and call stack could be easily reported via e-mail or logged to a file. Rabin also introduced the idea of making the assert notification conditional, giving the user the option to switch a specific assert off while still allowing other asserts to function. These are both excellent ideas that we will employ in our own replacement for assert.

Finally, the folks at Microsoft provided a set of functions in the DirectX library that are also incredibly useful. DXGetErrorString9() and DXGetErrorDescription9() can convert DirectX and Win32 error codes into human-readable strings. Using these functions, we can provide a specific type of assert macro to trap errors reported when DirectX or Win32 functions fail.

Using all of these ideas, we will craft a set of assert macros of our own. However, unlike Rabin and Robbins, we will not be using a custom dialog box. Because we want to build the assertion into our static Core library, we do not have access to application resources such as a custom dialog box template. Instead, we will continue using the built-in Abort, Retry, Fail message box provided by Win32, albeit a little differently than the standard assert macro uses it.

Our first step is to build the function that will construct and display the message box, and then return the user's choice to abort, retry, or ignore the assert. Unlike the standard assert macro, the buttons of our message box retain their true meaning. Whereas the Retry button of the standard assert is used to break into the code, ours will imply that the user wants to continue processing the application. The Ignore button will be used to ignore all future occurrences of the specific assert condition being tested. The Abort button will ask the user if he wishes to exit the application or break into the code. Using these button definitions, we get all of our desired functionality while still using the buttons of the standard abort, retry, fail message box intuitively.

Armed with the ability to trace through the current call stack and create a sting of its contents (the code for which can be found in core\stack_trace.cpp on the accompanying CD-ROM), we can now construct our assertion reporting function. Its responsibilities include gathering all necessary information, building an output string of the assertion failure, and presenting the user with the abort, retry, fail message box. The user's reply to the message box is translated into enumerated values that describe what to do next. The function is shown in Listing A.7.

ON THE CD

LISTING A.7   Reporting errors to the user.

```
// Assert function return values
enum ERROR_RESULT
{
    VR_IGNORE = 0,
    VR_CONTINUE,
    VR_BREAKPOINT,
    VR_ABORT
};

ERROR_RESULT displayError(const tchar* errorTitle,
                          const tchar* errorText,
                          const tchar* errorDescription,
                          const tchar* fileName,
                          int lineNumber)
{
    const   int     NAME_SIZE = 255;
    tchar moduleName[NAME_SIZE];

    // attempt to get the module name
    if (!GetModuleFileName(NULL, moduleName, NAME_SIZE))
    {
        _tcscpy(moduleName, _text("<unknown application>"));
    }
```

```
                        // if stack tracing is enabled,
                        // build a string containing the
                        // unwound stack information
        #ifdef _STACKTRACE
                const    int      STACK_STRING_SIZE = 255;
                tchar stackText[STACK_STRING_SIZE];

                buildStackTrace(stackText, STACK_STRING_SIZE, 2);
        #else
                tchar stackText[] = _text("<stack trace disabled>");
        #endif

                        // build a colossal string containing
                        // the entire error message
                const    int      MAX_BUFFER_SIZE = 1024;
                tchar    buffer[MAX_BUFFER_SIZE];

                int Size =
                    _sntprintf(buffer,
                                MAX_BUFFER_SIZE,
                                _text(  "%s\n\n" \
                                "Program : %s\n" \
                                "File : %s\n" \
                                "Line : %d\n" \
                                "Error: %s\n" \
                                "Comment: %s\n" \
                                "\nStack:\n%s\n\n" \
                                "Abort to exit (or debug), "\
                                "Retry to continue,\n"\
                                "Ignore to disregard all occurrences"\
                                " of this error\n"),
                                errorTitle,
                                moduleName,
                                fileName,
                                lineNumber,
                                errorText,
                                errorDescription,
                                stackText
                                );

                        // place a copy of the message into the clipboard
                        if (OpenClipboard(NULL))
                        {
                            uint32 bufferLength = _tcsclen(buffer);
                            HGLOBAL hMem =
                              GlobalAlloc(GHND|GMEM_DDESHARE, bufferLength+1);
```

```
    if (hMem)
    {
        uint8* pMem = (uint8*)GlobalLock(hMem);
        memcpy(pMem, buffer, bufferLength);
        GlobalUnlock(hMem);
        EmptyClipboard();
        SetClipboardData(CF_TEXT, hMem);
    }

    CloseClipboard();
}

// find the top most window of the current application
HWND hWndParent = GetActiveWindow ( ) ;
if ( NULL != hWndParent )
{
    hWndParent = GetLastActivePopup ( hWndParent ) ;
}

// put up a message box with the error
int iRet = MessageBox(hWndParent,
                      buffer,
                      _text ( "ERROR NOTIFICATION..." ),
                      MB_TASKMODAL
                      |MB_SETFOREGROUND
                      |MB_ABORTRETRYIGNORE
                      |MB_ICONERROR);

// Figure out what to do on the return.
if (iRet == IDRETRY)
{
    // ignore this error and continue
    return (VR_CONTINUE);
}
if (iRet == IDIGNORE)
{
    // ignore this error and continue,
    // plus never stop on this error again
    return (VR_IGNORE);
}

// The return has to be IDABORT,
// but does the user want to enter the debugger
// or just exit the application?
iRet = MessageBox ( hWndParent,
```

```
                          "debug the last error?",
                          _text ( "DEBUG OR EXIT?" ),
                          MB_TASKMODAL
                          |MB_SETFOREGROUND
                          |MB_YESNO
                          |MB_ICONQUESTION);

        if (iRet == IDYES)
        {
            // inform the caller to break on the
            // current line of execution
            return (VR_BREAKPOINT);
        }

        // must be a full-on termination of the app
        ExitProcess ( (UINT)-1 ) ;
        return (VR_ABORT);
    }
```

With the `displayError` function in place, we can now build the macro that will call it to report our assertions when they fail. This macro tests the condition supplied, and calls the `displayError` when the condition is not met. By incorporating brackets into the macro itself, the code will expand to create a local scope in which a static variable can also be contained. This variable is used to decide whether the assert failure should be reported to the user. When the user chooses to ignore all further errors caused by this assert, the internal static variable is set to prevent the message box from displaying again.

When the user chooses to debug the code in question, interrupt number 3 is signaled, which equates to a code break on Intel-based CPUs. The line `_asm{int 3}` causes the debugger, if present, to break into the code at the exact line containing the interrupt. Since our signaling of the interrupt is embedded in the macro, the debugger will display the line of code that contained our original assert condition. Source code for the `debug_assert` macro is shown in Listing A.8.

LISTING A.8   Controlling assertions with a macro.

```
#define debug_assert(x, comment) {\
        static bool _ignoreAssert = false;\
        if (!_ignoreAssert && !(x)) \
        {\
            ERROR_RESULT _err_result =  \
```

```
            displayError(_test("debug assert!"),\
            _text(#x), _text(comment), \
            __FILE__, __LINE__); \
        if (_err_result == VR_IGNORE) \
        {\
            _ignoreAssert = true; \
        }\
        else if (_err_result == VR_BREAKPOINT)\
        {\
            _asm{int 3};\
        }\
    }}
```

Unlike the standard assert macro, our `debug_assert` takes a comment string as well as the condition to test. This comment is passed on to the `displayError` function when the assert condition (x) fails. This allows the programmer to report meaningful text information inside the message box. For example, suppose you had a bit field of 32 members and you wanted to post an error anytime someone tried to request a bit outside the 0–31 range. The following assertion failure will display a message box whenever an invalid index is provided:

```
debug_assert(index>=0 && index<32,
        "invalid bit index requested");
```

The last piece of functionality to add is the use of the DirectX functions `DXGetErrorString9()` and `DXGetErrorDescription9()` to report human- readable strings from DirectX and Win32 error codes. To provide this functionality, we add a second function to convert an error code to a set of strings and pass them to the `displayError` function. To add a little more ease of use to this function, when it is called with an error code of zero, it will internally call `GetLastError` to determine the last known error code. This is useful for Win32 functions that return something other than an error code, but set an internal error code when they fail. Listing A.9 shows the source code for error reporting, and the macro that uses it.

LISTING A.9   Looking up Win32 and DirectX error codes and reporting them to the user.

```
ERROR_RESULT notifyError(uint32 errorCode, const tchar*
    fileName, int lineNumber)
{
    // if no error code is provided,
    // get the last known error
```

```
            if (errorCode == 0)
            {
                errorCode = GetLastError();
            }

            // use DirectX to supply a string and
            // description for our error.
            // This will handle all known DirectX
            // error codes (HRESULTs)
            // as well as Win32 error codes normally
            // found via FormatMessage
            const tchar* pErrorString =
                DXGetErrorString9(errorCode);
            const tchar* pErrorDescription =
                DXGetErrorDescription9(errorCode);

            // pass the data on to the message box
            ERROR_RESULT result = displayError( _text("Error!"),
                                            pErrorString,
                                            pErrorDescription,
                                            fileName,
                                            lineNumber);

            // Put the incoming last error back.
            SetLastError(errorCode);

            return(result);
        }

        #define debug_error(x) {\
                static bool _ignoreError = false;\
                if (!_ignoreError) \
                {\
                    ERROR_RESULT _err_result = notifyError((x), \
                    __FILE__, __LINE__);\
                    if (_err_result == VR_IGNORE)\
                    {\
                        _ignoreError = true;\
                    }\
                    else if (_err_result == VR_BREAKPOINT)\
                    {\
                        _asm{int 3};\
                    }\
                }}
```

COMPILE-TIME ASSERTS

Assertions that trigger during the execution of the application are very useful, but occasionally there are conditions we want to trap during compilation. These are usually traps we place within the code to catch ourselves from coding something destructive. Asserts where we verify the size of a given object, the count of certain objects, or other sensitive information, are vital to keeping ourselves in check.

One such example is bit flags. Suppose we have created a `cBitFlags` object with 8 bits of information to identify a game object such as a monster. In addition, we want to identify each bit within the bit flags separately using enumerated values. This way, we can inquire about the monster more easily to figure out what type it is. We might create an enumeration similar to the following:

```
enum eBitFlagIndices
{
    k_hasFangs = 0,
    k_hasClaws,
    k_smellsAwful,
    ..etc
    k_totalBitFlags,
};
```

As you can see, if we add eight `enum` values, they will be automatically numbered from 0 to 7, providing perfect index values with which to query the bit flags object. Likewise, the final value, `k_totalBitFlags`, will contain the total number of bit indices in the `enum`, eight. However, what if we revisit this `enum` at some point in the future and mistakenly add a ninth index value? Unless we check the index range elsewhere with asserts, our code will attempt to set and read a ninth bit in an 8-bit value, creating a bug. Even if we do perform a runtime assert to trap this case, we won't find it until we trigger the section of code that uses this `enum`. In short, some time might pass before we actually detect this simple bug.

A simple way to protect against such things is to add a compile-time assert to the code. In this particular example, we know that `k_totalBit-Flags` must be equal to or less than 8 for the bit flags object to perform within its scope of 8 bits. This is an easy value to test, but how do we do so during compilation time rather than at the point of execution?

The answer is to create invalid code. This way, the compiler will fail to build the application until we fix the problem. To build the bogus code, we use another macro that takes our conditional expression and converts it to invalid code when the condition is not true. We do this using a switch statement within the macro. The switch contains a case for values of 0, and one for a value based on our condition.

```
#define compiler_assert(x) {\
        const int _value = (x) ? 1:0;\
        switch (x)\
        {\
            case 0: \
            case _value: \
            default: break;\
        };}
```

When the condition (x) is true, _value becomes 1, giving us two perfectly reasonable cases within the switch statement. When the condition fails, however, _value becomes 0 and we have two redundant case statements within the switch. This creates invalid code that the compiler will catch and report as an error.

There are two limitations with this method, the first being the obvious condition that the condition being tested is something that can be determined at compile time. This includes the value of constants and sizes determined by the sizeof() operator. The second limitation is that the compiler_assert macro must still be used within a function that is being compiled. Keep in mind that template functions are not compiled unless they are actually used by other sections of the code. Therefore, compiler_assert macros placed in these sections will not be compiled and verified.

DEBUG TEXT MESSAGES

Quite often, we find the need to track the progress of the application through various functions and libraries. Perhaps we need to track the value of some variable, the state of some object, or the number of times a given condition happens. Performing this type of monitoring with assert macros would convert the application to a mess of message boxes and halting conditions. Instead, we'll add a robust debug message manager that allows us to output text strings to the user in order to monitor the application.

OutputDebugString performs the task natively, dumping whatever string is passed to it into the standard output window. However, it can be very limiting, especially if we want to output the value of some variable and need to build a custom string to do so. If we also want to log the string information to a file instead of passing it to the output window, we will need to create a separate solution to do so, and then decide at each message location whether the information should go to `OutputDebugString`, some log file controller, or both.

Instead, we will create a single debug message handler that allows us to build the output string on-the-fly, and categorize the string so the message handler can decide where to send it. We do this by providing 32 message types, designated by a bit field that is specified with each debug message. We can then plug in a listener, which we call a debug channel, that watches message types to flow into the debug message handler. These channels can then route the message to the output window, a file, or anywhere else we choose. This provides us with a great deal of flexibility when recording specific logs of engine performance data, user input, or error messages. It also provides us with a plug-in interface we can extend for future debugging needs, such as remote network monitoring.

First, we need to define what a debug channel is, and how it operates. Our implementation is little more than a virtual interface to handle the basics of message output. Since some channels might be linked to files or other external resources, we provide a common interface that allows the channel to be opened, written to, and closed. There is no distinction between opening a channel for overwriting or appending, the assumption being that all channels are opened once at the start of the application, written to for the duration of the application's lifetime, and then closed at the end. Each debug channel also needs to specify a set of bit flags for the message types it watches for. The basic class definition is shown in Listing A.10, along with a specific example of a message channel derived from it to post all messages to the standard output window. In the core header file `debug_channel.h`, there is also a specialized channel object called `cFileOutputChannel` that can be used to log messages to disk.

LISTING A.10 **The debug channel base class and a specific instance derived from it to output message to the standard output buffer.**

```
class cDebugMessageChannel
{
public:

    // a public set of bitflags used to filter messages
    u32Flags messageFilter;

    cDebugMessageChannel():messageFilter(0){}
    virtual ~cDebugMessageChannel(){}
```

```
private:

    // these functions are only called by the
    // cDebugMessageHandler object
    friend cDebugMessageHandler;
    virtual bool open(){return true;}
    virtual void close(){}
    virtual bool write(const tchar* pText){}
};

class cSystemDebugChannel : public cDebugMessageChannel
{
public:

    cSystemDebugChannel()
    {
        // accept all message types
        messageFilter = 0xffffffff;
    }
    ~cSystemDebugChannel(){}

private:

    // output all text to the standard output buffer
    bool write(const tchar* pText)
    {
        _tprintf(pText);
        _tprintf(_text("\n"));
        return true;
    }
};
```

Now that the basics are out of the way, we can build the message handler to receive all the input and route it accordingly. This is a simple class that accepts string input categorized by a set of message type flags, and then searches through a list of known listener channels for all members who need to be sent the message. We provide 32 message type flags, and up to 32 user-defined channels for routing the information. We limit ourselves to 32 so that we can store both sets of information, the message filter and the active channels, in 32-bit values.

The class interface allows for the user to add and remove active debug channels, activate or deactivate them, and output text messages to the active channels. By default, we construct the class with a built-in cSystemDebugChannel object (see Listing A.10) so it's ready for use immediately. Adding additional channels or changing the properties of the default system channel is up to the programmer.

The tricky part is being able to build the input string on-the-fly, which involves the use of ellipsis (. . .) arguments. Ellipses allow for a variable number of arguments to a function, which is the way string-building functions such as printf get their flexibility. Since we want the same flexibility, we will use the same method of allowing optional arguments. In fact, out text input function does little more than package the ellipsis arguments into the corresponding variable-argument list object (va_list) and pass them to a slightly different version of the printf to build our string.

Listing A.11 shows the text output functions. We build three functions to get the job done: one that actually does the work (processMessage), and two versions of an output function. The two versions allow us to send text output to the message handler with or without a message type flag. When the flag is omitted, an internal default message flag is used. This allows us to create simple macros such as TRACE to output text messages without requiring a message flag every time.

LISTING A.11   The three member functions of cDebugMessageHandler that handle receiving and processing text messages.

```
// route text input using the internal default message flag
void cDebugMessageHandler::output(const tchar* text, ...)
{
    // build the va_list of optional arguments
    va_list     arglist;
    va_start(arglist, text);

    // call the va_list version of output
    processMessage(k_defaultMessageFlag, text, arglist);

    // end the optional argument list use
    va_end(arglist);
}

// route text input using the message flag provided
void cDebugMessageHandler::output(uint32 messageFlags,
        const tchar* text, ...)
{
    // build the va_list of optional arguments
    va_list     arglist;
    va_start(arglist, text);
```

```cpp
        // call the va_list version of output
        processMessage(messageFlags, text, arglist);

        // end the optional argument list use
        va_end(arglist);
    }


// the function which handles the actual
// routing of text messages
void cDebugMessageHandler::processMessage(
            uint32 messageFlags,
            const tchar* text,
            va_list arglist)
{
    // are any channels currently open?
    if (m_openChannels)
    {
        // build our output string
        tchar   buffer[nMaxOutputStringSize+1];
        int Size = _vsntprintf(buffer,
                                nMaxOutputStringSize,
                                text,
                                arglist);

        // if a string was built...
        if(Size > 0)
        {
            // run through all the channels
            for (int i=0; i<nMaxChannels; ++i)
            {
                // if the channel is open
                // and it accepts this message type...
                if (m_openChannels.testBit(i)
        && m_channel[i]->messageFilter.testAny(messageFlags))
                {
                    // then send the message through
                    m_channel[i]->write(buffer);
                }
            }
        }
    }
}
```

CODE TIMING

Other than trapping errors and outputting text messages to ourselves to monitor the application, we also need a simple means to periodically test the efficiency of the code we are writing. Specialized performance monitoring tools such as the Intel VTune™ program or Compuware® DevPartner Profiler™ can provide detailed performance feedback, but we would still benefit from a profiling method that functions without the need for such external tools. There is also the occasional need for real-time performance feedback, where timing information for a specific function is only relevant during key situations. To provide high-level timing feedback, we will create a set of functions to monitor the speed of our application wherever we desire to do so. As with the error assertions and text output functions, we will do this via macros so that our final release builds will not contain any of this extra monitoring code.

A simple timer object is the first component of this profiling system. This class uses the `QueryPerformanceCounter` method to sample time values from the system. This is arguably faster (and more accurate) than other time sampling methods such as `timeGetTime` and `GetTickCount`, but not as efficient as using the target CPU's built-in performance monitoring counters. Because such CPU performance counters are vendor specific, we will avoid them for our basic timer class. However, the simple timer interface we will create will allow us to convert the timer to CPU-specific methods in the future should the need for greater accuracy arise.

The `cTimer` object provides this simple interface, allowing us to start, stop, pause, and un-pause a timer and read the time value at any moment. Time is reported in floating-point values as fractional seconds. We do this because this class object will be used for our code profiling, and for general-purpose timers within our application. Having a universal framework for time values makes using these timer objects more intuitive.

One specific type of `cTimer` object is the application timer, which we launch at the start of the application and let run until the program closes. At any time, we can then query the application timer to get the elapsed time spent executing our program. The `cApplicationTimer` class handles this for us. As a class based on `cTimer`, `cApplicationTimer` adds no new functionality other than to immediately begin a timing session upon construction, and terminate that session upon destruction. This allows us to create a global instance of this class object, simply named `applicationTimer`, which is created and destroyed along with the application. Getting the current time for any point in our code is then just a simple matter of calling `applicationTimer.elapsedTime`. The `cTimer` and `cApplicationTimer` class definitions can be found on the CD-ROM in the `timer.h` and `application_timer.h` files.

With the timer objects in place, the next method to define is how we will add timing operations to our code to monitor efficiency. To monitor a section of code over time, data must be tracked regarding the total amount of time spent in the code and the number of times the code was executed. An average execution time can be computed from this data. To provide more information, the minimum and maximum time samples recorded for all executions of the code will also be tracked. This gives additional insight into the maximum fluctuation in efficiency for the code being examined.

Listing A.12 shows the class object used to track this information, `cCodeTimer`. This class also contains a pair of pointers to a previous and next `cCodeTimer` object—allowing us to chain them all together into a linked list. Rather than using a fixed-size table of `cCodeTimer` objects, the linked list approach allows a more flexible number of code timers to be active throughout the engine.

LISTING A.12   The cCodeTimer object definition and key member functions.

```
class cCodeTimer
{
public:

    static cCodeTimer RootTimer;

    // Data Types & Constants...
    enum eConstants
    {
        k_maxNameLength = 32
    };

    // Public Data...

    // Creators...

    cCodeTimer(const tchar* name_string);
    ~cCodeTimer(){};

    // Operators...

    // Mutators...
    void beginSession();
```

```
    void endSession();
    void reset();

    void resetAllTimers();
    void outputAllTimers(u32Flags MessageFlags);

    // Accessors...
    float   averageTime()const;
    float   totalTime()const;
    uint32  totalCalls()const;

    float   maximumTimeSample()const;
    float   minimumTimeSample()const;

    const tchar* name()const;

private:

    // Private Data...
    cCodeTimer* m_nextProfile;
    cCodeTimer* m_lastProfile;

    float   m_totalTime;
    uint32  m_totalCalls;

    float   m_maximumTimeSample;
    float   m_minimumTimeSample;

    tchar   m_name[k_maxNameLength];
    float   m_startTime;

    static cCodeTimer* s_previousTimer;
};

// the constructor.
cCodeTimer::cCodeTimer(const tchar* name_string)
:m_nextProfile(0)
,m_lastProfile(s_previousTimer)
,m_totalTime(0.0f)
,m_totalCalls(0)
,m_maximumTimeSample(0.0f)
,m_minimumTimeSample(0.0f)
,m_startTime(0.0f)
{
    debug_assert(name_string,
```

```
                    "A name must be provided to the code timer");

        // record the timer's name
        lstrcpyn(m_name,name_string, k_maxNameLength);

        // append ourselves to the chain of timers
        if (s_previousTimer)
        {
            s_previousTimer->m_nextProfile = this;
        }
        s_previousTimer = this;
    }


// begin timing a section of code
void cCodeTimer::beginSession()
{
    ++m_totalCalls;

    if (!m_startTime)
    {
        m_startTime = applicationTimer.elapsedTime();
    }
}


// stop timing a section of code
void cCodeTimer::endSession()
{
    if (m_startTime)
    {
        float endTime = applicationTimer.elapsedTime();
        float sample = endTime - m_startTime;
        m_totalTime += sample;

        m_maximumTimeSample =
            maximum(m_maximumTimeSample, sample);
        m_minimumTimeSample =
            minimum(m_maximumTimeSample, sample);

        m_startTime = 0.0f;
    }
}
```

All cCodeTimer objects are held as static data within the code they are profiling. Placing these objects within the code pollutes the area being monitored, but for high-level profiling such as this, the cost should be minimal. A static member within the `cCodeTimer` object itself tracks a pointer to the last `cCodeTimer` object created, so new `cCodeTimer` objects can link to it and continue the chain. As monitored code is encountered, static `cCodeTimer` objects are created and extend the chain. Listing A.13 shows the macros used to create these static objects using names provided to the macro to construct the local instances of each `cCodeTimer`.

LISTING A.13   Macros used to embed a `cCodeTimer` object within the code being monitored.

```
// begin a profile session called [name] by
// creating a local static member called _ct_[name]
// and beginning a profile session with it
#define begin_profile(name) static \
    cCodeTimer _ct_##name(_text(#name));\
    _ct_##name.beginSession();

// end the profile session by name
#define end_profile(name) _ct_##name.endSession();
```

Monitoring a section of code is a simple matter of dropping the begin and end profile macros around the code and providing them with a matching name describing the code. For example, to profile the time spent in a loop, the following code could be written:

```
begin_profile(main_game_loop);
    while(!finished)
    {
            // run the game…
    };
    end_profile(main_game_loop);
```

Using the macros shown in Listing A.13, the compiler will expand this code to create a local, static `cCodeTimer` object, and profile the section of code desired.

```
static cCodeTimer _ct_main_game_loop("main_game_loop");
    _ct_main_game_loop.beginSession();
    while(!finished)
    {
            // run the game
    };
    _ct_main_game_loop.endSession();
```

To periodically query the values held within the code timers, the static function `outputAllTimers` can be called with a set of message flags. Internally, the `cCodeTimer` class will run through all objects held in the linked list and transmit their data as a string to the `cDebugMessageHandler` object. Using the message flag provided, the text output will be routed to the proper debug channel, allowing us to display the data in the output window, log it to a file—whatever we want. This provides a convenient way to take snapshots of application performance at runtime.

To further enable easy code profiling, another automatic class can be used to profile any given scope within the source code. Just as the `cApplicationTimer` object granted automatic use of a `cTimer` object over its lifetime, we can create a profiling object to manage code timing during its existence. By starting a profile session upon creation, and closing the session upon destruction, we can profile the amount of time spent while a given object is in scope—providing a profile of the scope itself. Listing A.14 shows the source code for this simple profiling class, `cScopeTimer`, and the `profile_scope` macro that makes use of it.

As with the other code timing macros, the `profile_scope` macro creates a static `cCodeTimer` object based on the unique name it is given. This object is static, so it is only created and added to the `cCodeTimer` linked list upon the first execution of this macro. The `profile_scope` macro also creates a temporary `cScopeTimer`, and passes it a pointer to the code timing object. As long as the `cScopeTimer` object remains active, the code will be profiled. As soon as the `cScopeTimer` goes out of scope and is destroyed, the profile session will automatically end. Therefore, placing a single `profile_scope` macro at the top of a function will profile the entire function from the point of the macro until the function returns.

LISTING A.14   The cScopeTimer object, and the macro used to automate its use.

```
class cScopeTimer
{
public:
    cScopeTimer(cCodeTimer* timer)
    :m_internalTimerLink(timer)
    {
        debug_assert(m_internalTimerLink,
            "A timer link must be provided");
        m_internalTimerLink->beginSession();
    }

    ~cScopeTimer()
```

```
    {
        m_internalTimerLink->endSession();
    }

private:
    cCodeTimer* m_internalTimerLink;
};

#define profile_scope(name) static \
    cCodeTimer _ct_##name(_text(#name));\
    cScopeTimer _ft_name(&_ct_##name);
```

REFERENCES

[Rabin] Rabin, S., "Squeezing More Out of Assert." *Game Programming Gems*. Charles River Media, Inc., 2000, pp.109–114.

[Robbins] Robbins, J. "Bugslayer." *Microsoft Systems Journal*. February 1999. (available online at *www.microsoft.com/msj/defaultframe.asp?page=/msj/0299/bugslayer/bugslayer0299.htm*).

[Wyatt] Wyatt, R. "Processor Detection and a Pentium III Update." (available online at *www.gamasutra.com/features/wyatts_world/19990709/processor_detection_01.htm*).

FLOATING-POINT TRICKS

Having a core set of numeric tools that deals with integer values is one thing, but the Gaia toolset must be as robust as possible. The whole point of spending the time to build a toolset for pushing bits around is to make our lives easier down the road, so we desire a consistent interface to deal with integer and floating-point numbers alike. The simple way is to have the floating-point versions of our numeric tools call out to the Standard C Math Library for support. For many of the numeric tools, this is exactly what we will do, but for a select few we will bypass the Standard C Library and create our own implementations.

Using floating-point numbers on a computer built to work in a binary fashion creates two issues with which to contend: speed and accuracy. Speed is a concern because while the Standard C Math Library contains every floating-point arithmetic operation we could ever need, many are too slow for frequent use. A dedicated Floating-point Processing Unit (FPU) is the only thing separating us from the days of fixed-point math libraries.

Accuracy becomes an issue when you consider that the computer cannot really represent floating-point numbers in the first place. What we get instead are approximations that deviate from their true values by some slight margin. As these approximated values are used together in math operations, the deviations are compounded, and the result can be slightly off from the value expected. The result? Equations you expect to return zero sometimes return tiny values like 1.0e-13, vectors you normalize end up with lengths slightly over or under a unit length, and bounding boxes you think are side by side overlap by incredibly tiny margins. It's enough to take the fun out of floating-point math.

In the numeric tools section of the core library, a few helpful utilities and macros will be added to address these problems. To do so, a basic understanding of the floating-point format is needed. The format is defined by the Institute of Electrical and Electronics Engineers, Inc. (IEEE), and has been adopted by most, if not all, computer processor manufacturers.

335

I'm not a big fan of reading through IEEE specifications, and I doubt you are either. Luckily for us, programmers treaded this path before and created ample documentation of the IEEE standard and tricks to abuse it.

EXAMINING FLOATING-POINT DATA

Floating-point data is held by the computer in a specific bit pattern designed for their storage. By peeking at the bits in this pattern, we can dissect a floating-point number and glean some key information about it. The format for an IEEE-compliant, 32-bit floating-point number is defined as a single sign bit followed by 8 bits of exponent and 23 bits of mantissa. Figure B.1 shows the bit pattern for single-precision floating-point numbers.

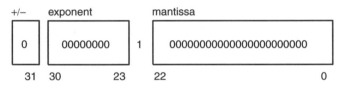
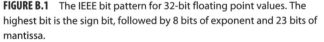

FIGURE B.1   The IEEE bit pattern for 32-bit floating point values. The highest bit is the sign bit, followed by 8 bits of exponent and 23 bits of mantissa.

Not many carbon-based life forms use exponents and mantissas to express values, so the format might seem a bit foreign at first. We will walk through an example and then explore some methods to work with the floating-point format without concerning ourselves with mantissas and exponents. The example will consist of converting a decimal value, 8.75, to a set of bits in floating-point format.

To convert a decimal value to the floating-point bit pattern, it must first be expressed in binary form. The value 8.75 is a little tricky to convert, because it contains a fractional value. Converting the whole portion, 8, is easy enough—it becomes the binary value 1000. To convert the fractional part (.75), remember that bit locations to the right of the decimal point represent the values 2^{-1}, 2^{-2}, 2^{-3}, and so on. These bit positions can also be thought of as ½, ¼, ⅛, and so on. Therefore, .75, which is the same as ½ (the first binary bit) plus ¼ (the second binary bit), becomes .11 in binary. The two values are then joined together to represent 8.75 in binary as 1000.11.

Converting to binary isn't much of a challenge, but the floating-point format is designed to hold the value in scientific format. To be exact, it's designed to reflect a normalized value in scientific format. That's quite a mouthful, but it's rather simple to create such a value. All that is required is to normalize the binary number. This is just a fancy way of saying "move the binary point to the right of the most significant bit, and record the binary point move as the exponent." This converts the value from 1000.11 to the equivalent, normalized, scientific-notation version 1.00011 x 2^3. This is the original value normalized by shifting the binary point three places to the left and recording the 3-bit move as the exponent.

When broken down into the component parts, 1.00011 x 2^3 can be read as a mantissa of 1.00011, an exponent of 3, and a sign bit of 0 (the value is positive). These are the three values needed to fill the floating-point data structure, but there are still a couple of hoops to jump through to build the final bit pattern.

First, the exponent must be expressed in biased form. Exponents can be positive or negative, but there are only eight bits provided to represent them within the floating-point data format. The IEEE format handles this by dividing the exponent value range into two halves: positive and negative. Consider that the 8 bits can hold 256 individual values (0 through 255). By splitting this range in half, one of the halves can be used for negative numbers and one for positive. The bias value is 127, since it is the halfway point that represents zero. Negative values fall in the range 0 through 126, and positive values are in the range 128 through 255. To store an exponent, simply add the bias to it to move it to the proper half-space. The exponent value of 3 (from the previous example) would be stored as 127 + 3 or 130, three units into the positive half-space.

Next is the straightforward task of creating the value stored in the mantissa. All floating-point mantissas are stored in normalized, binary form. You'll recall that to normalize a binary number, you simply move the binary point to the right of the highest bit that is set. This means that all normalized binary numbers will be in the format 1.x, where x can be any trailing number of bits. Since it is guaranteed that there is only one bit present to the left of the binary point, there is no need to store it. The floating-point data format only stores the bits of the mantissa to the right of the binary point. The single bit left of the decimal point is discarded, but will still be used in all floating-point calculations as the implied high bit of the mantissa. Given the mantissa of 1.00011 from the previous example, the bits actually stored would be 00011, followed by 18 bits of zero to pad out the 23-bit mantissa space.

Now, all three pieces of the floating-point data format are ready to go. The example input value, 8.75, has been converted to its normalized-scientific form, 1.00011×2^3. The exponent value, 3, generated by the normalization, has been biased to fit in 8 bits of space as the value 130, and the implied high bit has been removed from the mantissa. The final floating-point bit pattern can now be built by setting the sign bit (zero for the positive source value of 8.75), shifting the 8-bit exponent into position, and setting the mantissa bits. The result is shown in Figure B.2.

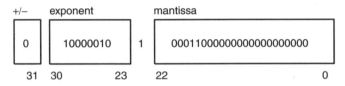

FIGURE B.2   8.75 converted to floating-point format 8.75 in binary form is 1000.11, or 1.00011×2^3 when normalized. This equates to a sign bit of 0, an exponent value of 3, and a mantissa of 1.00011. The exponent is biased to the value 130 (binary 10000010), and the high bit of the mantissa is removed for storage, leaving 00011 as the mantissa bits stored, padded out to fill the 23-bit mantissa space.

So, how can all this mantissa and exponent data be viewed in a simpler way? The key is to think of the stored components as a bit-shifting recipe rather than scientific notation. The 8-bit exponent value is 130, which converts back to the original exponent value 3 when the bias value is subtracted. This is the exact number of binary places the 23-bit mantissa value must be shifted to the left to get back the original value.

The mantissa bits are 00011 (plus 18 bits of trailing zeroes), which becomes 1.00011 when the implied high bit and binary point are replaced. If the binary point is shifted three places to the right, it will create the original value of 1000.11, or 8.75. Therefore, rather than thinking of floating-point values as a sign, exponent, and mantissa in scientific terms, they can be thought of as a sign bit, a shift count, and a value to be shifted.

Armed with this knowledge, we can look as some tricks that exploit the IEEE format. Some handy macros can be defined to perform the bit encoding and decoding tasks. These become the building blocks for the various tricks we will create.

```
// reinterpret a float as an int32
  #define fpBits(f) (*reinterpret_cast<const int32*>(&(f)))
```

```
// reinterpret an int32 as a float
#define intBits(i) (*reinterpret_cast<const float*>(&(i)))
// return 0 or -1 based on the sign of the float
#define fpSign(i) (fpBits(f)>31)
// extract the 8 bits of exponent as a signed integer
// by masking out this bits, shifting down by 23,
// and subtracting the bias value of 127
#define fpExponent(f) (((fpBits(f)&0x7fffffff)>23)-127)
// return 0 or -1 based on the sign of the exponent
#define fpExponentSign(f) (fpExponent(f)>31)
// get the 23 bits of mantissa with the implied bit
replaced
#define fpMantissa(f) ((fpBits(f)&0x7fffff)| (1<<23))
```

THE SIGN BIT

The first thing to notice is that the sign bit for floating-point numbers resides in the most-significant bit; exactly the same position as in 32-bit integer values. This means that the sign of floating-point numbers can be found by treating them as integer values. This can be done by aliasing a floating-point value as an integer, and then testing the sign of the integer value.

The samesigns() template function created in the last chapter can now be updated with this knowledge. For two floating-point numbers to have the same signs, they must have the same sign bit. Comparing their signs is just a matter of comparing sign bits of each value. To do this, the function converts each bit into a mask with a shift operation, and then simply compares the masks. The fpSign() macro is used to do the reinterpret_cast and shifting for us.

```
template<>
    inline bool SameSigns(float ValueA, float ValueB)
    {
        return (fpSign(ValueA) == fpSign(ValueB));
    }
```

Converting floating-point numbers to their absolute values is also trivial when using the sign bit. Up until now, the template function abs() used the Standard C Library function fabs(), but it's just as simple to do the work ourselves. To force any floating-point number to be positive, the sign bit must be cleared in bit position 31. By performing a bitwise-and operation with a mask containing the lower 30 bits, any floating-point number can be converted to its absolute value.

```
template <> inline float abs(float value)
{
    uint32 absValue = fpBits(value);
    absValue &= 7fffffff;

    return intBits(absValue);
}
```

CONVERSION FROM FLOATING-POINT TO INTEGER VALUES

The Standard C Library method to convert from floating-point to integer values is unbearably slow; something in the order of 60 processor cycles, depending on the platform and compiler. The other obstacle to overcome is that the ANSI C Standard dictates that fractional values are truncated when floating-point numbers are converted to integer values—which is not always the action desired. Both of these issues make the Standard C Library convention of converting float to integer values undesirable for the Gaia engine.

In the math library, pre-computed lookup tables will be used to avoid costly floating-point math routines such a sine and cosine calculations. In order to facilitate the use of a lookup table, a fast, reliable way to convert floating-point source values into integer table indexes will be needed. In addition, different rounding methods might be required when converting fractional values to their integer counterparts. A few tricky conversion methods for 32-bit floating-point values can address all of these needs.

The first step is to emulate the simple ANSI cast operation, truncating all fractional values of the floating-point source value to find the integer result. The steps are laid out in the function realToInt32(), shown in Listing B.1. Don't worry about the flipSign() macro just yet; its purpose will be explained as we examine the conversion process.

LISTING B.1   Converting 32-bit floating-point numbers to integers.

```
// flipSign is a helper Macro to
// invert the sign of i if flip equals -1,
// if flip equals 0, it does nothing
#define flipSign(i, flip) ((i^ flip) - flip)

inline int32 realToInt32 (const float& f)
{
    // read the exponent and decide how much we need to
    // shift the mantissa down
```

```
    int32 shift = 23-fpExponent(f);
    // read the mantissa and shift it down to remove all
    // fractional values
    int32 result = fpMantissa(f)>shift;
    // set the sign of the new result
    result = flipSign(result, fpSign(f));
    // if the exponent was negative, i.e. (-1.0 < f < 1.0)
    // we must return zero
    result &= ~fpExponentSign(f);
    // return the result
    return result;
}
```

Let's walk through this conversion to understand what it does. The first step is to determine the amount we will need to shift the mantissa. The exponent value would normally describe the position to place the binary point within the mantissa to reconstruct the floating-point value. Since the binary point currently resides above bit 23, shifting the mantissa value to the right by (23-exponent) steps will leave only the bits to the left of the binary point. The second step reads the mantissa value from the float value (replacing the implied 1 in the 24th bit) and executes the shift, producing an integer version of the source float with all fractional values removed.

If it was known that the incoming float value was positive, and that the value was not purely fractional (outside the range [−1.0, 1.0]), the function could stop here. However, for this function to handle general floating-point input, a few extra steps are required to handle negative numbers and numbers inside the [−1.0, 1.0] range.

To handle negative numbers, the flipSign() macro is used. This macro employs a handy trick to flip the sign of an integer value based on an input mask. The mask must be 0 or −1, which equates to having either all bits clear or all bits set. When all bits are clear, the macro has no effect. When all bits in the flip mask are set, the combination of bitwise-XOR and subtraction operations uses the mask to invert the sign of the input value i, changing it from positive to negative or vice versa. Because this is a bitwise operation coupled with a subtraction, it can occur much faster than multiplying the input value by −1 to invert its sign.

The realToInt32 function can take advantage of this macro because the routine has produced a positive integer value thus far, even when the source floating-point value is negative. If the source value is negative, the sign of the integer result must be inverted. Remember that the sign bit for a floating-point value is held in bit 31. If the floating-point bit pattern is shifted to the right by 31 places, it will be converted it to a mask of all 0s for positive values and all 1s for negative values. Coincidentally, this is exactly what the `flipSign()` macro needs. If the incoming source value is positive, an empty mask is created and the macro does nothing. If the incoming source value is negative, a full mask is created and the macro inverts the sign of the integer result.

The final step is to handle purely fractional values; values between −1.0 and 1.0. If the incoming value is within this range, the integer result computed up to this point will be wrong. The correct value to return is zero, since all fractional floating-point values between −1.0 and 1.0 equate to an integer value of zero when truncating. To test for this case, the same sign-bit-to-mask trick used for inverting the sign is used, this time using the sign of the exponent value to build the mask.

If a floating-point value is between −1.0 and 1.0, its exponent will be negative. If a mask is built from the sign bit of the exponent, it will be empty for positive exponents and full for negative exponents. If the mask is inverted, it can be used in a bitwise-and operation to convert the integer result into zero when necessary.

The result is a quick method to convert floating-point values to their equivalent integers. When compared to a standard typecast in C, this new method runs about five to six times faster. The method can also provide additional gains, since it does not use the floating-point unit at all. This leaves the FPU available to process other floating-point operations in parallel.

To handle other rounding methods, the `numeric_tools.h` header file also contains routines to convert between floating-point and integer values using floor, ceiling, and nearest integer rounding methods. These additional functions build upon basic methods defined here by determining which bits of the mantissa appear to the right of the binary point. This fractional value is used to decide whether the integer result should be incremented or decremented, depending on the rounding method used.

LIMITING FLOATING-POINT PRECISION

Floating-point numbers can have incredible precision—this can be both an asset and a curse. When working with tiny values, floating-point precision is perfectly suited to the task. However, when miniscule precision is not needed, it can cause trouble when you least expect it. Slight inaccuracies in floating-point math can sometimes lead to unexpected results. In the `numeric_tools.h` header file, we will add a function to help alleviate this problem.

Now that we understand how to read the IEEE floating-point format, we can use that knowledge to control the floating-point precision. In cases where precision must be limited, the fractional value can be read from the mantissa, and replaced with a lesser number of bits to truncate the precision. This will allow functions to control how many bits of precision (up to 23) are allowed to follow the binary point. Listing B.2 shows the method at work, taking a floating-point value and precision count as input and returning a rounded floating-point value.

LISTING B.2   Reducing floating-point precision.

```
float trimFloat(float input, int32 precision)
{
float result = input;
int32 exponent      = fpExponent(input);
int32 bias          = 23 - (exponent + precision);

if (bias < 1)
{
    return result;
}

if (bias > 24)
{
    result = 0.0f;
    return result;
}
int32 value         = fpBits(input);

if (bias == 24)
{
    value &= (1<<31);
    exponent = -precision;
    value += (exponent+127)<<23;
    memcpy(&result, &value, sizeof(value));

    return result;
}

_asm
{
    clc
    mov ecx, bias
    mov eax, value
```

```
        shr eax, cl
        adc eax, 0
        shl eax, cl

        mov value, eax
    };
    memcpy(&result, &value, sizeof(value));

    return result;
};
```

In the `trimFloat` method, a bit of inline assembly language is used to get the job done. Every once in a while, a situation arises that can be performed in assembly-language much more easily than in C++. In the assembly code, the mantissa is shifted to the right to push all unwanted bits out of the register. However, the last bit to get pushed out is the one that must be examined. Remember that each binary position represents half the value of the next-higher bit. This means that if the last bit we happen to push out is set, the entire value being trimmed off is greater or equal to half the value of the last bit we are keeping, and we must round up. Luckily, the last bit shifted out is stored in the carry flag of the processor. The next instruction, ADC (add-with-carry), adds the contents of the carry flag to our remaining value. If the last bit shifted out of the register was set ,the carry flag will also be set, and the add-with-carry operation will increment the remaining value in the register. If the last bit pushed out was clear, the carry flag will also be clear and the register remains unaffected. If the value within the register is then shifted back to the former position, the result will be a mantissa rounded to the precision desired.

This can be a very handy function to have in the tool chest. To control floating-point drift, values can be rounded to the precision desired. In addition, floating-point values can now be rounded to fixed precision increments easily. One such example would be in snapping rotation angles or timing values to fixed intervals.

CLAMPING FLOATING-POINT NUMBERS

Rounding floating-point numbers is useful in controlling the drift caused by error accumulation, but sometimes we simply need to ensure that a value is clamped to a certain range. Very often, values need to be clamped to the range [0,1], or pushed into the negative or positive range. In the `FloatTools.h` header, we define a few additional functions to make these types of clamping operations easy.

Forcing a value to the positive range (if f<0, set f = 0), is the easiest by far. Given that the sign bit resides in the 31st bit, we can easily to convert this bit into a mask. Applying the bit mask to the original source value with a bitwise-and operator will clear all negative values to zero. Forcing a value into the negative range (if f>0, set f=0) works much the same way: simply invert the bit mask to clear all positive values to zero.

```
float clampPositive(float input)
    {
        // if the value is negative, set it to zero
        int value = fpBits(input);
        int sign_mask = ~fpSign(input);
        return intBits(value & sign_mask);
    }

float clampNegative(float input)
    {
        // if the value is positive, set it to zero
        int value = fpBits(input);
        int sign_mask = fpSign(input);
        return intBits(value & sign_mask);
    }
```

Using these two functions, clamping can also be performed above or below any floating-point value. If the desired clamping value is first subtracted from the source value, the positive or negative clamping operation can be performed. The subtracted value can then be added back to the clamped value, resulting in a value clamped above or below the desired point. For example, to clamp a value below two (if f>2.0, set f = 2.0), a function similar to the following can be used:

```
float clampBelowTwo(float input)
    {
        float result = input - 2.0f;
        clampBelowZero(input);
        return (result + 2.0f);
    }
```

Apart from zero, the value most often clamped against is 1.0. The same method used in the example of clamping below 2.0 could be used, but there is a faster way. In the example method, offsetting the input value and then replacing the offset after the clamp is performed taxes the FPU twice, which is not ideal. Since clamping against 1.0 will happen more frequently, it makes sense to devise a more efficient method.

Thanks to the placement of the exponent in a higher bit range than the mantissa, we know that if one positive floating-point value is greater than another, its IEEE bit pattern will also be greater than the other when treated as integers. The floating-point value for 1.0 has a distinctive bit pattern of all zeros except for the lower 7 bits of the exponent (127<<23). This makes it fairly easy to test against. If any positive floating-point value has an equivalent bit pattern greater than (127<<23), then that floating-point value is also greater than 1.0.

Note that while this trick will also work when comparing two negative values, it will not function with a mix of negative and positive values. Since the sign bit resides in the highest bit position, negative floating point values will always be greater than their positive counterparts when treated as unsigned integers. This will cause our tests to fail if steps are not taken to correct for the sign bit.

```
float clampBelowOne(float input)
    {
        // if the value is greater than one, set it to one
        uint32 value = fpBits(input);
        uint32 mask = (~fpSign(input)) & 0x7fffffff;
        uint32 new_val = value & mask;
        new_val -= (127<<23);
        new_val >= 31;
        uint32 one = (127<<23) & ~new_val;
        value = (value & new_val) + one;
        return intBits(value);
    }
```

One case in which sign is not an issue is when values need to be clamped to the range [–1,1]. Such an operation would be useful in clamping normalized vectors to ensure that no floating-point precision drift pushes them beyond a single unit length. Because the only concern is whether the absolute value of the floating-point number is greater than 1.0, we can disregard the sign bit and clamp the positive and negative range at the same time.

```
float clampUnitSize(float input)
    {
        // if the absolute value is greater than one,
        // set it to one
        uint32 value = fpBits(input);
        uint32 abs_value = value & 0x7fffffff;
        abs_value -= (127<<23);
        abs_value >= 31;
```

```
        uint32 one = (127<<23) & ~abs_value;
        value = (value & abs_value) + one;
        return intBits(value);
}
```

FLOATING-POINT POWERS OF TWO

The last floating-point subject we will examine is rounding to a power-of-two value. This type of operation is not used very often for floating-point values, but having a speedy method in our numeric toolbox can't hurt. As with the floating-point to integer methods, our core library will contain versions of this operation that round to the nearest power-of-two, as well as find the next higher or lower power-of-two values. The functions can be found in the source\core\numeric_tools.h file on the CD-ROM.

ON THE CD

As usual, truncation is the easiest—so that is the example we will walk through. To convert a floating-point number to a power-of-two value is easy: simply dump the mantissa bits. Remember that the exponent value is taken from the scientific formula (mantissa^{2exp}), so if the mantissa is set to zero, all that is left is a truncated power-of-two value. Note that this truncation will also apply to negative values, returning negative results. An input value of 2.35 will return –2.0, but an input value of –2.35 will return –2.0. Strictly speaking, these are not valid powers-of-two, since 2 raised to any value could not become negative, but we will allow this functionality to remain.

The other caveat with this method is that it can also generate results from negative exponents. That is, when the exponent is negative, the method will return power-of-two fractions. Keep in mind that fractional values like ½, ¼, and ⅛ are valid powers-of-two, representing 2^{-1}, 2^{-2} and 2^{-3}, respectively. These values will be generated when the input value is a fractional value between –1.0 and 1.0.

```
float truncateToPowerOfTwo(float input)
    {
        // convert the value to an int
        int result = fpBits(m_float);

        // trim away the mantissa
        result &= ~((1<<23)-1);

        // convert back to floating-point as we return
        return (intBits(result));
    }
```

C

PROGRAMMING REFERENCE SHEETS

INTEL CPU IDENTIFICATION CODES

CPU Feature Flags reported by the CPUID instruction. Information provided by Intel documentation.

BIT	NAME	PURPOSE
0	FPU	The processor contains an FPU that supports the Intel387 floating-point instruction set.
1	VME	The processor supports extensions to virtual-8086 mode.
2	DE	The processor supports I/O breakpoints, including the CR4.DE bit for enabling debug extensions and optional trapping of access to the DR4 and DR5 registers.
3	PSE	The processor supports 4-Mbyte pages.
4	TSC	The RDTSC instruction is supported including the CR4.TSD bit for access/privilege control.
5	MSR	Model Specific Registers are implemented with the RDMSR, WRMSR instructions.
6	PAE	Physical addresses greater than 32 bits are supported.
7	MCE	Machine Check Exception, Exception 18, and the CR4.MCE enable bit are supported.
8	CX8	The compare and exchange 8 bytes instruction is supported.
9	APIC	The processor contains a software-accessible Local APIC.
10		Reserved Bit.

BIT	NAME	PURPOSE
11	SEP	Indicates whether the processor supports the Fast System Call instructions, SYSENTER and SYSEXIT.
12	MTRR	The Processor supports the Memory Type Range Registers specifically the MTRR_CAP register.
13	PGE	The global bit in the Page Directory Entries (PDEs) and page table entries (PTEs) is supported, indicating TLB entries that are common to different processes and need not be flushed. The CR4.PGE bit controls this feature.
14	MCA	The Machine Check Architecture is supported, specifically the MCG_CAP register.
15	CMOV	The processor supports CMOVcc, and if the FPU feature flag (bit 0) is also set, supports the FCMOVCC and FCOMI instructions.
16	PAT	Indicates whether the processor supports the Page Attribute Table. This feature augments the Memory Type Range Registers (MTRRs), allowing an operating system to specify attributes of memory on 4K granularity through a linear address.
17	PSE-36	Indicates whether the processor supports 4-Mbyte pages that are capable of addressing physical memory beyond 4GB. This feature indicates that the upper four bits of the physical address of the 4-Mbyte page is encoded by bits 13-16 of the page directory entry.
18	PSN	The processor supports the 96-bit processor serial number feature, and the feature is enabled.
19	CLFSH	Indicates that the processor supports the CLFLUSH instruction.
20		Reserved Bit.
21	DS	Indicates that the processor has the ability to write a history of the branch to and from addresses into a memory buffer.
22	ACPI	The processor implements internal MSRs that allow processor temperature to be monitored and processor performance to be modulated in predefined duty cycles under software control.
23	MMX	The processor supports the MMX technology instruction set extensions to Intel Architecture.
24	FXSR	Indicates whether the processor supports the FXSAVE and FXRSTOR instructions for fast save and restore of the floating point context. Presence of this bit also indicates that CR4.OSFXSR is available for an operating system to indicate that it uses the fast save/restore instructions.

BIT	NAME	PURPOSE
25	SSE	The processor supports the Streaming SIMD Extensions to the Intel Architecture.
26	SSE2	Indicates the processor supports the Streaming SIMD Extensions - 2 Instructions.
27	SS	The processor supports the management of conflicting memory types by performing a snoop of its own cache structure for transactions issued to the bus.
28	HTT	This processor's microarchitecture has the capability to operate as multiple logical processors within the same physical package. This field does not indicate that Hyper-Threading Technology has been enabled for this specific processor. To determine if Hyper-Threading Technology is supported, check the value returned in EBX[23:16] after executing CPUID with EAX=1. If EBX[23:16] contains a value >1, then the processor supports Hyper-Threading Technology.
29	TM	The processor implements the Thermal Monitor automatic thermal control circuit (TCC).
30		Reserved Bit.
31	SBF	The processor supports the Signal Break on FERR feature. The FERR signal is asserted if an interrupt is pending and STPCLK is asserted.

DIRECT3D HLSL DATA TYPES

Variable types available in HLSL vertex and pixel shaders.

SCALAR DATA TYPES	DESCRIPTION
bool	Boolean values that can be set to true or false.
int	32-bit signed integer.
half	A half-precision, 16-bit floating point value.
float	A full-precision, 32-bit floating point value.
double	A double-precision, 64-bit floating point value.
VECTOR DATA TYPES	**DESCRIPTION**
vector	A vector of four float values.
vector<t, num>	A vector containing *num* members of scalar *t* values.

MATRIX DATA TYPES	DESCRIPTION
matrix	A matrix of 16 float values in a 4x4 grid.
matrix <t, row, col>	A matrix of type *t* values in a grid of size *row* by *col*.

OBJECT DATA TYPES	DESCRIPTION
string	An ASCII string.
pixelshader	A Direct3D pixel shader object.
vertexshader	A Direct3D vertex shader object.
sampler	An object describing the use and filtering of a texture.
texture	A Direct3D texture object.

VECTOR TYPEDEFS	DESCRIPTION (# REPRESENTS VALUES BETWEEN 0 AND 4)
bool#x#	Defined as vector <bool, #>. Example: bool4.
int#x#	Defined as vector <int, #>. Example: int4.
float#x#	Defined as vector <float, #>. Example: float4.
half#x#	Defined as vector <half, #>. Example: half4.
double#x#	Defined as vector <double, #>. Example: double4.

MATRIX TYPEDEFS	DESCRIPTION (# REPRESENTS VALUES BETWEEN 0 AND 4)
bool#x#	Defined as matrix <bool, #, #>. Example: bool4x4.
int#x#	Defined as matrix <int, #, #>. Example: int4x4.
float#x#	Defined as matrix <float, #, #>. Example: float4x4.
half#x#	Defined as matrix <half, #, #>. Example: half4x4.
double#x#	Defined as matrix <double, #, #>. Example: double4x4.
double#x#	Defined as matrix <double, #, #>. Example: double4x4.

Direct3D HLSL Expressions

The following is a list of the numeric and conditional expressions supported by the High-Level Shader Language (HLSL) for vertex and pixel shaders.

OPERATOR	USAGE	MEANING
+	value+value	Addition of each component.
-	value-value	Subtraction of each component.
*	value*value	Multiplication of each component.
/	value/value	Division of each component.
%	value%value	Modulus of each component.
=	variable=value	Assignment of each component.

OPERATOR	USAGE	MEANING
+=	variable+=value	Addition and assignment of each component.
-=	variable-=value	Subtraction and assignment of each component.
*=	variable*=value	Multiplication and assignment of each component.
/=	variable/=value	Division and assignment of each component.
%=	variable%=value	Modulus and assignment of each component.
++	variable++	Postfix increment of each component.
—	variable—	Postfix decrement of each component.
++	++variable	Prefix increment of each component.
—	—variable	Prefix decrement of each component.
-	-value	Unary minus of each component (negation).
+	+value	Unary plus of each component.
!=	value != value	Inequality test each component.
!	!value	Logical not each component.
<	value < value	Less than each component.
>	value > value	Greater than each component.
<=	value <= value	Less than or equal to each component.
>=	value >= value	Greater than or equal to each component.
==	value == value	Equality test each component.
&&	value && value	Logical AND each component.
||	value||value	Logical OR each component.
?:	float?value:value	Conditional operator.

DIRECT3D HLSL INTRINSIC FUNCTIONS

The following is a list of the intrinsic functions provided by HLSL for vertex and pixel shaders.

FUNCTION	DEFINITION
value abs(value a)	Absolute value of each component.
acos(x)	Returns the arccosine of each component of x. Each component should be in the range [–1, 1].
all(x)	Test if all components of x are nonzero.
any(x)	Test is any component of x is nonzero.
asin(x)	Returns the arcsine of each component of x. Each component should be in the range [–pi/2, pi/2].
atan(x)	Returns the arctangent of x. The return values are in the range [–pi/2, pi/2].

FUNCTION	DEFINITION
atan2(y, x)	Returns the arctangent of y/x. The signs of y and x are used to determine the quadrant of the return values in the range [–pi, pi]. atan2 is well defined for every point other than the origin, even if x equals 0 and y does not equal 0.
ceil(x)	Returns the smallest integer that is greater than or equal to x.
clamp(x, min, max)	Clamps x to the range [min, max].
clip(x)	Discards the current pixel, if any component of x is less than zero. This can be used to simulate clip planes, if each component of x represents the distance from a plane.
cos(x)	Returns the cosine of x.
cosh(x)	Returns the hyperbolic cosine of x.
cross(a, b)	Returns the cross product of two 3-D vectors a and b.
D3DCOLORtoUBYTE4(x)	Swizzles and scales components of the 4-D vector x to compensate for the lack of UBYTE4 support in some hardware.
ddx(x)	Returns the partial derivative of x with respect to the screen-space x-coordinate.
ddy(x)	Returns the partial derivative of x with respect to the screen-space y-coordinate.
degrees(x)	Converts x from radians to degrees.
determinant(m)	Returns the determinant of the square matrix m.
distance(a, b)	Returns the distance between two points a and b.
dot(a, b)	Returns the dot product of two vectors a and b.
exp(x)	Returns the base-e exponent ex.
value exp2(value a)	Base 2 Exp of each component.
faceforward(n, i, ng)	Returns –n * sign(dot(i, ng)).
floor(x)	Returns the greatest integer that is less than or equal to x.
fmod(a, b)	Returns the floating-point remainder f of a / b such that a = i * b + f, where i is an integer, f has the same sign as x, and the absolute value of f is less than the absolute value of b.
frac(x)	Returns the fractional part f of x, such that f is a value greater than or equal to 0, and less than 1.
value frc(value a)	Fractional part of each component.

FUNCTION	DEFINITION
frexp(x, out exp)	Returns the mantissa and exponent of x. frexp returns the mantissa, and the exponent is stored in the output parameter exp. If x is 0, the function returns 0 for both the mantissa and the exponent.
fwidth(x)	Returns abs(ddx(x))+abs(ddy(x)).
isfinite(x)	Returns true if x is finite, false otherwise.
isinf(x)	Returns true if x is +INF or –INF, false otherwise.
isnan(x)	Returns true if x is NAN or QNAN, false otherwise.
ldexp(x, exp)	Returns x * 2exp.
float len(value a)	Vector length.
length(v)	Returns the length of the vector v.
lerp(a, b, s)	Returns a + s(b − a). This linearly interpolates between a and b, such that the return value is a when s is 0, and b when s is 1.
lit(ndotl, ndoth, m)	Returns a lighting vector (ambient, diffuse, specular, 1): ambient = 1; diffuse = (ndotl < 0) ? 0 : ndotl; specular = (ndotl < 0) || (ndoth < 0) ? 0 : (ndoth * m);
log(x)	Returns the base-e logarithm of x. If x is negative, the function returns indefinite. If x is 0, the function returns +INF.
log10(x)	Returns the base-10 logarithm of x. If x is negative, the function returns indefinite. If x is 0, the function returns +INF.
log2(x)	Returns the base-2 logarithm of x. If x is negative, the function returns indefinite. If x is 0, the function returns +INF.
max(a, b)	Selects the greater of a and b.
min(a, b)	Selects the lesser of a and b.
modf(x, out ip)	Splits the value x into fractional and integer parts, each of which has the same sign and x. The signed fractional portion of x is returned. The integer portion is stored in the output parameter ip.
mul(a, b)	Performs matrix multiplication between a and b. If a is a vector, it treated as a row vector. If b is a vector, it is treated as a column vector. The inner dimension acolumns and brows must be equal. The result has the dimension arows x bcolumns.
noise(x)	Not yet implemented.

FUNCTION	DEFINITION
normalize(v)	Returns the normalized vector v / length(v). If the length of *v* is 0, the result is indefinite.
pow(x, y)	Returns x^y.
radians(x)	Converts *x* from degrees to radians.
reflect(i, n)	Returns the reflection vector v, given the entering ray direction i, and the surface normal n. Such that v = i - 2 * dot(i, n) * n.
refract(i, n, eta)	Returns the refraction vector v, given the entering ray direction i, the surface normal n, and the relative index of refraction eta. If the angle between i and n is too great for a given eta, refract returns (0,0,0).
round(x)	Rounds *x* to the nearest integer.
rsqrt(x)	Returns 1 / sqrt(x).
saturate(x)	Clamps *x* to the range [0, 1].
sign(x)	Computes the sign of *x*. Returns −1 if *x* is less than 0, 0 if *x* equals 0, and 1 if *x* is greater than zero.
sin(x)	Returns the sine of *x*.
sincos(x, out s, out c)	Returns the sine and cosine of *x*. sin(x) is stored in the output parameter s. cos(x) is stored in the output parameter c.
sinh(x)	Returns the hyperbolic sine of *x*.
smoothstep(min, max, x)	Returns 0 if *x* < min. Returns 1 if *x* > max. Returns a smooth Hermite interpolation between 0 and 1, if *x* is in the range [min, max].
value sqrt(value a)	Square root of each component.
step(a, x)	Returns (x >= a) ? 1 : 0.
tan(x)	Returns the tangent of *x*.
tanh(x)	Returns the hyperbolic tangent of *x*.
tex1D(s, t)	1-D texture lookup. s is a sampler or a sampler1D object. t is a scalar.
tex1D(s, t, ddx, ddy)	1-D texture lookup, with derivatives. s is a sampler or sampler1D object. t, ddx, and ddy are scalars.
tex1Dproj(s, t)	1-D projective texture lookup. s is a sampler or `sampler1D` object. t is a 4-D vector. t is divided by its last component before the lookup takes place.

tex1Dbias(s, t)	1-D biased texture lookup. s is a sampler or sampler1D object. t is a 4-D vector. The mip level is biased by t.w before the lookup takes place.
tex2D(s, t)	2-D texture lookup. s is a sampler or a sampler2D object. t is a 2-D texture coordinate.
tex2D(s, t, ddx, ddy)	2-D texture lookup, with derivatives. s is a sampler or sampler2D object. t, ddx, and ddy are 2-D vectors.
tex2Dproj(s, t)	2-D projective texture lookup. s is a sampler or sampler2D object. t is a 4-D vector. t is divided by its last component before the lookup takes place.
tex2Dbias(s, t)	2-D biased texture lookup. s is a sampler or sampler2D object. t is a 4-D vector. The mip level is biased by t.w before the lookup takes place.
tex3D(s, t)	3-D volume texture lookup. s is a sampler or a sampler3D object. t is a 3-D texture coordinate.
tex3D(s, t, ddx, ddy)	3-D volume texture lookup, with derivatives. s is a sampler or sampler3D object. t, ddx, and ddy are 3-D vectors.
tex3Dproj(s, t)	3-D projective volume texture lookup. s is a sampler or sampler3D object. t is a 4-D vector. t is divided by its last component before the lookup takes place.
tex3Dbias(s, t)	3-D biased texture lookup. s is a sampler or sampler3D object. t is a 4-D vector. The mip level is biased by t.w before the lookup takes place.
texCUBE(s, t)	3-D cube texture lookup. s is a sampler or a samplerCUBE object. t is a 3-D texture coordinate.
texCUBE(s, t, ddx, ddy)	3-D cube texture lookup, with derivatives. s is a sampler or samplerCUBE object. t, ddx, and ddy are 3-D vectors.
texCUBEproj(s, t)	3-D projective cube texture lookup. s is a sampler or samplerCUBE object. t is a 4-D vector. t is divided by its last component before the lookup takes place.
texCUBEbias(s, t)	3-D biased cube texture lookup. s is a sampler or samplerCUBE object. t is a 4-dimensional vector. The mip level is biased by t.w before the lookup takes place.
transpose(m)	Returns the transpose of the matrix m. If the source is dimension mrows x mcolumns, the result is dimension mcolumns x mrows.

DIRECT3D HLSL SAMPLER SETTINGS

The following is a list of the values that may be specified when building texture samplers for HLSL shaders.

SAMPLER STATE	TYPE	ACCEPTABLE VALUES
AddressU	dword	WRAP = 1, MIRROR = 2, CLAMP = 3, BORDER = 4, MIRRORONCE = 5
AddressV	dword	Same as AddressU.
AddressW	dword	Same as AddressU.
BorderColor	float4	A color value. The vector contains REBA values from 0-1.
MagFilter	dword	NONE = 0, POINT = 1, LINEAR = 2, ANISOTROPIC = 3, PYRAMIDALQUAD = 6, GAUSSIANQUAD = 7E
MinFilter	dword	Same as MagFilter.
MipFilter	dword	Same as MagFilter.
MaxAnisotropy	dword	Maximum anisotropy value. Default value is 1.
MaxMipLevel	int	Maximum mipmap level to use from 0–n, where n is the number of mipmaps available. The largest texture is index 0. The smallest texture is index (n–1).
MipMapLodBias	float	A bias value applied to the mipmap level chosen. The default is 0.0.
SRGBTexture	bool	Set to true (non-zero value) when the texture being sampled is in sRGB format (gamma correction 2.2). See the DirectX SDK for more information on Gamma.
ElementIndex	dword	When a multi-element texture is assigned to the sampler, this indicates which element index to use. The default value is 0.

RECOMMENDED READING

Following is a list of references cited in the book, along with some additional material we recommend for further reading.

MATHEMATICS

Lengyel, Eric. *Mathematics for 3D Game Programming & Computer Graphics.* Charles River Media, 2002.

Gribb, G., and K. Hartmann. "Fast Extraction of Viewing Frustum Planes from the World-View-Projection Matrix," (available online at *www2.ravensoft.com/users/ggribb/plane%20extraction.pdf*).

3D PROGRAMMING

Deloura, M., *Game Programming Gems.* Charles River Media, Inc., 2000.

Deloura, M., *Game Programming Gems 2.* Charles River Media, Inc., 2001.

Treglia, D., *Game Programming Gems 3.* Charles River Media, Inc., 2002.

Watt, A. *3D Computer Graphics.* Addison-Wesley, 1993.

Watt, A. and Watt, M. *Advanced Animation and Rendering Techniques.* Addison-Wesley, 1992.

Microsoft DirectX9 Development FAQ, (available online at *http://msdn.microsoft.com/library/en-us/dndxgen/html/directx9devfaq.asp*).

Engel, W. *ShaderX.* Wordware Publishing, Inc. 2002.

Wenzel, C. "Ocean Scene," (available online at *http://meshuggah.4fo.de/OceanScene.htm*).

ACADEMIC RESEARCH

Perlin, K. "Making Noise: Tutorial and History of the Noise Function," (available online at *www.noisemachine.com*).

Perlin, K. "Improving Noise." *Computer Graphics*, Vol. 35 No. 3 (available online at *http://mrl.nyu.edu/~perlin/paper445.pdf*).

Preetham, A. J., P. Shirley, and B. Smits. "A Practical Analytic Model for Daylight." Siggraph proceedings 1999 (available online at *www.cs.utah.edu/vissim/papers/sunsky*).

Hoffman, N., and A. J, Preetham. "Rendering Outdoor Light Scattering in Real Time," (available online at *www.ati.com/developer/dx9/ATI-LightScattering.pdf*).

Fournier, A, and W. T. Reeves. "A Simple Model of Ocean Waves." *Computer Graphics*, Vol. 20, No. 4, 1986, pp.75–84.

Peachey, D. "Modeling Waves and Surf." *Computer Graphics*, Vol. 20, No. 4, 1986, pp. 65–74.

Mastin, G. A., P. A. Watterger, and J. F. Mareda. "Fourier Synthesis of Ocean Scenes." *IEEE CG&A*, March 1987, pp. 16–23.

OTHER USEFUL WEB SITES

The author's Web site: *www.mightystudios.com*
The ATI developer Web page: *www.ati.com/developer/*
NVIDIA developer relations Web page: *http://developer.nvidia.com/*
FlipCode: *www.flipcode.com*
GameDev: *www.gamedev.net*
GamaSutra: *www.gamasutra.com*
USGS Geological Data: *www.usgs.gov/*
Virtual Terrain Project: *www.vterrain.org*

TOOLS AND UTILITIES

3DEM, Visualization Software, LLC: *www.visualizationsoftware.com/3dem.html*
T2: Texture Generation Program: *www.petra.demon.co.uk/Games/texgen.html*

E

ABOUT THE CD-ROM

The CD-ROM included with *Real-Time 3D Terrain Engines Using C++ and DirectX 9* contains all of the files necessary to compile the engine discussed in the book. It also includes the source code and executables for the demonstrations mentioned in each chapter. All model, texture, and effect files are also provided. Special thanks to Christopher Barrett for his help in creating some of the models and textures found on the CD-ROM

CD FOLDERS

SOURCE: All of the source code is contained within this folder. Subfolders are provided for each section of the engine, and for each individual demo program. A bin folder contains precompiled executables for each demo, along with all the media required to run them.
DIRECTX: The entire DirectX 9.0 SDK. To install the SDK, follow the instructions provided in this folder.
TOOLS: We have included a set of tools to aid in building your own terrain. Check the homepages listed for each tool to download more recent versions when available.

The first is a version of T2 by Keith Ditchburn. This useful texture generation program can construct texture maps for any terrain given a set of parameters. More information can be found at *www.petra.demon.co.uk/Games/texgen.html*.

The second application is 3DEM from Visualization Software, LLC. This program is capable of converting real-world terrain information from a variety of sources into height maps for use in a terrain engine. More information and support for this product can be obtained from *www.visualizationsoftware.com.* This Web page also lists locations to download free terrain data for use with the program.

SYSTEM REQUIREMENTS

Windows 2000/XP:

- Pentium III Processor, 1GHz+
- DirectX 9-compatable video card providing hardware-accelerated, programmable vertex and pixel shaders (NVIDIA GeForce 3 or higher, ATI Radeon 8500 and beyond)
- CD-ROM/hard drive
- 128MB RAM (256MB recommended)
- 500MB of free disk space to install the DirectX SDK, the sample source code, and the tools provided

SOFTWARE REQUIREMENTS

Microsoft Visual Studio.NET or Microsoft Visual Studio 6.0 is required to edit and compile the source code provided. Other editors and compilers might be compatible, but have not been tested.

INSTALLATION

To use this CD-ROM, make sure that your system matches at least the minimum system requirements. Each tool provided has its own installation instructions, and you should contact the developer directly if you have any problems with installation. The source code folder can be copied directly to your hard drive for editing with a program of your choice.

UPDATES AND ERRATA

Be sure to visit the Web sites of Charles River Media (*www.charlesriver. com*) and the author (*www.mightystudios.com*) for any updates or errata associated with this book and the included source code.

INDEX

Quadtrees (*cont.*)
  power-of-two, 106–107
  slow searches, 111–117
Quaternion
  D3DXQuaternion object, 21
  rotation, 20–21
Query performance counter, 327
Queues
  priority, 163
  render, 82–95, 141, 146, 264

R
Raleigh light scattering, 257, 258, 261
Random terrain. *See* Textures
RandomChannelNoise, 215
Real Time Stamp Counter, 307
Real to integer conversion, 340
Recommended reading, 359–360
Refract function, 48
Render
  effect files and rendering procedures,
    27–33
  entry, 83–95, 141
  meshes, 26–27
  method resources, 75–76
  passes, 218
  queue, 82–95, 141, 146, 264
  sky. *See* Sky rendering
  terrain sections, 146–150
  water, 287–292
Renormalization and bump map, 251–254
Resources
  cModelResource, 264
  cResourcePoolItem, 72–73
  data pools, 63–68
  disableResource, 73
  managing shared data, 62, 68–72
  model, 78–81
  render method, 75–76
  resource base class, 72–74
  resource code, 70–72
  restoreResource, 73
  texture, and surface materials, 74
RGBA color and pixel shader, 50
Right-handed coordinate system, 9–11

ROAM (Real-Time Optimal Adapting
    Mesh)
  algorithm, described, 154–157
  building display geometry, 165–168
  buildTriangleList, 165
  cRoamTerrain, 160–161
  cRoamTerrainSection, 160–162, 165, 166
  cTriTreeNode, 160–162
  displacement value, 155–156
  distance, scale, and limit values, 157
  error metric, 156–157, 160, 171
  implementing, 159–165
  LOD popping, 194
  split decisions, 157–159
  vertex and index buffers, 165–168
  See also Terrain geometry
Robbins, John, "Bug Slayer", *Microsoft System Journal*, 314
Rock texture, 201–202, 203, 216
Rotation
  gimbal lock, 21
  quaternion, 20–21
  vectors, 16
Roughness scale, 123–124
Row-major format of matrices, 17

S
Sample application framework, 5–8
Samplers
  HLSL, 48–50
  SetSamplerState, 48
Satellite terrain data, 121
Scalar data types, 45, 351
Scaling vectors, 13
Scenes
  cModelResource, 264
  cSceneModel, 264
  nodes and objects, 81, 103–104
  organization, 100–103
  sectors, 102–103. *See also* Quadtrees
  space partitioning, 100
Scenes, outdoor
  ambient light, 243–247
  animating water, 277–286
  approximating outdoor light, 254–261

Y
Y-axis coordinates, 9–12

Z
Z buffer and ambient lighting, 244–247
Z-axis coordinates, 9–12

Numbers
3D Computer Graphics (Watt), 18

3DEM, Visualization Software LLC, 121, 361
16-byte memory alignment, 4–5
32-bit floating-point values, 336

Symbols
: (colon) and semantics, 46
... (ellipsis) arguments, 325